the go-Girl guIde

Surviving Your 20s with Savvy, soul, and style

julia bourlaNd

CB
CONTEMPORARY BOOKS

Library of Congress Cataloging-in-Publication Data

Bourland, Julia.
    The go-girl guide : surviving your 20s with savvy, soul, and style / Julia
Bourland.
        p.   cm.
    Includes index.
    ISBN 0-8092-2476-3
    1. Young women—Conduct of life.   2. Young women—Life skills guides.
3. Single women—Conduct of life.   4. Single women—Life skills guides.
I. Title.
HQ1229.B62   2000
646.7'0084'22—dc21   99-59379
                                                                                CIP

Cover design by Jennifer Locke
Cover illustrations copyright © Tracey McGuinness
Interior design by Amy Yu Ng

Published by Contemporary Books
A division of NTC/Contemporary Publishing Group, Inc.
4255 West Touhy Avenue, Lincolnwood (Chicago), Illinois 60712-1975 U.S.A.
Printed in the United States of America
International Standard Book Number: 0-8092-2476-3
        03   04   05   ML   19   18   17   16   15   14   13   12

Contents

Acknowledgments   vi

The Author's 20s   viii

Introduction: *Rooaaarrrr!!!!!!!*   x

Part I: Our Careers

1 "What the F%@#!!! Am I Going to Do with My Life?"   3
The Soul-Search Train * The Career Psychics * Internship
Insight * Occupational Guidebooks * The Insiders * The
Trial-and-Error Approach

2 The Job Hunt   19
Tunnel of Horror * Getting Set Up * Vibing the Company *
Paper Coquetry * The First Interview * The Rejection Factor
* Considering Commitment * Negotiating the Offer

3 The Entry-Level Initiation   43
The Induction * Culture Shock * Bonding with the Elders *
The Ultimate Elder * Tribal Speak * Rising Through the
Ranks * The I Hate My Job Syndrome * Beyond Entry Level

Part II: Our Love Lives

4 The Mating Frenzy   69
Getting to the Starting Line * Ladies, Start Your Engines *
And the Race Begins (The First Date) * Laps Two and Three
* Red Flag Alert * Safety Hazards * Staying on Track * The
Final Lap: Are We Dating Yet?

5 Adventures in Couplehood   93
   Lesson#1: Self-Preservation ✽ Lesson#2: Communication ✽
   Lesson #3: Conflict Resolution ✽ Lesson#4: Romance
   Maintenance ✽ Long-Distance Dating ✽ When It's Time to
   Dump a Guy ✽ Getting Over a Breakup ✽ On Taking
   Minibreaks ✽ Moving In with Mr. Maybe ✽ Swapping Vows

6 You Sexy Thing   123
   Let the Cannonballs Fly! ✽ Choosing Our Comrades in Bed ✽
   The One- (or Two-) Night Stand ✽ The Sex History Talk ✽
   Our Sexual Health ✽ A Word or Two on Birth Control

7 The Upredictable Female Orgasm   145
   Truth #1: All Women Climax Differently ✽ Truth #2:
   Orgasms Don't (Pardon the Pun) Come Easily ✽ Truth #3:
   Our Partners Need Pointers on What Turns Us On ✽ Truth
   #4: Intercourse, Alone, Doesn't Cut It (At Least, for Most of
   Us) ✽ Truth #5: Not All Orgasms Have the Same Oomph ✽
   Truth #6: The Mind Has More Verve than a Vibrator ✽ Truth
   #7: Orgasms Aren't Proof of Good Sex ✽ The Libido Crash
   and Revival

Part III: Our Body and Soul

8 Emotional Theatrics   163
   The Identity Crisis ✽ That Self-Loathing Feeling ✽ "I'm So
   Stressed Out!" ✽ "Is There Anybody Out There?" ✽ Moving
   101 ✽ When You Have the Blues ✽ Rage ✽ Envy ✽ A Mental-
   Health Checkup

9 The Body-Image Demons   195
   The Value of Being Cute ✽ Real Women and the Airbrushed
   ✽ Ads That Promise the Universe ✽ The Roots of Body-Image
   Blues ✽ The Scapegoat Factor ✽ The Body Morph ✽ One
   Week Without Obsessions ✽ A Wardrobe You Love ✽
   Bathroom Scale Torch ✽ Mirror, Hateful Mirror! ✽ Exercise
   and Proper Fuel ✽ Body Image and the Bedroom ✽ The Mind
   Factor

10 That Whacked-Out Body Feeling   211

Our Size and Shape * Our Faces * Our Skin * Our Hair *
Our Digestive Systems * Our Reproductive Systems * Our
Feet * Exercise Guidelines * Nutrition Guidelines * Screening
Tests to Get Right Away

Part IV: Our Support Group

11 Family Knots   243

Who *Are* These People (And What Did They Do with My
Parents)? * Cutting the Cord * Unresolved "Issues" * Sibling
Rivalry No More! * Sharing the Nest * Home for the
Holidays and Other Visits * The Bizarre Role Reversal *
Starting a Family of Our Own * On Becoming Friends

12 Our Surrogate Family   269

The Maintenance Factor * Downsizing the Circle * Forging
New Bonds * Mixing Boyfriends into the Stew * Grouping
the Gang

Part V: Our Finances and Other Loose Ends

13 Financial Chaos   289

On Being Dirt Poor * Our Budget * The Price of Fun *
Money Etiquette * Getting Out of Debt (And Staying Out) *
Saving for Retirement * The Crisis Fund * Investing Extra
$$$ * One Final Taxing Matter

14 Loose Ends   323

Our Birthdays * Theme Music * The Three-Month Marker *
Top 10 List of Things to Do in Your 20s * Keep On Movin'

Go-Girl Resources   329

Index   333

Acknowledgments

*O*h gosh. Where do I begin? First and foremost, I owe immense gratitude to all the 20-something women I interviewed while writing this book. Your experiences, hilarious stories, candid wisdom, and enthusiasm for the project gave me the needed inspiration and insight to write about our collective 20-something experience. I've changed all your names to protect your privacy, but you'll recognize your stories.

Within this group of amazing women, I owe special thanks to my running mates—Jill, Kate, Alyssa, and Lois—for all those great women talks during our long miles and postworkout workouts, for reading parts of the manuscript, and above all, for helping me through my first marathon this year! I swear I'll catch up with y'all down at Ocean Beach one of these days. I'll bring the Gu.

Equally indebted am I to all the counselors, professors, psychologists, career consultants, dating and relationships experts, sex therapists, and financial advisers, many of whom I've quoted, who graciously dedicated their time for an interview about all the issues specific to us 20-something girls. Your professional savvy has given this guide weight and strength I couldn't possibly have provided on my own, and for that I'm deeply grateful.

Galaxy-wide gratitude goes to my three new superheroes, editor Matthew Carnicelli, sidekick Erika Lieberman, and agent Liz Ziemska, for their uncanny insight and amazing powers to make *The Go-Girl Guide* a reality.

The same goes to my girlfriends Jennifer, Christine, Holly, Nicole, Annie, Angie, Chloe, and Faerol, who encouraged and inspired me throughout the writing process. My debut into adulthood would have been a complete disaster (not to mention a total bore) without each and every one of you.

Hugs and kisses to my family back in Dallas for all that fantastic encouragement—and a special high five to Dorothy and Darcy not only for being the greatest little sisters a girl gets to brag about, but also for giving me extra incentive to write this guide. (You're going to *love* your 20s.)

My love to Larry for being the most perfect boyfriend on the planet. I never could have pulled off the scary task of writing *my first book!!!* without your undying encouragement, constant support, and awesome back rubs. I absolutely adore you!

Above all, deep thanks go to my oldest sister, Laura, who fearlessly braved the 20s just 15 months my senior, dutifully sharing the lessons she learned along the way. Thank you, *meine schwester*, for being the most nonjudgmental and steadfast sounding board for every single decision I've made during my 20s (and my entire life, for that matter), and also for just being so cool! You will always be my number one role model.

The Author's 20s

Age 20: Midcollege identity crisis. Still obsessing over the Freshman 15 and dodging perverse inquiries about future lifelong plans. Angst, angst, angst!

Age 21: "Of age" lacks luster when you've had a fake I.D. since you were 18. Bars and clubs oozing with obnoxious loser guys. Fret over how long it will take to pay off mounting student loans. Have first *real* orgasm!

Age 22: Ponder spirituality during study abroad in Indonesia. Decide to worship the sun. Take semester leave of absence and spend three months on the beaches of Thailand. Become a lifeguard at college pool upon return.

Age 23: Graduation prompts untimely identity crisis. Fifty résumés to local newspapers for a reporting position solicit 50 rejections. Minimize expenses by eating Top Ramen every night and sharing a dilapidated flat with three strangers in San Francisco's Chinatown. Lose 10 pounds.

Age 24: Miraculously secure an editorial assistant position with a national magazine, but become quickly disillusioned by lack of responsibility. Consider getting an M.B.A. Enter a series of bleak relationships with men. Girlfriends disgusted by the amount of time dedicated to odd array of boyfriends.

Age 25: Start scrutinizing face for wrinkles. Continue entry-level misery and tumultuous relationships. Seek therapy. Decide to pursue a career in psychology.

Age 26: Promotion! Move into a *studio*. Rent doubles. Cut costs by eating cereal for breakfast *and* dinner. Therapy probes "issues" with food. End an ill-fated relationship.

Age 27: Transfer to New York City with job. Another promotion! Start a 401(k) plan. Snag a smart, sexy boyfriend (but still tormented by self-doubt, bad body image, and "boundary issues" from childhood). Find a gray hair.

Age 28: Return to California, and move in with smart, sexy boyfriend. Reform career plans and become a freelance writer. Try to ignore eight pounds gained over past year. Take up yoga.

Age 29: Run a marathon to prove athletic vitality. Promise knees never to run another marathon. Begin writing *The Go-Girl Guide . . .*

Introduction
Rooaaarrrr!!!!!!!

Lately, your moods are in perpetual flux. On good days, self-esteem soars: you're entrusted with a challenging project at work, the guy you met the night before sends you flowers "just because," and you squeeze in spinning *and* yoga at the gym. Other days, you welter in the meaninglessness of your job, the babe you met last week who begged for your number *still* hasn't called, and you surrender your night at the gym to a two-hour-long phone call from your best friend analyzing your recent hibernation. Emotional exhaustion is too great to bear.

Your body is acting in strange, unpredictable ways. An undeniable tummy begins to protrude from your abdomen. Of course, no one but your most empathetic friend sees it, but still. You meticulously watch what you eat and therefore have somehow been grossly cheated! Pms seems to be getting worse; horrifying acne invades your lower cheeks and chin. You need glasses—a double blow to your fragile ego, since the new specs magnify the teeny wrinkles forming beneath your eyes. And suddenly, you can't digest any of your favorite foods without (a) diarrhea; (b) constipation; or (c) uncontrollable gas all night long.

Career aspirations oscillate wildly. Self-inflicted doubt about your career choice gnaws at you, and you wonder in vain/anger/resignation why you went to college if your job requires merely learning how to add toner to the copy machine. Once you have that golden five years' experience on your résumé and responsibility begins to increase (trust me, it does), a second wave of life-purpose questioning haunts your every thought. You wonder if having a baby might not be more fulfilling than the daily grind, until you remember that you're a far cry from motherhood without even a boyfriend to boast of, at which point you convince yourself that you'll be infertile by the time you're ready to get pregnant.

Financial security is a joke. You're up to your eyelashes in student loans and unavoidable credit-card debts. After all, you have to buy *some* furniture and cooking stuff—not that you'll ever use it—for your first apartment, as well as a semiprofessional wardrobe that doubles as sexy going-out-after-work outfits. You're plagued with guilt for not setting aside money for retirement and feel terribly resentful about your entry-level salary that forces you to shop at (*eek!*) a discount clothing store. For a fleeting moment, you wonder how much topless dancers really do make, until you realize you'd probably have to invest in silicone implants, and then writhe in shame for having even considered such an objectifying (though lucrative) act.

Relationships are undergoing major reconstruction. Parents don't quite know how to deal with you now that you're an adult, resulting in familial tension that everyone tries to pretend doesn't exist. Mom, approaching menopause, acts increasingly controlling/annoying/incomprehensible every time you talk to her. Dad, you decide, is the root of all your intimacy issues. Power struggles with siblings erupt as you timidly discard your "big" or "little" sister role and test the waters of mutual respect. Friendships, too, undergo mutations, since work and dating demands leave less time for reminiscing about high school or college days. Adding to the overall connection-confusion are fierce desires to find a mate (or, at most, an ever-ready sex machine to accommodate your hungry libido). But dating in the 20s is more complicated than ever.

Sometimes you just want to Rooaaarrr!!!!!!!

But try to relax and enjoy it. Twenty-something turbulence is all part of the flight—to adopt an airplane analogy—toward becoming an emotionally rich, sexually fulfilled, professionally successful, financially secure woman. While the trip, at times, may send your stomach and head spinning (think of the 20s as a decade-long bout of PMS), a few strategic maneuvers will guarantee smooth flying, despite all the changes that are propelling your body, soul, career, finances, and relationships into a nosedive. That's where I can help.

Having just tiptoed through the most foreboding of all birthdays, number 29, I've learned a thing or two about navigating the gusty airways of adulthood, which I'd like to share with you. (For a background check, see preceding author profile.) *The Go-Girl Guide*, however, isn't limited to my personal expertise. This comprehensive survival guide to the first decade of adulthood is a compilation of savvy advice and wisdom from nearly 100 20-something women and dozens of experts who know a thing or two about what it takes to transform into a woman. Our cumulative experience and realistic advice will guide you through every phase of the most bizarre and thrilling 10 years of your life. Don't at all feel obligated to read it cover to cover—just jump right in to whatever topic grabs your attention for some quick reassurance, a couple of pointers, and, hopefully, a chuckle or two. Then, grab a seat, recline, and prepare for takeoff instructions: *The Go-Girl Guide* will tell you everything you need to know to make the most of this hair-raising decade of transition.

PART I

Our Careers

1

"What the F%@#!!! Am I Going to Do with My Life?"

*T*he very first lesson of our great debut into adulthood is to ignore this question entirely, because it will haunt your consciousness throughout the decade. If you panic every time it disrupts your peaceful thoughts (which are rare anyway, so protect them as fiercely as you do that carton of ice cream you keep half-hidden from roommates in the freezer for emergencies), you will surely go insane. Besides, there's something I need to tell you right off the bat: Most of us won't know what we're going to do with our lives until our mid to late 20s, after we've had some work experience. And even then, the vision is still a blur.

In fact, only a teeny percentage of women can genuinely boast of having reached career enlightenment during their 20s. They are typically the same annoying bunch who have known without a doubt since second grade that they will become doctors, kindergarten teachers, or NASA scientists when they grow up. And don't you just loathe them?

I was definitely not of that breed. It took me four internships, ranging from politics to travel writing; several part-time jobs as diverse as teaching swimming to inner-city teens and recruiting Hmong translators for a multilanguage advertising agency; a countless number of rejections from full-time newspaper reporting positions; and a snail's-pace ascent up the editorial ranks of a national baby magazine (with periodic fantasies of getting an M.B.A., a master's in psychology, or a similar token of professional achievement) to figure out that what I really wanted to do was write.

Once that lightbulb *dinged*, it took a tremendous amount of encouragement from friends to actually quit my stable editing job and wade into the murky (not to mention financially ambiguous) depths of freelance writing. All along the way, I tormented myself with the question of where my career whims might ultimately lead. Sometimes I still think that all I want to do with my life is go live with orangutans in Sumatra, but I figure my fragmented ambitions will all harmonize one of these days. Isn't that what the 30s are supposed to be about?

In this decade, our task is simply to determine four career-related ambiguities: (1) what skills we like to use, (2) what field or industry gets us excited, (3) what type of lifestyle we'd like to enjoy (meaning how much money we want to make and how many hours we're willing to dedicate to making it), and (4) what type of work environment and style best suit our personality—for instance, whether we like working alone, in teams, for a start-up in a cyber-chic loft in a hip part of town, or in a corporate cubicle wearing conservative suits and spanning time at the computer between coffee breaks. Once we determine where we stand on these critical issues, the closer we will be to career enlightenment.

There are several strategies for helping us figure out these occupational unknowns, and we'll get to them in just a minute. But first, let's discuss a more important matter—the emotional chaos that dogs us relentlessly at the dawn of our careerhoods, threatening the very soul of our search for purpose.

THE SOUL-SEARCH TRAIN

Trying to figure out our purpose in life is like taking a long, bumpy ride on Amtrak, and word around the track is, the train doesn't stop until we retire. Besides being an unsettling thought in general, career ambiguity is hard for most of us to accept because it makes the 20-something emotional wreckage we're already carrying around that much heavier.

Unlike the more predictable decades ahead, the 20s are racked with stressful changes: leaving college and all our college friends, starting life in a new city, trying to find an apartment that we can actually afford and that doesn't have mice or roaches or sketchy next-door neighbors, moving back in with our parents (God forbid), falling in love (God, please), and taking all those life-altering risks that will forever change the course of our future. With so much change underfoot, even the most well adjusted among us can become slightly crazed, which is partially why the whole notion of soul-searching during this time is a very bad idea any way you look at it.

The emotional upheaval, unfortunately, doesn't come to a screaming halt when we get our first jobs (though, come to think of it, our introduction to the working world does make most of us want to scream). In fact, the anxiety about our future track continues right on through the decade at a steady pace, flaring up at times of career crossroads, like when we don't get the job/promotion we wanted, or when we wake up one morning and experience a rare flash of clarity in which we realize we'd rather haul trash than spend another day sitting beneath florescent lighting, staring at our screen saver and wondering what more important people are doing.

When we fall in love, another 20-something emotional whistle-stop, well, that too can add a chink to our track as we begin to imagine our future with a steady mate and (oh gosh!) babies, which may transform our high-speed bullet train on the fast track into a low-speed locomotive that chugs from home with caboose attached to hip. By the way, since the topic of motherhood and professionalhood is going to come up a few times in the next couple of chapters, let's get one thing straight: Women who want to dedicate their lives to raising a family are just as awesome and hardworking as those who want to dedicate their lives to a career or who want to attempt both, but the next few chapters mainly speak to the career-mode crowd. So, if professional enlightenment doesn't apply to you right now in your life, skip on over to Chapter 5, "Adventures in Couplehood," which probably will. The rest of us will catch up with you later.

Those of us who've been riding the soul-search train for a few years and are used to the bumps, the sudden stops, the backtracking, and, most of all, the characteristic turtle's crawl have learned several truths about career satisfaction. I'll attempt to narrow those truths down here in the briefest of sentences: Feeling intellectually challenged and having a good amount of responsibility in our first few jobs is key for soul satisfaction. Respect from our bosses and coworkers is right up there, too. So is feeling adequately compensated for our work (but don't hold your breath on that one). Working in a friendly and personality-conducive environment helps. Most of all, we must like doing the things we do. If you're not sure what drives your engine, try looking back at your past for clues to how you like spending your time and what has given you feelings of success.

Maggie, 29, director of development for a nonprofit volunteer center in Dallas, for example, realized through some of the volunteer work she had done in college that working for a nonprofit would bring her career satisfaction. So far, she says, it has: "I felt a connection with some of the fund-raising projects I was involved in at college, such as raising money for the Special Olympics and various philanthropy organizations on campus. These activities helped me realize how important it is for me to feel passionate about what I do."

Once you've taken stock of past glories, make a list of the top 50 things you like to do, suggests Marie, 27, of New York City, who has done her fair share of soul-searching in the three fields she's explored so far—consulting, fashion, and public relations. "The list helps identify what you value. Mine included making plans, meeting new people, putting out fires, and traveling, which helped me figure out that I need a job that's constantly moving and involves working with other people." The list and a quick assessment of our past glories are good starting points to figuring out the distant destination of your soul search. But if you need some extra help in getting on some sort of a track—and most of us do—the following are a few aggressive strategies worth pursuing.

THE CAREER PSYCHICS

I've never seen a psychic, but judging from what I hear from friends who have paid 10 bucks to get their cards read or palms interpreted, psychics can be delightful distractions from the rigors of life in an escapist kind of way. They can actually even be helpful in giving us a few things to ponder when we're at a crossroad. Likewise, career counselors—the palm readers of the professional world—are good sources to tap as we attempt to clear the haze that's clouding our career crystal balls.

As with a psychic, it would not be wise to base decisions about our future solely on what a career counselor sees in our stars, because he or she or the stars could be dead wrong. Besides, we alone have the power to know where our true calling lies. What's more, our calling is proba-bly going to change several times during our 20s. Forewarnings aside, good career counselors know the right questions to ask as we attempt to figure out what to do with our lives. They also know a great deal about all the various professions and fields that could possibly make good matches for our skills and work-related values. So, a few counsel-ing sessions are definitely worth considering at every stage of our quest for career enlightenment (although, good luck finding one as cheap as a 10-dollar psychic!).

If you are still in college or have free or discounted privileges to your alma mater's career center resources, by all means, take advantage of them. "That's part of what you're paying for at a university," says Beth, 29, of Washington, D.C. Now a trade association lobbyist and website coordinator, she admittedly blew off career counseling services when she was in school and spent her first job search unsuccessfully sending résumés to random advertising and PR firms listed in the D.C. yellow pages, which her dad's friend had photocopied and faxed to her. (She eventually got her first job, which she's had ever since, through an ad in the paper after she moved to the area.)

In addition to offering job search strategies, résumé critiquing, and emotional support in general, career counselors have all sorts of rituals and procedures for helping us figure out our calling. Some techniques can be helpful, while others are good for a laugh—something all of us desperately need as we make our first formidable moves in the world of work. The most popular venue of professional channeling is career assessment tests, including the Myers-Briggs Type Indicator, the Strong Interest Inventory, and the John Holland Self-Directed Search (SDS), which is available on-line (www.self-directed-search.com/).

These tests are designed to organize our disparate career inclinations (landscape photographer? earth sciences professor? fly fisherwoman tour guide?) and help identify patterns we may not be aware of, such as wanting to work with nature or instruct groups of people. Theoretically, the tests make it easier for us to see how our interests, values, personality, and skills might all fit together in one profession. Some even provide a few suggestions for potential jobs based on our preferred skills, ideal work environments, and working style.

These assessments may be good for getting us to think about our passions and priorities, but it's important to realize that they're not Magic 8 Balls. When I took them in college, one of my top occupational matches turned out to be the cheery job title of funeral director. I don't recall writer being on the list, actually. Let's move on.

INTERNSHIP INSIGHT

If you're still in school and you haven't done the work-for-free apprenticeship ritual, a.k.a. The Internship, *what are you thinking?* Get on it right away, because internships are one of the best ways for us to get realistic insight to the fields we're interested in and the types of work we like to do. They also give us experience with which we can fatten up our résumés when the time comes to hunt for a job, but I'm skipping ahead. If you are already out of school but stuck in a meaningless job, doing the temp circuit, or living off handouts from doting grandparents, you should consider getting at least a part-time internship in whatever profession intrigues you. If you must wait tables at night, work the early early shift at the local coffee shop (which will at least get you good and caffeinated for your long day ahead), or live with three roommates in a cheap part of town to support your explorations (as I did when I graduated from college and had a part-time job but wanted to do an internship at a U.S. senator's local office), go ahead and join the club. It's not as tragic as it sounds, especially when all your friends are doing the same thing.

Internships give us more of an opportunity to do non-assistant-type work than, say, an entry-level job (at least in theory). This makes them an excellent way to spend your early experimentations in nine-to-five living during this highly emotional time when our futures are so uncertain and our egos so fragile. More important, they often turn into real paying jobs. Shelley, 23, an associate editor at a fitness magazine in New York, got her first job this way: "When I was still in college in Tampa, I took on an internship at a local weekly magazine for about six months. Soon after I left, I heard of an opening for a full-time staff position. They were looking for someone who had five years' experience, but because I had interned there, they knew I could do the work, and they hired me."

When perusing the internship listings in the paper, from professional associations, or posted on the campus career center bulletin board, look for one that's related to either your major or the field you think you want to go into, so you'll get a realistic taste of the work involved in your field of interest, advises Judith Sommerstein, a career consultant and alumnae counselor at the University of California, Los Angeles.

Then, if you still have extra time to kill, do an internship that sounds fun but is completely different from anything you ever thought you'd want to do, suggests Ramona, 24, a law student in New York City. As an undergrad, she knew she wanted to go into law but had a gut feeling that she should try something different. "I volunteered at the local police department and helped set up a community-based family violence prevention program that improved police training and community education on domestic violence," she says. "That experience really developed my interest in criminal justice and race and gender issues. It gave me a focus for what type of law to pursue." As happened with Shelley at the fitness magazine, Ramona's internship also turned into a full-time job when she graduated.

Keep in mind that internships require a Zenlike mind-set; make sure you're in the right mental mode before taking one on. Otherwise, you will likely feel utterly resentful and bitter about the fact that you are working for free. This is more maddening if you are struggling financially, which we all are when we're doing internships, are we not? It can be excruciating if the internship turns out to be horrible and boring, which many do. During these times, remind yourself that an internship is part of the dues we have to pay to get a job that requires more intelligence than answering phones all day long. Then meditate on the fact that you're getting experience and references in return. Also, realize that 99 percent of all internships involve some assistance-type work. And finally, soothe yourself with the reality that the internship is not your real job and will probably end soon anyway.

Note: If you're doing *only* clerical tasks, you're clearly being taken advantage of. Talk to your supervisor, detailing what you'd like to do more of—attend meetings, take on your own project, interact with clients, or whatever. So that you'll look competent and professional, come up with a plan that lays out how your time might be more fairly spent during the hours you so eagerly and graciously devote to the company. You'll need this negotiating-for-more-responsibility practice for your first job. But there I go jumping ahead again.

OCCUPATIONAL GUIDEBOOKS

If you're clueless as to what jobs are even out there for those of us with zero or just a couple years of work experience, resist the urge to panic. All you need is to catch up on some career-oriented reading. This is not exactly pleasure reading (at least, it never was for me). The object is to get a sobering view of all those glamorous careers we see on nighttime TV dramas and consequently think (or hope) our first jobs will resemble.

The *Occupational Outlook Handbook* is a good reference book to start with. This resource, regularly updated by the Bureau of Labor and available in website form (http://stats.bls.gov/ocohome.htm), offers a detailed and, more important, *realistic* description of all the possible occupations that exist in the United States. The brief write-ups include a sketch of all the various jobs' typical working conditions; the type of training, degree, or qualifications we need under our belts to even be considered for them; how most people arrive at these positions and claw their way up the career totem pole; and what salaries we can expect for starters (needed for negotiating our compensation during the job search).

Industry-specific resource books are also worth a good flip-through in the business or career sections of most large bookstores. I found one called *Opportunities in Psychology Careers*, part of a series of career

The Myth of Higher Education

Unless you've taken time off between high school and college and gained real work experience to guide your academic pursuits, or unless your lifelong passion has been to enter a field that requires a technical or professional degree—such as engineering, computer programming, law, or medicine—college tends to introduce us to so many interesting ideas, ways of thinking, and disciplines that many of us feel more lost coming out than we did going in.

Truth is, the academic world and the world of work are separate universes. Most of us will end up taking jobs throughout our career that are totally unrelated to what we studied in school, especially if we earned liberal arts degrees. For that reason, if you're still in college and you haven't chosen a major, pick a subject that excites you, not one that's going to get you a good job, because the only jobs that are good are the ones we feel excited about. If you've always been drawn to creative disciplines, immerse yourself in them now. Use internships and part-time jobs to develop marketable skills for your résumé and to give you direction on how you might turn your passion for the arts, for instance, into a passionate livelihood. Don't waste precious college money on courses that will "prepare" you for the working world, because no college course can do that.

Graduate school won't help us figure out what we want to do with our lives, either. If you choose to believe the myth that it will, you may be in for a postdegree decade of debt and an identity crisis if, upon graduation, you *still* feel clueless about your future. If you're not sure what you want to do, take time off between academic programs to work in the field you think you'd like to pursue before jumping into bed with your books for another few years. And, by all means, really investigate the graduate programs you're considering and know exactly what you're getting into, advises Brenna, 27, of Washington, D.C. She went directly from undergrad to a doctorate program in English with visions of *Dead Poets Society*—type teaching, but she soon realized that she didn't fit into the culture of subspecialization and missed collaboration insanely.

Even if you are sure about the program and what you're going to get out of it, say many 20-something women who have earned advanced degrees, why not take time off to explore other options? Getting work experience will probably deepen your appreciation for the program and resources, as well as give you a tighter focus on what you want to learn. Experience may also improve your application for getting into a graduate program in the first place. One exception: If you know exactly why you're going to grad school and where the degree will take you, you're on full scholarship, or money is not an issue, then go for it! You've got nothing to lose.

books published by VGM Career Horizons, extremely helpful during my brief therapy-inspired desire to become a psychologist during my early-20s career-angst days. The book detailed all the various psychology-related jobs I might have enjoyed had I been willing to take out a gazillion more dollars in student loans and get a graduate degree in psychology. After reading this book, I was earnestly able (not to mention eager) to scratch psychologist off my careers-to-try checklist, because the reality of the job of a clinical therapist and the typically minuscule starting salary were nothing close to what I wanted to explore. I recommend picking up a copy of the book dedicated to whatever field you're considering—it can really help narrow your options.

If you're intrigued by a certain industry—finance, fashion, high tech, the environment—but don't know much about the companies within the field, skip on over to your library's periodicals or business section and peruse the myriad shelves of trade publications and industry magazines or newsletters. These will give you a sense of what jobs are available. And finally, read every article in your local paper that pertains to the fields that get your adrenaline pumping, taking note of recent industry trends, up-and-coming companies, and interesting-sounding people who are doing something you might like to do someday. You will attempt to get informational interviews with these contacts, which leads me to the next, and most crucial, step to take in your train ride to enlightenment.

THE INSIDERS

I mentioned that we all have glamorized images of certain careers. Lawyers, for instance, sing and dance in the office unisex bathrooms, moan about their love lives instead of work, and win every case. Emergency room doctors stay up all night working minor medical miracles and still look irresistible come sunrise. Undercover detectives investigate the most intriguingly sordid subjects and always manage to worm their way out of perilous situations with ease.

Unfortunately, real-world vocations aren't quite so exotic, but you won't know that until you get the "insider" scoop. Career transition strategist Joyce Scott, of Austin, says the fastest way for a woman to figure out if a certain career is a good match for her is to talk to at least three women in the field: one who loves her job, one who hates her job, and one who is retired. "Find out why these women feel the way they do about their work, and weigh their answers against your career objectives," she says. "The retiree will be able to tell you what critical skills are required for the job and what the position has been like for her in the long term."

As you approach the insiders, who might be friends, family members, professors, college alumnae, former coworkers, or sorority alumnae if you were a sorority girl, you don't necessarily need to set up a formal meeting, although doing so will give you good practice for interviewing when you start your job search. If you know exactly what to ask, a 10-minute phone call can offer just as much valuable insight. Here's a list of questions that those of us who've become familiar with this routine deem worth asking in order to get a candid picture:

- **What's your day-to-day like?** The idea is to find out what responsibilities you might have in a certain job (retyping your boss's memos or writing your own reports?), the skills you'd employ (researching? analyzing data? schmoozing?), and how you'd go about doing the work in question (via the teamwork approach or the alone-with-your-computer-in-a-generic-cubicle approach?) Note: If the insider you're speaking with is in a high position, be sure to ask what someone at your level would be doing day to day.

- **What do you like and dislike about your job and the industry in general?** Since you may get a bitter and disgruntled Linda Tripp–type answer from one insider, be sure to ask all of your insiders the same questions, but especially this one.

- **How did you get where you are today, and if you had it to do over, would you take the same route?** This is a particularly good source of insider scoop when you're thinking about your big-picture career strategy. For instance, if someone asked me this about the magazine biz, I would tell her to not do what I did (which is start in San Francisco at a magazine that had very little opportunity for upward mobility) but instead move to New York directly after graduation, because opportunities in the heart of the publishing industry are obviously much more abundant, as is the chance to move quickly up the ranks.

- **I've heard . . . (whatever it is you've read or discovered in talking to other people that you found interesting or discouraging about the profession). Has that been true in your case?** This is another juicy tidbit that you can't get from books. Just keep in mind once again that there are as many opinions as there are people you speak with, which is why it's a good idea to yak with as many insiders as you can for a more accurate, collective view.

- **I've read that the range of salaries for my level is. . . . Does that sound right? What might I expect after 2, 5, and 10 years?** Not only will salary reality help you determine whether a certain career path is right for you, but it will also help you negotiate a salary if and when the time comes.

- Which industry publications are the best sources of information for learning more about all the companies in this field? Start reading these immediately.

- How has your career been affected by starting a family (if applicable)? Babies may be far from our thoughts when all we want right now is a challenging job, but if family is definitely in your future, it won't hurt to find out how progressive an industry or a particular company is concerning working mothers' needs. Just a thought.

- And if you're gearing up to start a job search, go ahead and ask a few specific questions about the company your insider works for: How is your company different from others in the field? What is the office culture like (formal, flexible, young, conservative, cutthroat)? What three top companies in the industry might be ideal to start with and why? Would you mind reviewing a copy of my résumé? Of course, ask for feedback on your résumé only if you are sold on the profession. No sense wasting anyone's time—especially those who are helping us out.

While you're interviewing for information, keep track of your conversations. Also ask for addresses so you can send brief notes of gratitude. A thank-you note is an important gesture, since these contacts will become the base of your networking once you have a sense of what you want and are ready to embark on an actual job search, which I know I keep mentioning, and I promise I'll get to that nightmare ritual in just a bit.

As you interview, tune in to mentorship potential—a contact with exceptional vision and wisdom in this field—whom you might call in the future for advice on particular job opportunities and decisions. Mentors are invaluable resources for those of us just starting out, so don't be shy about asking for future contact. Says Joyce Scott: "You're not asking them for a long-term engagement. You're just asking for advice. Tell the person that you were impressed by him or her and would like to know if you could call again if you have any more questions." Better yet, ask for the person's E-mail address; in most cases, using E-mail makes quick requests for advice less intrusive and easier for everyone involved.

The worst someone could do is say no, and I doubt anyone will. If your contacts are like most of us who've been in the working world a few years, they'll appreciate the opportunity to reflect on their careers, brag when appropriate, and most of all, take a nice little deviation from normal afternoon tedium.

THE TRIAL-AND-ERROR APPROACH

After finding a comfortable seat on the soul-search train (remember, you'll be hanging out here for a while), visiting with the career mystics, and engaging in various consultations with the insiders, there comes a point when we have to give up the idealistic notion of knowing where we're going and just hop onto the track—*any* track that seems like a reasonable route to the unknown future. This is because when all's said and done, the most effective way to get in touch with our purpose in life is through good old-fashioned trial and error. By that, I mean trying out a profession to see if it fits (and if it doesn't, getting on another track). Don't dwell in the train station waiting for divine intervention to tell you where to go. That takes too long, and, believe me, you'll get antsy— especially when your friends pass by waving.

"Women are often so afraid they're going to pick the wrong job or graduate program that they become paralyzed and aren't able to make any type of career move," says Judith Sommerstein, of UCLA. "But the 20s are the time in life when women should be taking risks. It's OK to fail; that's how we find out what job is right for us."

Claire, 27, of New York, is a perfect example of successful track hopping. Having graduated from college with a degree in psychology, she started her soul search as an intern at the French consulate because she wanted to explore possibilities in foreign diplomacy. When the red tape and office-bound reality of that glamorous-sounding job hit home, she switched tracks and took a job as a sales associate at a high-end clothing store. This position was fun at the time and gave her needed space to gear up to her next career move, which was into the accounting side of advertising, a field that had always intrigued her.

There, she quickly realized that she was on the wrong side of the business and wanted to do something more creative with her career, so she took a year off to explore acting (a lifelong passion), supporting herself with hostessing jobs at night. When acting didn't give her the fulfillment she was looking for, she applied to graduate school in psychology, which she had always imagined herself doing one day. However, after her applications were in, she realized she'd miss the creativity that she also wanted in her professional life, so she went back to advertising. This time, she got a position in the creative side of the business, where she could combine all of her passions and talents—sales, dramatic persuasion, and psychology. And that's where she is now, loving her career choice.

But all her track hopping wasn't without insecurity. It's taught her a lesson, she says: "When I started working, I had very little trust that I would make the right decisions and had lots of fear and anxiety over what I should do. I felt that I had to make the 'right' decision, and that provoked all kinds of anxiety as I was making changes in my career choice. I learned that the most important thing you can do is be true to yourself from the get-go. If I could do it over again, I would trust in the process of life more and not feel the deep need to control everything. I would have more faith in my decisions. The fear of making the wrong decision—and dwelling on that fear—was far worse than when I started taking steps into the unknown."

Beyond the obvious fear of failure, going after our passions can be difficult for other reasons. Parents, for instance, may want to play a heavy-handed role in our occupational decisions, which can be especially distracting if they're still helping out with the rent now and then. The pressure to pursue a certain career may be overt ("When are you getting a *real* job?") or a little more subversive ("Do whatever will make you happy, but it'd be great if you became a doctor."). Hard as it may be, do yourself a favor and don't listen to them.

"You have to find something that makes *you* happy," says Shelby, 28, who works in the distribution department of a San Francisco clothing company. "After I got a graduate degree in speech and hearing science, I took a sales job at a clothing store. My family and friends kept asking me why I was *there* instead of doing something related to my degree, and that made my confidence plummet. I told them that I had made smart decisions in the past and I was making the right choice now, too." Two promotions later, Shelby works with planners and merchants distributing clothing to stores around the country, using the research and number-crunching skills she developed and loved using in grad school.

The moral is: Trust your decisions, no matter how many eyebrows are raised about your choices. If your parents threaten to cut you off financially if you don't pursue the career choice of *their* dreams, take a temp job and skip directly to Chapter 11, "Family Knots," where we'll discuss how to deal with such parents. This may be hard and could possibly stir up a lot of familial conflict—after all, our parents *just want what's best for us*—but we're the only ones who really know what might make us satisfied in the grand scheme of life. Besides, they will get over their need to control in due time, so take the leap as soon as you're ready.

One last thing: If you get on the wrong track for whatever reason, don't freak out. We all get turned around at some point. Calmly look for the next detour, and trust yourself that you'll make the right move as soon as you can see the new and better track. You will eventually find the right route. Take Gabrielle, 28, who works in retail in Chicago. She knew she wanted to be involved in the fashion industry since she was 13 years old, but all through college and the postcollege career scramble, she felt compelled to pick a career that was considered more professional. She majored in history, did some political internships, took a state government job, then went to law school for a year. "I completely lost a sense of what I wanted to do," she says. "It wasn't until I quit law school and took a clothing retail job that paid $7 an hour, and realized that I *loved* my job, that I felt it was OK if I wasn't a doctor, or a lawyer, or a superwoman businessperson—I was happy!"

And so will you be. Until then, relax, sit back, take in the scenery, and keep your eyes on all the tracks. You'll eventually find the right one for you.

2

The Job Hunt

*M*ost of us undergo several job searches during our 20s, but the first one is always the most gruesome, mainly because we're not prepared for the amount of work and emotional energy involved in actually snagging a position (cross our fingers, hope to be reborn famous) that will set us on the track toward a fulfilling career. Looking for a job, in fact, is just as exhausting and nerve-racking as looking for love. Some of the same criteria even apply. Similar to the way we seek out a mate who has common interests and values, we must look for a job that captivates our intrigue and challenges our growth. And, like a good significant other, a company that's fun, that's inspiring, and that likes to spend money on us is always a bonus.

Luckily, there are a slew of rituals to help guide us through the hunt. We'll get into the specifics in just a minute, but first, let's talk briefly about our mental health, which is just as much a player in the search for a job as a well-endowed résumé.

TUNNEL OF HORROR

To reinvoke the soul-search train from the previous chapter, the job hunt is like being in a black tunnel. We can't see the end light and are surrounded by eerie noises and things popping out at us as they do in haunted house train rides. In fact, the job search is one of the most frightful legs of the soul-search journey, dredging up as much emotional anguish as trying to find a mate. Olivia, 27, an associate engineer at an engineering consulting firm in northern California, describes the process most appropriately: "Looking for a job is a nightmare. It's got to be one of the worst things on the face of the Earth."

Part of the reason why the search is so horrible is that it typically lasts much longer than most of us are comfortable with. Companies may take months to hire (for unexplainable reasons, since we're obviously perfect candidates!), but their hesitations don't mean we are not qualified to do the work in question, and they certainly don't mean we're incompetent. Cold feet on their part could indicate a number of conditions: (1) The company is not in a hurry to fill the position; (2) The loser who is hiring never gets anything done anyway, so the stalling is absolutely no reflection on our capabilities to do the work; (3) The hiring powers that be want to feel out the pool of candidates very slooww-lllyyyy because they enjoy torturing us. The best advice is to prepare for all the uncomfortable feelings that go along with waiting, because everyone feels anxious, depressed, and rejected during the hunt. As with dating, if you don't accept the emotional upheaval as part of the ritual, self-confidence will plummet to an all-time low. Don't worry, I have a few tricks for keeping morale high. So, pay attention because you will need them.

If you're feeling anxious, identify the main source of your stress, and then design an immediate plan for curbing it. If lack of money is your main concern, join a temp agency or get a part-time job while you're looking for full-time work. You don't want to feel financially forced to accept a position that's clearly not right for you. Temp jobs are an excellent way for you to get a sense of what's out there in the world of work and add real experience to your résumé. (They are also a great way to expand your pool of potential friends, especially if you are new to an area, because you'll get lots of exposure to all sorts of new people.)

If anxiety results from waiting for companies to call you back, invite you in for an interview, decide if you're right for the job (all this while you're trying to ignore that burning question, "Why would they want to interview other people when I'm perfect for the job?"), fill your free time with activities that make you feel good about yourself. Keep your mind active too, advises Elena, 23, a marketing assistant in San Francisco. "I spent two months between my first two jobs, and my confidence was shot," she recalls, "so, I started volunteering at various organizations. Knowing that I was helping people and making a difference kept me from dwelling on my job search. If I hadn't had that, I would have gone crazy."

GETTING SET UP

Emotions aside, one of the first challenges of the hunt is finding all the sexy, available jobs out there. That is where the insiders from the previous chapter become so important. They can introduce us to the hiring gods. Who knows, they may even be able to set us up for an interview or two. Like being set up on a date, getting a lead through a personal referral, as opposed to responding to an ad in the paper or going to a massive job fair (the singles bar of the working world), puts us at a tremendous advantage. Not only are most opportunities passed on through word of mouth, but also, having a personal connection makes us look a thousand times more desirable than all the rest of the desperate job-seekers of the world, simply because we've passed the "she's cool" screening test.

That's why networking with insiders, as revoltingly power-suitish as the word *networking* sounds, is one of the components to career success and therefore a skill that we must all learn to perfect early on in our 20s. There are five essential rules of networking:

Rule #1: Everyone You Meet Is a Potential Contact
Simone, 28, started her career doing political events planning, progressed to paralegal work, and is now a law student in New Orleans. She got her first job through a chance encounter, she says: "After I graduated from college, I moved to Washington, D.C., and met a woman at a party who worked on the Clinton campaign. She helped me get a

volunteer position for the Democratic National Convention, and three weeks later, I was on the payroll." As you meet potential contacts, be gutsy about asking for job leads, advises Claire, a creative assistant at a New York City advertising agency and another fearless networker. When she was working as a sales associate at a high-end clothing store and wanted to get into advertising, she began asking clients she was assisting if they knew anyone in the advertising business she could talk to. One of her clients turned out to be the president of a small advertising agency, and she ended up getting a job at his company.

Rule #2: Leave No Lead Unturned

Always follow up on those job leads that your friends, relatives, and insiders pass on to you, no matter how depressing or corny the job sounds, advises Melissa, 28, a public relations consultant for a children's art project in a Houston hospital. She got her first PR job through a referral from her uncle. Her take: "Even if the lead turns out to be for a job that's not right for you, the contacts you make could lead you to another position that's really great." (These scenarios are sort of like those blind dates where we end up falling for the roommate instead.) Besides, if you don't follow up on the leads, you'll feel like an ingrate (and may look like a flake) when your friend, relative, or insider asks if you acted on the suggestion and you have to say, "Not yet," tail between your knees.

Rule #3: Get Your Friends to Help Spread the Net

Think of networking as a communal project: the more workers you can get involved in your net, the more job leads you'll catch. Ask your close friends to do some of the networking for you. If they meet someone who's in the field you're dying to join, ask them to mention amazing *you*, and to pass the person's name and number on to you.

Rule #4: Work the Associations

Join your local alumni organization and professional associations for the field in which you're interested. Better yet, volunteer for a committee position, which will give you extra access to valuable contacts, while simultaneously plumping up your résumé. These contacts are especially useful if you're in the field already but are looking for your next move. "Some companies will pay for your membership, so take advantage of that and go to the meetings and social events," says Beth, 29, a trade association lobbyist and website coordinator in Washington, D.C. She belongs to a couple of member organizations. "It's a great opportunity to meet other people in your field, and they can actually be kind of fun."

Rule #5: Do the Maintenance Work

Keep in touch with contacts who are helpful during your job search, advises Olivia. "I kept a folder with names of all the people I spoke with when I was looking for my second job out of school. After six months or so, I contacted them again and said, 'It's been six months, and I'm still interested in your company . . .' Sometimes, after a certain amount of time went by, your contacts forget how they originally came to know you, so you become more like an old friend instead of a pesky person who wants a job."

VIBING THE COMPANY

At risk of taking the job-seeking/mate-seeking analogy too far (but I can't resist, so indulge me), the next stage in our job search is to start scamming, and by that I mean checking out, head to toe, the companies we think we might be interested in. You could also call this step "researching," but that's so boring. Vibing is one of the most effective strategies of the whole job search, because if we don't thoroughly check out the companies we're planning on contacting for an interview, the results—having nothing in common, no shared interests, ill-matched values—could make a first meeting (and any long-term commitment that might carelessly result) a disastrous affair, not to mention a waste of time, which I'm sure you don't have to spare.

The process of vibing is not complicated: Start by asking the organization's human resources or public relations department to send you company information. Or try searching for information about the organization on the Internet (I've listed a few good sites in the "Go-Girl

Corporate Matchmakers

Headhunters typically recruit for upper-management positions and, therefore, don't usually seek out those of us who are unproven in the working world. But there are recruiting agencies that do specialize in sending less-experienced applicants like us to companies that are hiring. They're worth giving a call if you need the extra support. Many large corporations also have in-house recruiters in their human resources departments.

The thing to keep in mind about corporate matchmakers, though, is that they are often trying to meet a quota or earn a finder's fee if a company they refer you to ends up taking you on. They tend to hype up every job opening they send your way and to take little concern whether it's right for you, so don't get caught up in their enthusiasm— and they *are* some of the most enthusiastic professional Cupids populating the planet. Personally, I think they are great for getting you in the door, but that's about it. I tend to lack respect for them otherwise for my own reasons:

When I was working as an editor, I was approached by an in-house recruiter for a beauty editor position at another magazine. As part of the publishing industry standard hiring process, I endured a series of interviews and completed a massive edit test that involved writing a couple of articles, editing another, and coming up with all sorts of story ideas. After weeks of leaving those "I'm just checking to see if you've made a decision, because I'm still interested" messages, I was flatly rejected. A few weeks later, I received a call from the same recruiter who had contacted me about the opening a month before to tell me about a job that was *perrrrfect* for me—beauty editor for the same magazine I'd been losing sleep over. After I told her that I'd been interviewing with them (upon her referral!) for the past month and was rejected, I heard a mad shuffle of paper, followed by a curt explanation that I didn't have the right background for that position. Just goes to show how attuned they are to the hiring gods!

Resources" section at the back of this book) or in local industry resource directories, which are available in many libraries or at your city chamber of commerce. These directories offer descriptions of many of the companies in your area that are affiliated with a particular industry. Those industry trade magazines and newsletters I mentioned in the previous chapter are also worth perusing for potential companies to contact. So, knock yourself out.

As you read descriptions of the various companies' missions, client lists, products, employee culture, and overall goals, your objective is simple: to determine if you like what you see, especially in terms of company values. "To determine a company's values, look for clues in the company myths, rituals, customs, and heroes," advises Beverly Potter, Ph.D., author of *Overcoming Job Burnout: How to Renew Enthusiasm for Work*. "Pay attention to the buzzwords you keep coming across or hearing in interviews. These words can also tell you about company culture." For instance, if one of the rituals is wearing navy suits (something to note among female employees during an interview) and you keep reading weird military phrases in company literature, it's safe to conclude that the office is conservative and run with an iron grip. If, on the other hand, one of the office customs is to host happy hour every Friday afternoon in the company "billiards room" and words such as *teamwork* and *company spirit* keep popping up in the office lingo, the work culture promises to be a chummier place. Remember, if you don't vibe with the values that your sleuthing has uncovered, you will be miserable in any long-term engagement. Take this part of the job search seriously. Knowing exactly what you're getting into can prevent unnecessary heartache.

PAPER COQUETRY

The cover letter and résumé are to the job hunt what flirting is to the search for a mate. Like those pay-attention-to-me comments we so casually toss into the conversation when we meet a guy we want to impress (you know the kind: "When I was backpacking through Alaska by myself . . ." or "After I graduated Phi Beta Kappa . . ."), these ritualistic offerings have but one purpose: to seduce a prospective employer into calling us up for an interview.

For best results, we must carefully tailor our written flirtation to appeal to each unique job we seek. For instance, if the position we want happens to be in the wine industry, it's to our advantage to include that summer we spent pruning grapevines in Napa, but not the following fall when we protested the wine industry's exploitation of migrant grape pickers. Otherwise, our seduction will backfire and our effort to secure an interview will be about as fruitful as trying to charm an environmental activist whose only mode of transport is a one-speed bicycle by flashing him the keys to our gas-guzzling SUV.

This does not mean we have to completely revamp our résumés each time we pursue a job. "The different versions of your résumé and cover letter can have the same content, but they must have a slant that appeals to the company," says Shirley Weishaar, director of Mills College (my alma mater!) Career Center, in Oakland, California. "This insider approach shows an employer that you know what they're all about and what the job entails, and that you've got the perfect background to fit in." It worked for Simone when she moved to Washington, D.C., to get a taste of politics after she graduated from college: "I created two résumés—one with a Republican slant and one with a Democratic slant—and got interviews with both political parties."

The slant approach also helped Brenna, 27, get into the door of the health-care consulting firm she works for in Washington, D.C. "My cover letter was tailored to the company. I read all of the organization's PR material, talked to three people who worked there, and then wrote the company using the language I had picked up," she says. "The position was very writing intensive, so in my letter, I said that based on everything I had read about how much the company valued rhetoric and ideas, I believed I could add value because I had spent the past three years in graduate school studying how composition happens. Then I articulated my own theory of writing. When I walked into the room at my interview, the guy looked at my cover letter and résumé, looked at me, and said, 'You are exactly what we need.'"

Since the sole purpose of the cover letter is to entice prospective employers to take a peek at your résumé, it must explain (1) why you want to work for that particular company; (2) how your past experience and skills make you the perfect candidate for the current opening (cite examples); and (3) how your unique talents and personal attributes can benefit the company's mission. This is where the vibing you do at the front end of the job search becomes so important. Otherwise, how will you know what the organization's mission is and whether or not you'd make a good match?

There's just one catch: If you can't honestly address these three points in your cover letter, cross this job possibility off your list. You are not right for the position, you probably won't get it, and if by chance you do receive an offer, you won't like your job, so don't waste your time, girlfriend. Move on to greater expectations!

Once you've created a seductive cover letter, your goal is to design a head-turning résumé to deliver the punch, sealing an invitation for an interview. Stick to the chronological format, with education or training certification on top, advises UCLA alumnae counselor and career consultant Judith Sommerstein. "This signifies that you're a recent grad, which makes employers less critical that you don't have much work experience." Include your major and any pertinent classes or training that may relate to the job you're after. Also mention any study-abroad programs you have participated in (these *always* get attention from prospective employers), special honors, awards, and academic achievements. If you were a stellar student, don't be shy about your GPA. Brenna, for instance, manipulates her résumé so that the first thing anyone sees is her 4.4 out of a possible 4.0 undergrad GPA. Who wouldn't do a double take with such brazen evidence of a hard worker (the real sex appeal of our paper coquetry)?

Next, adhere to the guidelines you read about in all those résumé-writing books. List previous employment, starting with your most recent job, including the names of the company or organization you worked for, your title or position, and the dates of employment. Follow these listings with a description of your accomplishments, using impressive active verbs. If you have tangible statistics or percentages that cite your achievements on the job, include those as well. Also highlight any accomplishments in previous internships, volunteer work, or leadership positions you held on campus or with community organizations. Add

The Scannable Résumé

Many companies electronically scan (scam?) résumés to weed out ones lacking the key words or phrases mentioned in the job listing. Those that include the specific skills and experience requirements are then reviewed by real people. So, if you're responding to a listing of an opening for which you'll likely be competing against hundreds of other job seekers, call the company and ask if they require scannable résumés. If the answer is yes, do a little cosmetic surgery on your traditional résumé:

- Include the same buzzwords used in the job description, especially those relating to specific skills.
- Use standard typefaces, such as Courier, and a 12-point font, with no italics, boldface, underlining, tabs or indentations, or graphics.
- Saved it in ASCII text.
- Printed it on plain white paper—background patterns may confuse the computer.

any membership affiliations you have and a brief description of other special talents or personal attributes that might make you more attractive. Finally, list all your skills, including the computer programs you know and foreign languages you speak—that is, if you can do so honestly. When I embarked upon my first job search, I put "fluent in German" at the bottom of my résumé. After all, I had taken three years of the language in high school. As bad luck would have it, one of the women I interviewed with was from Austria, and when she saw my little point of braggery, she proceeded to interview me *auf Deutch*! Needless to say, I wasn't offered the job.

THE FIRST INTERVIEW

If our paper flirtation was a success, we've aroused our prospective employer's interest and convinced the reader that we have the background and appropriate skills to perform the job in question. What remains to be seen, and what can be determined only in an interview, much like a first date, is whether our personality and interaction style match the company's. Employers also, obviously, want to make sure that what we said in the résumé is true, which they will attempt to confirm through a series of nerve-racking questions.

Our goal in the process (besides trying to woo the company) is to check out our potential supervisor and working environs as thoroughly as we would a potential mate. "Finding a culture you'd like to be a part of is the most important thing to look for in your first job," says Beverly Potter. "You can learn skills in any environment, but if you want to be successful, you need to be at a place in which you'll flourish and go on to do better and better. A good fit sets up a cycle of success." Following are some interviewing strategies that those of us who are familiar with this whole song and dance have learned along the way.

First Impressions Mean Everything

Our foremost objective during a first meeting is to present our prospective employer with the image of us at our professional best, as defined by that position. That means that every anecdote we recount, every experience we elaborate upon, every vision we conjure of ourselves must illustrate that we are a leader, manager, organizer, motivator, creator, adventurer, or whatever other personality characteristic or skill is required for the job. "This is not a time to be humble," says career transition strategist Joyce Scott. "There's no humility in business."

Learning to toot our horns or, should I say, blow our own whistles (remember, we're still riding the soul-search train) takes practice. Doing so effectively requires an acute understanding of what the company in question is looking for. So, if you somehow managed to snag an interview without vibing the company, do so before the meeting. You won't be able to convince a prospective employer that you're the answer to the company's problems if you aren't clear what the company values, how it is responding to industry trends, who the nasty competitors are, and what the company's mission or philosophy is all about.

The next step is to work on style. Though it seems that companies are becoming increasingly casual, you can't commit a fashion blunder by wearing a suit. The suit doesn't necessarily have to scream corporate bore, but it must look professional as a token of respect for the person you're meeting. If you're interviewing for your first job, you probably don't have a closet full of suits to choose from. But if you're lucky, you have a same-size friend who can lend you at least two, because you will likely have several interviews (on different days) with a company that's serious about hiring you. Until you get the job, which may indeed turn out to be California Casual as far as style is concerned, in which case any interviewing suits you buy may disappear further and further into the depths of your closet, you may be living off your credit card, and you don't want to overuse the plastic. Until a steady paycheck is on the way, and until you know what you'll need, avoid buying. If your friends aren't the right size, purchase a generic black jacket (that can work with a matching black skirt or pants), and alternate between the two "suits," wearing remarkably different shirts beneath to disguise the fact that you're too broke to elaborate on professional attire.

Etiquette is another component to a good first impression. "If you don't have a lot of work experience, the way you conduct yourself in the interview will really stand out," says Barbara Pachter, business communications trainer and coauthor of *The Prentice Hall Complete Business Etiquette Handbook*. "Start the interview with a handshake. There are gender components to this tradition, and as a result, some people won't extend their hands to women, so make sure you do—it's a sign that you're a professional." Then, pay attention to body language.

Sit up straight, and look your future employer in the eye, advises Simone. "It's hard to do, especially with older businessmen. I have to consciously think about it, but it shows that you're honest and that you have the ability to deal with them." After every interview, shake hands again (another sign of professionalism), then go home and immediately ravage a bag of chips to console yourself over the whole horrendous charade.

Get Personal (But Not Too Personal!)

"Getting a job ultimately boils down to chemistry," says Mills College career counselor Shirley Weishaar. You can be the smartest and most qualified person, but if your personality, values, humor, and style don't mesh with the company culture, you're not going to get the job. This is often one of the cruelest aspects of the job search, because rejection is so damn personal! (Don't worry, we'll talk about rejection momentarily.) Truth is, if your heart doesn't beat to the company pulse and your interviewer picks up on that before you do, the person is actually doing you a favor by not hiring you, because you would likely hate your job almost immediately, anyway.

Hopefully, all that previous vibing you've done on the company has given you some insight that you would fit in and enjoy working there. But what you probably don't know from your research is whether or not you would like your potential boss. This is an important consideration, because if you don't have a reasonable manager who's interested in your ambitions and who wants to help you advance in your career, you may come to loath both your boss and your job. So, during the interview with your potential boss take notes on how he or she is making you feel: confident? inexperienced? belittled? challenged? Then, pay attention to your gut reaction. Remember that no matter how much you want or need the job, a supportive boss is key to your having a positive initiation into the working world.

If you begin to feel the interview heading toward a conversation rather than a question-and-answer-session, then relax a little, says Brenna. "Not only is the interviewer getting answers to the questions, but he or she is also getting to know you, which is a good sign." If, on the other hand, your interviewer begins to hone in on your skills, you should become concerned and try to relate to your interviewer in a more personal way. Sneak in comments that indicate what you value, what you've found challenging in the past, what your goals are, and what your work ethics consist of.

Your objective is to give your potential employer a sense of who the real you is, as opposed to the résumé you. One caveat, advises Elena: "You don't want to blab about things that aren't related to your career goals. If you're going to work with the person who's interviewing you, there will be time for personal stories later on."

Don't Freak Out if You Bomb a Question

We all fumble during interviews. When it happens, keep your cool and try to immediately erase the blunder from your short-term memory. You can fret and sweat later, but your primary concern at the moment is to make your interviewer forget your weird answer and dazzle him or her with other encouraging attributes about yourself. When I was searching for my first job out of school, one the of the many interviewers I met along the way asked what faults I had that might inhibit my performance. I went blank. Completely blank. Couldn't think of one bad thing to say about myself. So, I sat there looking like an arrogant idiot, getting increasingly more red in the face. I ended up assuring him that I did have faults . . . but could I get back to him on that one? The rest of the interview was a disaster. Not only had I practically soaked through my shirt, but also I was distracted from the following questions because I was still trying to come up with a fault in the back of my mind and had lost every ounce of confidence I had when I walked in.

If you're asked a question that throws you for a loop, don't stutter or spew out a ridiculous answer as I did. Stop and say, "Let me think about that question for a minute." You will appear thoughtful and reflective, and your answer will definitely be more articulate than mine. If you're asked a question about the industry or business you don't know the answer to, admit your ignorance up front. Then, immediately ask what the answer is, so you'll appear conscientious and eager to learn.

If you got the interview despite the fact that you lack a certain skill or degree that the job announcement listed as a requirement, not to worry. Unless the law requires specific certification, many companies are willing to overlook certain "requirements" if you are right for the job in other ways. But just in case, prepare ways to spin potential questions that are directed toward your lack of appropriate background. For instance, if you lack a graduate degree, which the job listing said is required, point to the work experience you've had instead, and give examples of how that experience has prepared you for the job you seek. If you don't know a certain computer software program, highlight all the other technical skills you know, and give examples of how quickly you picked up the last technical tool you mastered.

Whatever you do during the interview, don't make up an answer that you're not sure about or tell an outright lie, advises Nicki, 24, a study-abroad program coordinator in a New Orleans. "I once told a half-truth in an interview and got caught," she admits. "The job was selling textbooks to college professors, and before the interview, I was supposed to have gone around to a few campuses and approached professors about these books. I did actually call a few of my old instructors, but I didn't really make the rounds. During the interview, they kept pressing me about it, and finally it came out that I hadn't really gone on campuses. They wouldn't let up on me. I was so embarrassed, I counted the minutes until the interview was over."

If you feel that you're blowing it, keep in mind that there are bad interviewers out there. If you're not making a connection, it might be because the interviewer is a non–people person. Don't automatically assume that you're the one who's making this the most uncomfortable experience since the invention of underwire bras. Or you might just be having an off day. "Some interviews, you'll be really nervous and have no rapport at all, but it's not the end of the world. The more interviews, you go on the more you realize that," says Shelley, 23, an associate editor at a fitness magazine in New York.

And if you really screw up on an answer, you can always redress it in a thank-you letter following the interview. That's what Brenna did when she thought she had blown one of her interviews. "I sent the guy I interviewed with the typical 'Thank you for your time' note, but I also said that I actually think I messed up answering one of his questions and wanted the opportunity to reanswer it in the letter," she says. She got the job.

Arm Yourself with Questions

"It's important to come prepared with a set of questions," says career consultant Judith Sommerstein. Not only do companies expect this, but also you'll appear uninterested if you don't have any. What to ask? Anything concerning job responsibilities you're not clear about. For instance, what percentage of your job will involve administrative work, since most entry-level positions include clerical tasks. Of course, you don't have to let on that you don't like this aspect of the job, but it's better to know now than after you've accepted the offer. Find out who you'll report to, and ask if you can meet everyone you'll be working with directly (this is to assess potential personality conflicts or supervisor overload). Also, find out if you'll have advancement opportunities, what the typical time line for promotions at your level is, who determines promotions and salary increases, and how often your performance will be reviewed. You'll want to know all this before you accept a job that may lead nowhere or give you a bad taste of the working world, which is not a great way to kick off your career.

Keep in mind a few things that you don't want to ask upon first meeting. "One woman I interviewed with asked me if I had any questions, and so I asked about benefits," recalls Shelley. "She really pulled an attitude and said, 'You don't need to know about that now.'" Typically, salary and benefits inquiries should be posed only after you receive an offer for the job. In the early stages of interviewing, you want to appear to be concerned only about whether this job is a good career move for you (even though money and benefits are the foremost burning questions in our minds).

Remember References

Come armed with a few names of praising professors, academic advisers, former bosses, coaches, volunteer coordinators, or anyone else who's not related by blood or last name and who will tout your achievements. Let your references know ahead of time that they may receive a call from your prospective employers, and remind them of a few projects you worked on, your level of responsibility, what you accomplished, and how your contribution influenced the project or company. No matter how much of a star you were in the past, these people may have forgotten all you've done for them, so be sure to remind them of your wonderful deeds.

End with a Good Note

After each interview, write a perky thank-you letter either handwritten or typed. This functions similarly to those "I had a *great* time last night" phone calls you make after an incredible date. Take the opportunity to, once again, explain why you're the best candidate for the job (if you decide you want it, that is), and send it that day. Then, go on with your life and plan a million other activities to keep your mind off the phone, because you'll probably not hear back from the company for weeks. Even so, check in every week or thereabouts after the interview, letting them know you're still available and interested. It can't hurt.

THE REJECTION FACTOR

Rejection, as I mentioned before, is one scary thing most of us experience during our job search, much as we do in the world of dating. Me, I was Rejection Queen during my first (and second, and third . . .) attempts to find a job. (Notice, I work for myself now, where I will be rejected no more!) Truth is, rejection is actually a good thing. If we are rejected for an opening, it does not necessarily mean we lack competence; it simply means that someone else out there was more qualified or better suited temperamentally for that particular job. It is not our loss, as much as it feels like it. It is simply the route we didn't take.

The best way to deal with rejection is to confront it head-on. If you don't get a job you interviewed for, be gutsy and find out why. It may be that you were the second choice, and that the job went to someone who had five years more experience than you or an insider connection. The interviewer may also be able to offer you tips on how you might improve your candidacy (remove an uncomplimentary reference from your list, get more experience in a particular area, tone down the self-important attitude during future interviews).

That said, the real reason to find out exactly why you were rejected is that doing so will make you feel more in control over the situation. That, in turn, will make you feel at least a bit better about yourself. If you're like me, the knowledge will also prevent you from conjuring up all sorts of horrible reasons why you were not chosen, all of which are probably highly exaggerated in your mind.

One last thing. During this time of professional uncertainty, many of us are vulnerable to depression. Now is the crucial time to get emotional support from friends—especially those who are going through the job search too, who will be great for commiserating—family, or anyone else who can remind you how great you are.

CONSIDERING COMMITMENT

Two of the greatest thrills in the 20s are having the person who makes your stomach do flip-flops ask you to date exclusively and having the prospective employer you've been trying to bait offer you a job. Both call for breaking out the champagne, and both require serious consideration.

If you've gotten an offer, it's always wise to take a few days to a week to mull it over if you have any reservations. In case you're wondering, it's totally acceptable to tell a prospective employer that you're delighted by the offer and would like a few days to think it over. Don't make excuses; don't apologize. If the company reps pressure you to tell them yes or no because they need to wrap this sucker up immediately (meanwhile, they've been sitting on your application for weeks), try to compromise on a deadline and then ask yourself if you really want to work for such a nightmare organization.

There are two reasons for thinking over the offer: One, if you've been interviewing elsewhere and would prefer to work for another company that's been stringing you along, letting the preferred prospect know about the offer may get the decision maker to act, advises Jacki, 28, a San Francisco sales associate in telecommunications software. She received five offers after she informed all the companies she was interviewing with about the first offer she'd received. Two, you want to make certain that this job will be a stepping-stone for you, even if you're not sure about your ultimate destination. Our first few jobs must be challenging and allow us to learn new things; otherwise we'll be miserable. High-paying, high-profile, great-benefits jobs that lack intellectual challenge and opportunities for growth are the occupational equivalents of tall, dark, and handsome: though seductive, they won't make us happy in the long run.

So, when you're considering an offer, ask yourself the following key questions:

- Will the job be a challenge?

- Will I have a respectable amount of responsibility?

- Are there opportunities for leadership?

- How many hours will I be working, and am I OK with this?

- Will I *love* at least 60 percent of the day-to-day tasks?

- Do I believe in the company's product/philosophy/values?

- Is this a supportive and stimulating environment?

- Do I fit in with those who work here?

- Have I met everyone I'll be working for, and was there mutual respect?

- Can I learn from my prospective boss?

- Does my supervisor communicate well and respect me? Or intimidate me?

- Is there an opportunity for advancement? What's the time line?

- Where will this job lead?

- Can I live with the amount of money they're offering? If not, is there any room for negotiation? (Remember, you must have enough to cover rent, student loan and credit card repayments, living expenses including basic essentials, clothes, entertainment, and a vacation at least once a year—but ideally twice, because you will need it, and the obligatory trip back home for the holidays isn't always the most ideal form of relaxation.)

NEGOTIATING THE OFFER

Most entry-level salary offers are negotiable, unless, like government jobs, they are based on a fixed scale. Negotiable offers are generally determined by a variety of factors, including how much the company has allotted for the position (which is usually based on professional standards, the size of the company, and its geographical location, with smaller companies in rural locations getting the butt of the deal), your level of education, your experience, how well you've convinced your interviewer that you're more desirable than the other applicants, whether you have a competing offer, and what benefits are also being offered, such as a health-care plan, paid vacation days, and company matching in a 401(k) plan. These benefits must be weighed when you're deciding if the compensation is adequate, since they are expensive for the company to provide and are valuable assets for us, even though we feel we should be entitled to them all, plus a rocket salary.

....

Go-Girl Guidance "Silence is one of the best tools for negotiation," says career transition strategist Joyce Scott. When you've been told the salary range and then been asked how much money you'd like, state the amount, and then shut up," she says. "Give anyone a few minutes of silence and he or she will talk."

....

Typically, your interviewer will ask you at some point during one of the many get-togethers how much money you'd like to make. Try not to answer with a number. I was told by several more experienced job-seekers when I was hunting for my first job that the person who names a number first is the one who loses. And you know what? I've tested that theory, and it's valid. That's because once you name a number, your interviewer will either agree to it, or may even talk you down (rarely does an employer try to talk you up). So, blow over any requests for an exact salary until you've received an exact offer to consider. For instance, you might say: "I'd like to be fairly compensated at market value for a person with my experience and skills, but I'd prefer not to discuss numbers until there's an offer on the table. Right now, I'm more interested in determining if this job will be intellectually challenging and provide me opportunities to learn and grow." (*Blah!* it may sound, but it works.)

Once you've got that offer, you'll have more bargaining power. Your future employers have made it clear that they want you and are probably eager for the hiring ordeal to be over with, which gives you the upper hand. As you consider the compensatory pros and cons, keep in mind that most entry levelers are shocked by the paltry amount our first jobs typically pay. "So many recent grads—especially those with liberal arts degrees—think that because they spent so much money on their education, their starting salaries should be between 35K and 40K," says

Shirley Weishaar. "But that's just not the norm in nontechnical fields. Everyone has to start at an entry-level base and pay his or her dues."

Before you begin the negotiation, you must know three things: (1) what most companies are willing to pay for whatever position you're haggling over, (2) what you'd like in an ideal world, and (3) what you're willing to settle for. All that research that led you to the grand finale of an offer should have given you some idea of what you're worth in the marketplace, but if you forgot to find out (or avoided the topic when talking to insiders), call your contacts back. Find out what the typical salary range is by talking to people in the field who *really* know how much you can ask for, suggests Claire, who has compared salaries with coworkers at her level and has always come out ahead. She attributes this result to having the guts to ask for a higher amount than was offered. "Remind yourself that you're worth what you're requesting, and ask for the higher amount with confidence," she says. "So many women don't realize that what they want is within the realm of what they can get. If you're confident, people will believe you're worth what you're asking for."

Roses and Chocolate

Benefits, the nonmonetary employee compensation, are the roses and chocolates of the hunt for a job. Here's what every girl should know about some of the typical (and often confusing) benefits that many companies offer. Keep in mind that the specifics will vary tremendously among companies. You can get the details from human resources or the office manager.

Health Care

Companies aren't legally required to offer group health care, but if they do, you may be able to choose from several plans, including the traditional indemnity plans, managed-care HMOs (health maintenance organizations), or PPOs (preferred provider organizations). You will likely have to pay a percentage of the premium, which will come out of your paycheck, and, depending on your specific plan, a deductible or copay-ment when medical services are needed. Some companies let you set up a pretax spending account, in which a predetermined portion of your salary is funneled into a special account before being taxed. You can then draw upon this fund to cover any out-of-pocket medical expenses (or dependent-care costs in some cases) that your health-care plan doesn't cover. The benefit of having this spending account is that you won't be taxed on any of the hard-earned cash you must spend on health-related causes. The downside is that if you don't use the money in this fund by the end of the year, you'll forfeit it to Uncle Sam, so cal-culate wisely. Also, if your company offers dental coverage, go ahead and sign up; the cost is nominal and also comes out of your paycheck. Your teeth will thank you for it.

401(k)

The 401(k) is a tax-deferred retirement fund, which means part of your salary, before being taxed, is placed in a special retirement account where you can invest your money with the idea of making it grow. This is one benefit that every woman should take advantage of if offered. (You can read more about why in Chapter 13, "Financial Chaos.")

The immediate benefit of starting a 401(k) plan, depending upon how much of your salary you designate to the plan (and there are lim-its determined by the Internal Revenue Service), is that it may help lower your annual income taxes, because your taxable income will be less. Some companies may also match your contribution—dollar for dol-lar in some cases—which is basically giving you free money. But keep in mind, some employers won't give you access to the amount they match before a certain period of time has passed, a condition known as *vesting*. If you decide to leave the company before you are vested, you may lose the amount they gave you. This little catch is obviously designed to give you incentive to stay. If you do decide to leave, how-ever, you'll always have full ownership of the money you, yourself, con-tributed to the plan.

The long term benefit of a 401(k) plan is that when you retire, you will have some savings to fall back on, since our country's social security system is now looking pretty bleak. If you leave your company, many 401(k) plans can be rolled over to another company's retirement savings plan or to an individual retirement account (IRA).

Stock Options

If your company's stock is highly valuable (or could be in the future), stock options are a great benefit. They enable you to purchase this stock usually without paying a commission or broker's fee. If your company offers an employee stock ownership plan (ESOP), which, as its name suggests, means that company stock is owned by the employees, the company will either sell its stock to you at a discounted rate or give it away within a tax-qualified plan. Like a 401(k) plan, an ESOP is typically transferable, so you can roll these tax-deferred stocks into an IRA if and when you leave the company.

Profit Sharing

Profit sharing is another type of retirement benefit in which company profits are distributed among employees through individual tax-deferred savings accounts. Like ESOP and 401(k) plans, profit sharing plans are typically portable if you leave the company, and the only contribution that you as an employee must make is to help ensure that the company is profitable by doing the best job you can.

Vacation

There are no federal requirements for a company to give employees paid vacation days, but this is one benefit that can often be negotiated when you receive an offer. The standard paid vacation for the first year is one week, and two weeks after that, but many enlightened companies offer more. Some businesses require that you accrue vacation days, meaning that you work a certain number of days at the beginning of each calendar year before you can take time off, but department managers are often willing to overlook these policies.

Bonuses

Extra money is always, well, a bonus. But the reality of a bonus is that this money is taxed just like the rest of our salary. A $500 bonus can be a huge disappointment once the Fed sinks its teeth into it. If you're negotiating for a signing bonus, be sure to specify the after-tax amount you desire; otherwise, you'll wonder why you wasted the brain power.

Education Funds

Some companies reimburse employees for work-related classes or workshops and, in some cases, tuition for a related professional degree. Take advantage of these. The money is there to be spent, and a lot of older employees with families don't have the time to avail themselves of this opportunity. It's an excellent way to keep up with new technology, refine certain skills, or get that M.B.A. you've been thinking about, all of which will help you get to the next level in your career.

3

The Entry-Level Initiation

*I*f you've made it to your first job, you deserve a big, fat congratulations! Now you can jovially look back at your fearless endurance aboard the bumpy soul-search train and at your skillful maneuvering throughout the hunt. (But remember, you'll board that sucker many times in life, so consider your first job a brief recess in which to stretch your legs.) Maybe you can even laugh about those hideous times. (Oκ, wishful thinking.) The bottom line is that you're employed, and that means one thing: You rock!

You are now entering a new phase in life, an initiation into the world of work. Like most other initiation rituals, this stage doesn't automatically entitle you to all the benefits and celebrity you clearly deserve. Unfortunately, most employers still regard us as initiates into the nine-to-five "tribe," just a grade above the desperate-job-seeker status we only recently escaped. In fact, most of us will be treated as neophytes until our first promotion or second job, whichever comes first. This usually takes about a year and a half to two years, and it's a grueling couple of years due to several factors.

For one, we often don't know what we're doing at work and, consequently, screw up more than we're used to, which could make anyone uncomfortable and insecure. Adding insult to injury, many supervisors put us through a rigorous hazing process that involves making us do brainless tasks for hours on end simply because we're at the bottom of the totem pole. (It's also my secret suspicion that such bosses, due to reasons for which they should promptly seek therapy, are testing our dedication to the tribe by subjecting us to emotional torture, with overtime beyond the call of duty and no reward system to make it all worthwhile).

What's more, many of us feel unproved, undervalued, and isolated from the more stimulating work that intrigued us about the industry in the first place, which doesn't help our morale. The working world annoyingly refers to this initiation period as a time in which we must "pay our dues," after which we are fully accepted as members of the working elite. The whole thing smacks of robbery, if you ask me.

But let's get a little perspective here: We *are* in our first jobs, and our first everything is always emotionally traumatizing. Besides, there's one thing worth knowing and repeating to yourself during moments of work-related anguish: Our first jobs are nothing like our future careers.

Our first jobs are simply a modern adaptation of an ancient ritual left over from the apprenticeship days in which we must appear to worship the elders who exceed us in rank and experience. Through countless interviews with career experts and 20-something women who have mastered the initiation, I have uncovered a few tactics that will not only help guide you through this formidable rite of passage, but also help you get ahead. Let's discuss them, shall we?

THE INDUCTION

The first few weeks of every new job are critical for establishing our role (and forming our attitude) within the tribe, so there are a few things to think about even as early as the first big day on the job. Many companies offer official training programs through which experienced tribe members pass on the details of our job to us. These organized programs are exceptionally groovy because they give us a fixed role during those first few awkward days of not knowing what to do with ourselves (and not knowing anyone in the office). This is the best time to ask as many questions as possible, so don't be afraid that you'll pose a stupid one and look unqualified for the job. If you don't inquire now, you won't learn how to conduct all your daily rituals or tribal customs, and two months down the line, you *will* look unqualified for the position, as well as reek of incompetence. Heed my advice and ask, ask, ask.

If you weren't given a formal job description upon being hired (lack of direction is common, by the way), write one up within the first few days of employment based on everything you were told during the interviewing process regarding what you'd be doing, including your daily, weekly, and long-term responsibilities. Also write down the names of all the people you work for and associated duties, including how your job contributes to their goals. Then, go ahead and throw in your own personal objectives just to remind your supervisor(s) that you have some.

Next, ask your main boss for a 10- to 15-minute meeting to go over the description. Since our performance on the job is typically based on how we measure up to this goal-oriented description of our purpose in the tribe, it's imperative that everyone involved agrees upon how we're supposed to be spending those long hours between our morning cappuccino and happy-hour splash.

There's one more benefit to having a written job description: This little piece of paper is our arsenal if senior coworkers try to dump their dirty work on us, a common occurrence among entry-level initiates. Getting stimulating and challenging work from the higher-ups is one thing, but if an elder coworker who we are not supposed to be working for wants us to write a tedious report here and fax a document there, or do more than an occasional favor, forget about it. Stick to what's on your job description, and don't accept their requests, advises Nicki. Now a study-abroad program coordinator at a New Orleans university, she has had such an experience with senior coworkers. She explains the pitfalls: "Standing up for yourself is hard to do when you're just starting out and so grateful to have a job, but it's important to be firm. After doing meaningless tasks for people you're not even supposed to be working for, you'll find that they will start expecting help from you all the time, and you'll be taken advantage of." And that's the last thing we need when we're just starting out.

CULTURE SHOCK

Blending into the working culture is a bit like trying hard not to look like an American tourist in Paris, where our alien dress and foreign behavior will earn us only snotty looks and zero respect. Because we are unproven initiates into the working tribe, we must attempt to assimilate into the culture quickly so that we'll at least *appear* to be full-fledged members. Doing so will earn us more reverence among the higher-ups and accelerate our initiation process. This in turn will help soothe our egos, which are usually pretty deflated by the fact that we're at the bottom of the totem pole.

Assimilation begins by adhering to the company dress code, which shows our elders that we are capable of representing the tribe with the image they'd like to project. If we don't reflect that image, we certainly won't have the opportunity in the near future to project it. Note: If this image makes you gag, you're probably working in the wrong culture; so, you might want to consider such things as tribal garb, superficial as they may be, before you start interviewing for your next job. Also note: Older coworkers—men and women (but in my experience, it's always been the women)—may scrutinize your attire and make comments about your dress and/or figure if what you're wearing is form fitting, and sometimes even when it is not. To appear professional and to avoid such comments, don't wear clothing that your mother might object to (or at least cover up the strappy tanks and fitted dresses with a business-type jacket whenever you're in the office).

The second step in acclimating to the nine-to-five tribe is to follow office behavior protocol, which either is based on common etiquette sense, like knowing not to tell your boss what you *really* think of her management style, or is easily picked up by observing those who are already well assimilated into the culture, like noting that the best way to get a point across in a group meeting is by interrupting whomever is talking (unless, of course, that person is the company president). However, there are two rules of work etiquette that career experts say many of us 20-something women, being novices in the world of work and the more emotional and socially preoccupied gender, are particularly vulnerable to violating. Let's briefly discuss them:

Rule #1: Don't Take Personal Problems to Work

If you do, you might as well have "RECENT GRAD" tattooed across your forehead, because no one will take you seriously. What makes sticking to this rule hard is that personal dramas often slip out when we're least expecting them during this hazardous decade of high trauma and hormonally induced outbursts. Our PMSing roommate, for instance, calls and accuses us of eating her chips the night before (which we didn't), so, naturally, we're defensive about the accusation, and others overhear. Or we break up with our boyfriend and run into him having lunch the very next day with a very unhip chick, and we're shaken beyond repair. Or our mom calls us right before a serious deadline and complains that we never have time for her anymore, and then wants us to do her a favor.

These are all perfectly valid reasons for any girl's emotional wattage to blow a fuse, but we mustn't let our professional associates become aware of the internal drama sabotaging our emotional health. "No one is paying you for your emotions," says career transition strategist Joyce Scott. "When you bring problems about your boyfriend or friends into the office, you're giving your coworkers and boss the impression that you have poor judgment, or that you're not responsible, or that you can't handle the pressure. Those impressions aren't going to get you a promotion." All in all, the best thing to do when such mental meltdowns occur—and they will—is to calmly head toward the bathroom, covering your face with a tissue (scream, "Allergies!" if anyone asks), and break down in the privacy of a stall. Then, compose yourself and get on with the rest of the day, knowing that you can work out your angst with the punching bag at the gym or purge your woes that night while floating in a bath of optimism-inducing essential oils.

Rule #2: Avoid Office Gossip

As juicy and entertaining as talking about your coworkers can be during a sluggish week, don't get tangled up in the vine. "A lot of young women believe that they will be liked if they participate in office gossip, but gossip is damaging," says career coach Laura Berman Fortgang. "You may fall out of favor with the gossips, and then they'll talk about you." This, of course, is one more reason why you should keep your personal traumas far away from office ears.

Talk to coworkers about work projects, movies, and the nontragic events in your life, but don't discuss hectic personal problems that could (and probably will) be leaked into the rumor circuit. If the buzzing starts in your presence, try to change the subject or simply say, "You know what? I'd rather not talk about the transvestite that was just hired in accounting." So you won't appear alien or antisocial, turn the focus of the discussion back onto the gossips. Ask them something about themselves—their projects, their family, their hair. If they're like most cluckers, they won't notice the abrupt shift in conversation, so hungry are they for conversation that will boost their own esteem.

BONDING WITH THE ELDERS

Making affiliations with those who are high in the ranks of our nine-to-five tribe is a time-honored strategy for rising above the lower tier, where most of us initiates are begrudgingly paying our dues. Befriending the higher-ups is not something most of us find particularly natural, but we must learn and practice if our ascent out of entry-level hell is to be a relatively quick and painless climb, since promotions come from above. "Younger crews tend to clump together at events and meetings, which is not necessarily bad, but it's important for young women not to cling to a clique all the time, or they will be labeled a young counterpart and possibly be taken less seriously," says Fortgang. Of course, that doesn't mean we should boycott friendships with our peers—after all, we've got to have *some* fun at work, or we will go crazy—but it does mean that we need to make an effort to forge bonds with the higher-ups as well, intimidating as it may be to strike up a conversation with someone who (a) is busier and more successful than we, (b) has a granddaughter our age named Bunny, and (c) couldn't care less about our personal career aspirations.

One way to break the ice with a higher-up you'd like to get to know is to volunteer to work on a project with him or her. Such an undertaking will enable you to work closely for an extended period of time, which will give your superior ample opportunity to get to know you and your brilliant talent and vision. Offering to assist an elder who's under deadline or going on vacation also will give you an opportunity for personal interaction that you might not otherwise be graced with. Not only do such affiliations with experienced coworkers make our day-to-day duties more stimulating, but also, higher-ups are great sources to tap for professional feedback on our ideas and work. This informal evaluation is especially helpful if the critiques we normally receive from our supervisor(s) are next to nothing, as is often the case when we're stuck in the entry-level bunkers. "If you develop rapport with the people you work with, they'll be more open to sharing tips with you, so it will be easier for you to learn and succeed," says Beverly Potter, author of *Overcoming Job Burnout*

The connections we make in the office inevitably help us advance our careers in the long run, too. If our coworkers leave the company for a better opportunity at another firm, for instance, we've instantly gained a valuable connection at a new company if and when we decide it's time to move on to bigger and better professional challenges. If a bond forms between you and an elder, there's also a good opportunity for a mentorship-type relationship to develop, and we all know how much that can help us in our careers. We'll talk about mentors more, but first, an important caveat.

Do Not Bond Too Deeply (If You Know What I Mean) with Coworkers of the Opposite Sex

Sure, more and more companies are condoning office-sprung love, as long as the extraprofessional relationship doesn't interfere with work, and one of you doesn't supervise the other. And with such long hours on the job, how else are we ever going to find a mate? But before you leap into the lap of the babe in the cube next door, be aware that there could be disastrous side effects to dating someone who you must see and interact with every day.

If the relationship status leaks into the stew of office gossip, it could conjure up weird jealousies and ill feelings among your coworkers, especially if you break the rules and work directly under your office-born lover. On the other hand, if your romance is kept a secret, it may conjure up weird jealousies and ill feelings within yourself, especially if your midnight cowboy ignores you during the day, flirts with other coworkers, or is in the unfortunate position of having to tell you what to do. And if you can't take the closet romance (or him) anymore and decide to break the whole thing off, or worse—you get dumped!—the breakup-aftermath fiasco will be in your face eight or more hours a day. You'll be emotionally screwed until one of you leaves the job.

There are, of course, exceptions. Molly, 27, a human resources director in Philadelphia, for instance, discretely dated her manager (who is now her husband), with hardly any problems. Her advice: "Totally separate your personal from your professional lives, and keep your emotional egos outside the office door."

THE ULTIMATE ELDER

Ahhh, the fabled mentor. Most companies, unfortunately, don't anoint mentors to guide us through our initiation. This is too bad, because most of us could use the extra advice, insider tips, and feedback— especially if we're working in traditionally male-dominated professions. While the women's movement, thanks to our moms' generation of pioneers, has opened up so many opportunities for female initiates, we all still face inequalities, especially in terms of salary compensation and advancement. Sexual harassment and gender discrimination also proliferate in the world of work, particularly, it seems, for those of us who just got here. And none of this makes the initiation any easier for us.

That's why finding an inner-office adviser, ideally a woman, who can share professional knowledge and advocate our advancement up the ranks is key to kicking off our careers successfully. An in-house mentor is also great for giving us perspective when entry-level angst begins to take over our better sense. Nicki's mentorlike coworker, for instance, once saved her from a passionate decision to quit when one of her bosses persisted in asking her to do demeaning tasks that weren't part of her job: "I typed up a letter of resignation and gave it to her to look over," Nicki recalls. "She put it in the shredder and told me to think about it." Through the help of another supervisor, she was eventually relieved of her duties for the egomaniac who had no respect for her job position.

Because most offices lack established mentorship programs, the majority of us will have to seek them out ourselves. Approach an experienced coworker (even if her experience exceeds yours by only a few years) and ask if you can meet with her periodically to get feedback and career advice, say Cynthia, 23, who has three mentors at her job, running the public service department in public interest law at a Boston law school. She advises: "Explain your expectations and suggest lunch once a month to discuss what you're doing."

If no one in your office has the time or desire to mentor you, don't take it personally. Seek a professional adviser elsewhere—a former professor, a past internship supervisor, one of the many contacts you encountered during your job search, or an affiliate at a professional organization. Some professional associations have established mentorship programs in which younger members are matched up with experienced workers.

TRIBAL SPEAK

Learning to communicate like a successful tribal member is like picking up a new language for many of us, especially if your only experience in exchanging ideas and information is through gabbing with friends or dissecting complex and esoteric concepts with professors who are masters of elaboration themselves. Of course, the language you must learn depends on where you end up working, but according to some career experts, there's one universal truth: Relaying information in a clear, concise manner is necessary to our success, because our manner of communication is one of the most immediate ways by which our bosses and coworkers evaluate our competence on the job.

"The way we communicate gives people insight into who we are and how we think," says executive career coach Lois Frankel, Ph.D., author of *Jump-Start Your Career*, who has done research on women's credibility in the workplace. "Women tend to explain themselves more than men. We're apt to give long-winded explanations, which has the effect of muting our message and making us appear more insecure. The more words you use, the more you soften your meaning and the further you distance yourself from the person you're speaking to."

Frankel coaches women to practice speaking to colleagues about work-related subjects in short, crisp sentences. Here's an example she gives: If you've got a great idea, don't cushion it by asking your boss if she might have time, at her convenience, to maybe listen to a couple of suggestions on how to approach project such-and-such. Instead, tell her: "I've got a great idea for tackling that project: we can do a, b, and c." Also, suggests Frankel, when you're asked a question (such as what time you'll be done with a certain report that's already late), give the bottom line first—"It will be done by 4:30 P.M."—instead of explaining why you haven't yet completed the report (because your necessary sources didn't call you back until 3 P.M.). According to Frankel, "This forces you to immediately address the question and relay the most important information up front. After you've done that, you can provide the who, what, where, when, and why."

One last thought (there are so many!): Don't do what many women are apt to do—take the blame for mistakes you aren't responsible for, like missing the FedEx messenger because your boss gave you the stuff to mail one minute before the final pickup, or not being able to turn in a memo on time because your computer became possessed and is currently being tranquilized by the technical support people. "Women are constantly apologizing for things that are not their fault," Frankel says. "When we take the blame and say we're sorry all the time, we're diminishing our credibility and power."

RISING THROUGH THE RANKS

Besides learning a few new skills and doing what our job descriptions dictate, most initiates have one thing on our minds: rise above entry level ASAP! Not to be the bearer of bad news, but here's a reality check about the whole promotion process: You will probably be ready for a rise in rank long before the tribal elders deem you worthy of rising. In fact, you may have to prove that you possess the knowledge and skills to do more advanced work by taking on all the higher responsibilities a good six months before you receive an official promotion with raise.

This, at least anecdotally, is often the case. So, get over bitter feelings and outrage about this particularly cruel aspect of the initiation right now. There's not much you can do about it except perhaps watch the evening news, which will convince you that you've got breast cancer *and* that some politically turbulent nation in Southeast Asia will soon nuke the entire globe, thereby diminishing the weight of your own pathetic work-related neurosis. That said, there are a few skills—or "arts"—that, when perfected early on in our careers, can greatly assist our effort to get ahead.

The Art of Assertiveness

Being assertive is not exactly a behavioral trait most of us were taught growing up. Although this is changing somewhat for our little sisters' generation, with competitive sports now considered cool among young girls (thank you, Mia Hamm!), many of us were raised to perfect opposite behaviors—to compromise, collaborate, and above all, think about others before ourselves. Boys, on the other hand, often have had more opportunities through aggressive sports and through a socially prescribed acceptance of boys' aggressive natures to practice the art of assertiveness early on. That preparation ultimately helps them succeed in the world of work, where aggression—as in seeking more responsibility—is the means to moving ahead. So, the first step in rising through the ranks is to learn how to aggressively seek more responsibility if you haven't yet mastered the art.

The simplest way to get more interesting work is to push for it from everyone in the office, which is something I did at my first job as a magazine editorial assistant. It was a horrendously clerical position in which I had so much free time that I was amazed the company even hired me. After telling my boss point-blank that I felt completely unchallenged, I got the green light to seek more interesting work from other departments and coworkers. Within a week, I was fact-checking articles from the magazine's research department, editing the magazine index (a completely brainless task, but better than sitting at my desk waiting for my boss's phone to ring), and writing articles for various editors. Conclusion: The quest for better work is entirely in your hands. "You have to take responsibility to ask your boss how you're doing and to get more work," agrees Maureen, 28, who works in PR in San Diego. "If you don't say anything, you may go through a whole day of doing nothing. People will let you just sit there if you don't speak up."

If your boss is reluctant to allow you more challenging work due to unsupported fears that new assignments might compromise your present duties, ask for more responsibility on a trial basis, suggests Simone, 28, who has worked in political events planning, done paralegal work, and is now a law student in New Orleans. "Show up early and stay late if that's what it takes to get more interesting work," she says. Once you've passed the trial, you'll probably get more permanent duties.

As you amass new responsibilities, always clear the extra work you take on with your boss. And whatever you do, don't disregard the mundane tasks you were originally hired to do, advises Olivia, 27, an associate at an engineering consulting firm. "A lot of us have the tendency to blow off the little tasks in our job that we don't like doing, but if we do our work well, people will notice and give us more and more responsibility." No matter how much other important work you're taking on, if you don't perform your primary responsibilities, you will not be rewarded for the extracurricular achievements you've mastered splendidly.

Another tactic for getting more responsibility is to develop an expertise. Simone reports: "When I was working as a paralegal, we did a lot of securities work. During some of my research, I came across a securities website, downloaded the information, and made a booklet for the partners at the firm. After that, everyone thought I was an Internet guru, so I always got research assignments to do on the Web." She offers a word of caution about attempting to take on more work: "Be selective about what you take on. Only work on something that makes a visible change in the office. You want to be sure the extra work is going to take you to the next level." Don't do what many women, according to executive career coach Lois Frankel, fall into the trap of doing—volunteering for behind-the-scenes projects that won't give them the necessary skill level or visibility to get ahead. Remember, this is *your* extra time and effort, so make sure all the extracurricular duty is high profile and, above all, that it counts.

The Art of Self-Promotion

Another skill many of us aren't particularly savvy about practicing in our daily lives is self-promotion (although you probably have some inherent knack at it since you need it to get a job in the first place). The ability to toot our own horns is essential to rising through the ranks, because no one is going do it for us.

There are countless ways to self-promote without sounding too braggadocious or annoying; here are a couple of low-key tactics worth absorbing immediately:

1. **Ask for critiques**. When you finish a project, ask your supervisor for a 10-minute critique of your work. To your supervisor, you will appear conscientious and eager to improve, while what's really going on is that you're forcing him or her to acknowledge what you're working on and how well you're doing, which will keep your work and progress in the forefront of your boss's mind.

2. **Casually mention your greatness**. At least once a month, initiate informal conversations with your head boss and mention the projects you're working on and boast of your achievements—even though doing so feels very unnatural. For instance, you can say, "Hey, did you hear that I . . . ?" If you don't sing your own glories, your boss may never know about the amazing work you're doing. This becomes even more important if your head boss is not your supervisor, because (shocker!) your immediate manager may not pass on all the details of your recent contributions and ideas.

3. **Don't downplay your achievements**. This is something women, in particular, are apt to do, says Frankel. "If someone compliments you on a job well done, don't respond by saying that you were just lucky or at the right place at the right time. That diminishes your power,"

she says. "Instead, say, 'Thanks! I worked really hard for that, and I'm very pleased with the outcome.'"

4. **Let people know when you're doing them a favor.** Being socialized as helpers, many of us are used to bending over backward to assist others and not receiving any of the credit. This posture doesn't help our mission to rise above the ranks. If someone asks you to help out with something extra, let the person know in a low-key way that you're going out of your way to help, Frankel advises. For instance, if someone drops an expense report in your box at 4 P.M. and wants his check processed that day, let him know that you're going above the call of duty to help: "Gee, it's four o'clock. It's going to put me behind schedule, but I'll stay late and make sure this is processed today, since you need it." Whatever you do, don't tell him that the favor is no problem, or you'll get endless future requests *and* zero credit for your exceptional dedication.

5. **Use your reviews for ultimate promotion.** Use the formal review process to keep your boss further informed about all your accomplishments and to push for more responsibilities that will prepare you for next level. Before each formal review, write down all your successes since you last discussed your performance, and present your boss with a list of your short-term and long-term goals. Don't be afraid to use these formal meetings to ask outright where your job is heading. Says career transitionist Joyce Scott: "Tell your supervisor, 'I'd like to talk to you about my career progression. My reviews have been excellent. Where is this job leading?'" You'll appear ambitious to your boss, and you'll get a better sense of what the company has to offer you.

6. **Jump on in-house opportunities to get ahead.** One of the weirdest realities of the whole promotion process, in my opinion, is the fact that we have to ask or apply for promotions. Call me ignorant, but when I was going through my career initiation, I had naively assumed that promotions were natural rewards to which we were entitled for doing good work, similar to getting academic honors at

school (not that I ever did, but a girl can imagine). Turned out that's just not the case in the strange rituals of the working world.

"All of my past promotions had an interview process," says Maggie, 29, director of development for a nonprofit volunteer center in Dallas. "Each time, I had to meet with the department heads and discuss my skills and explain how I would improve the department." If there is an opening in the office, take advantage of your insider position and talk to the person who's leaving, suggests Beth, 29, of Washington, D.C., a trade association lobbyist and website coordinator. "When I found out about an opening in another department, I asked the woman who was leaving for advice on interviewing with her boss. She told me what they were looking for and which strengths to emphasize. That helped me get the job."

The Art of Negotiation

Learning how to negotiate is another ticket to success in the world of work. This communication skill makes us better equipped to convince the higher-ups to give us a raise, anoint us with a new title, send more stimulating projects our way, agree to a more flexible schedule (in the event motherhood calls), or allow us to go on an extended vacation (in the event we decide we want to learn how to scuba dive in Costa Rica for a month).

In the same way we negotiate our starting salaries, getting additional perks on the job requires knowing two things: what we want and what's reasonable for us to ask for. If what we want is a raise (and who doesn't?), we will need to show evidence that what we desire is a reasonable amount to request. Contact the human resources departments of competing companies, local professional organizations, or the *Occupational Outlook Handbook*, which I mentioned in Chapter 1, to get an idea of the general pay range for employees with similar experience and skills. Many career websites also have general salary scales to help figure out your worth, and I've listed a few in the "Go-Girl Resources" section at the back of this book. If our salary is, in fact, short of market value, this knowledge will help fuel the effort to get more money.

The next step is to prove to our employer how valuable we are to the company. Otherwise, why would the honchos care if we're underpaid or we leave to go work for the competition? "Make a case for yourself," counsels Stephanie, 26, of San Francisco, who has always been able to finagle more money from her employers (her first raise was $6,000). "Find out how much it would cost the company to replace you (what others in your position in the industry are making, how much it would cost to hire a recruiter to fill your position, plus the cost of a temp for the meantime). Next, remind your manager of your expertise, which a replacement won't have and will have to be trained for. Then, if you can, put a dollar amount on some of your specific accomplishments."

She cites her own experience: "When I was negotiating for my first raise, I reminded my boss of certain events that I had planned, which the company would have had to hire an events planner for had I not stepped in. Then I pointed to specific jobs I had worked overtime to complete, which saved the company from having to spend money on a temp. The thing to keep in mind is that negotiation is a business deal. Walk in with confidence, know that you're worth what you're asking for, and don't approach your boss when you're emotional or defensive. Remember, you can get another job, and you need that attitude while you're making your case."

The Art of Advancing

Once you've gotten that first promotion, your world will change. You have passed the initiation and are now considered a valuable member of the working world. As you enter the brave new territory of an "experienced" worker, keep in mind that if you've been promoted within the same department, ego-trippy coworkers may come to you with requests to do things that you used to do but are no longer responsible for. Try not to accept this work—even if you're not busy and can do it. No matter how much you like the person, it's important to set the record straight from the beginning that your job has changed and you're no longer doing your old duties. Refer your coworker to whomever has taken over your old task.

As you explore your new status, be sure to get (or create) a clear-cut job description of your new responsibilities so that everyone will know what your promotion entails. Then enjoy your progress, girlfriend. You're on your way to a brilliant career. Before we put this chapter to bed, however, let's discuss just a few more issues we can expect to face.

THE I HATE MY JOB SYNDROME

Job hatred is an office-born illness that most of us catch sometime during the early years of our initiation. The sickness typically comes and goes in bouts; nevertheless, we feel like hell when it hits. (I've been told we get relapses throughout life, but they *can't* be worse than our first exposure!) Symptoms include gut-wrenching anger and resentment from being overworked, undervalued, and underpaid; extreme feelings of worthlessness and plummeting self-esteem; stress-related ailments, such as stomachaches, headaches, acne, and muscle tension; and, for some, weight gain or loss. The cause of this syndrome may vary, and in order to recuperate, we must deal directly with the source of our distress. There are typically four:

Cause #1: A Lame Supervisor

Maybe it's our age, but it seems as if most of us have outrageous bosses at some point during our 20s, and most of us, being new to the working world, also don't quite know how to deal with them. A demeaning boss not only will make our days miserable but also often has the uncanny ability to deplete every ounce of self-esteem within us.

Take Nicki's boss, for instance, who once asked her to shrink down the entire *New York Times* to five by five inches so he could hide the paper in his Bible to read during the church sermons his wife dragged him to. Or take 26-year-old lawyer Tory's former boss, who berated her with condescending insinuations that she could never do real estate law because women are "retarded with numbers," *and* who had the audacity to ask how she could be "so smart and so fucking stupid at the same time." Then there are the ego-trippy bosses who dump a stack of papers on our desks at a quarter to six and expect the documents to be completed (a job that will take hours) by the time they take that first sip of coffee the following morning. And let's not forget the maniacal corporate-climbers who are so protective of their positions that they won't delegate any interesting work to us—or give credit to our accomplishments when credit is due. Finally, there are the bosses who have convulsive-like fits when we make the most innocent of mistakes. These are the worst of all.

As much as we'd all love to scream, "*I hate you!*" at such supervisors before repeatedly slamming an office door in their faces, a more professional approach would be to communicate our dissatisfaction and attempt to change the situation. For instance, if a boss has the habit of talking to you in a demeaning way, tell him or her: "Previously I've stood here when you yell at me, but your behavior is not reasonable. I'm leaving the room now, and we can talk when you can do so without yelling at me," suggests career coach Laura Berman Fortgang. "In these incidences, the only chance you have at keeping your sanity is to draw the line in the sand."

Remember, you may need a recommendation from this person down the road, so keep your emotions between yourself and your friends, and release your anger at the gym. Don't keep it bottled up inside. Then, direct your mental energy toward making your work situation more bearable. For starters, try to pinpoint what about your boss is making you so angry: the work he or she is asking you to do, the way you're being asked to do it, his or her communication or work style in general? Once you've got a clear idea of where the problem may lie, outline several ways to improve the situation. Then schedule a meeting to discuss your complaints one-on-one. Whatever you do, don't bring up the controversy when you're boiling. Wait until you are calm so that you can figure out why you're upset and offer solutions to fix the problem.

Standard business etiquette dictates that we always approach our antagonist directly before going to a third party for help. If the problems persist after you've had a talk and you still feel that you are being unjustly treated, approach your boss's boss, the office manager, or a human resources associate for advice. Begin looking for a new job only if change seems like a lost cause. Until then, fantasize about retaliating in innocuous ways, like Simone, who started ordering extra mayonnaise on her boss's sandwiches, which she had to order for lunch every day.

Cause #2: Nightmare Coworkers

Rude, catty, back-stabbing coworkers are certainly not the norm, but a few bad seeds seem to sprout in every office, notably in the entry level ranks, where the competition for getting ahead is so fierce. Nasty coworkers may just be unhappy about their own lives and therefore want everyone else to be, but their unattractive behavior could also stem from jealousy that they harbor toward you, simply because you're young, new, talented, and hip, and they aren't! If you establish a mentorlike relationship with a higher-up, for instance, a coworker at your level may feel threatened that you may usurp him or her in the insidious race up the ranks. And if you do advance, envy may provoke gossip and back stabbing about how you got there, unfair and untrue as the rumors may be.

If a coworker is directly trying to sabotage your success or move into your territory, confront him or her immediately, laying out what behavior you will and won't accept from your peer. Jacki, 28, a San Francisco sales associate in telecommunications software, concurs that standing up for yourself the moment a coworker crosses a boundary is crucial to maintaining your integrity and respect in the office. Once, another associate tried to steal a sales deal from her. She told him off in front of their coworkers and got her client territory and office-wide respect back.

If you can't establish a tolerable working environment, tell your boss about the situation, and present a couple of ways in which the conflict may be resolved: for instance, you and your nemesis can work on different projects, or you can move to another part of the office or transfer to a separate department where you won't have daily interaction with the monster.

If your trouble with bonding has more to do with the fact that you just don't connect with your coworkers, don't try to mold your personality to match theirs, advises Claire, 27, a creative assistant at a New York advertising agency. As she puts it, "It's more wearing on the soul to try to befriend people you don't relate to." Instead, concentrate on getting your work done, talk to the people you can tolerate—there must be *someone* in the office—and if the situation is making you miserable and resolution seems afar, it may be time to look for a new job with an environment that's likely to draw the type of people that you have more in common with.

Cause #3: Too Much Work, Too Little Satisfaction

We all have to put up with some of that dues-paying "monkey work," as Nicki calls the tasks you could train a monkey to do, during the first couple of years of our initiation. This makes us more prone to workaholism, not to mention depression, so it's important to make sure your life is balanced. "Try to stay positive and think about the things outside of work that keep you going," says Rosie, 26, who works for a marketing research company in Los Angeles but keeps her world outside of work spiritual through hiking and rock climbing. "Realize that you will go through ups and downs during the first few years of work, and remind yourself that there will be an end to what you're doing. Sometimes I work on projects that keep me up until 2 or 3 A.M., so I have to stop and consciously think that this is one project and it will be over."

Also, concentrate on the things you like about your job, advises Melissa, 28, a public relations consultant for a children's art project in a Houston hospital. She says: "When I get frustrated, I think about the kids with cancer who I'm helping through my work. Then I keep my nose to the grindstone and get my stuff done as quickly as possible, so I can go home and enjoy my life. On bad days, I tell myself, 'Tonight, I'm going to yoga, then to dinner with my husband.'" Also, suggests Shelley, 23, an associate editor at a fitness magazine in New York, it helps to remind yourself that everyone goes through the entry-level nightmare and that it will soon be over: "It's so frustrating because we feel that we have so much talent. But try to remember that once you get through the first few years of work, you'll never, *ever* have to do the entry-level stuff again."

Cause # 4: Hostile Work Environment

Being young and female, many of us are prey to the power-seeking, control-freaking, sexually perverted lichens of the working world, and consequently, we are often the victims of sexual harassment. Marcie, 26, of New York, had a taste of this during her first job as a screenplay analyst for a major cable network:

"I was just out of college and was hired by one of the big networks in Hollywood to read scripts and write reports. The executive story editor, who was in his 50s, became very palsy with me and started asking me to coffee and dinner. My instincts were telling me that the guy was being too friendly, but my brain was saying that this was normal networking and what you did in Hollywood.

"The last time I went out with him socially, he told me that he had a lot to offer me and wanted to take our relationship up a level. I asked him if he was suggesting that we get romantically involved, and he said yes. Panicked, I told him that I was involved with someone else. A week later, I was handing in a report to him, and he told me that he had to let me go—one of his uppers didn't like my work.

"I was so flabbergasted by what had happened that I was too afraid to investigate his claim. I was just starting out in the film industry and was afraid that if I dared complain of sexual harassment to higher authorities, my not-yet-even-blooming career in the film industry would be over forever. I also blamed myself; I thought maybe I had given this guy the wrong signals because I had gone to dinner with him. Then, I felt that I must not have talent as a writer at all and was hired only because the guy had wanted to sleep with me."

There's a wide range of definitions and a lot of gray area for what constitutes sexual harassment. The most obvious incidences are unwelcome sexual advances or requests for favors as a condition of employment and/or future opportunities. If you think you're a victim of sexual harassment, the first thing to know is that there are state and national laws protecting your right to work in an environment free of hostility and harassment. (You can probably get a copy of these laws through your company human resources department, or contact the Equal Employment Opportunity Commission.) The second thing to know is that it's important to follow your company's sexual harassment policy, which should be stated in the bylaws. The third thing to know is that it's vital to tell the harasser that his (or her, but woman-to-woman harassment isn't as common) conduct is unwelcome and must stop. Many young working women unexpectedly confront this problem. Remember that you're not alone and that you did nothing to provoke the aggression. However, it is important to do something about it. Talk to your human resources department immediately if the harassment continues after you've expressed your complaint, and seek appropriate help. (See the "Go-Girl Resources" section for a good book on the subject.)

....

Go-Girl Guidance *If you hate your job, look for a new one as soon as your instincts tell you, advises Olivia, 27, an associate at an engineering consulting firm. It's a lesson she learned the hard way: "I knew my first engineering job wasn't right for me after three months, but everyone in the field who I consulted said I should stay at my first job for at least two years because that's the way you play the game. Looking back, I feel that I wasted two years. The only game you need to play is the one that's fun for you."*

....

BEYOND ENTRY LEVEL

Believe it or not, there will come a day when you too shall rise above entry-level demoralization. With determination and perseverance, this will likely happen sometime by your mid 20s. Having endured the hazing rituals—the long hours, the condescending looks from competitive coworkers, and all the endless, brainless tasks—you will emerge a wise, valued member of the nine-to-five tribe. And after five years of experience, all sorts of doors will open up.

Remember the soul-search train? Well, around the time the afore-said doors start swinging open, all those maddening thoughts about your purpose in life will begin to swirl around you once again. During those few years prior to turning 30, your whole life undergoes a major reevaluation, as mine did when I hit 28 and decided not to put this writing career on hold any longer. If I can offer any sort of condolence, it's this: Don't be afraid of these thoughts, but by all means, honor them! You'll find that they won't sting as sharply as they did when you were 21 and straight out of school and feeling so vulnerable. If anything, the entry-level initiation toughens our emotional skin, and these questions don't feel so threatening to our sanity. In fact, they're a little exhilarating, because our first few years of experience have taught us success and given us confidence in ourselves that we didn't have before.

Remember, we've got a lifetime of career choices and decision making ahead. Don't get obsessed with trying to make it all happen today, because, frankly, you probably won't. The career you've been dreaming of will eventually take form. As it does, the clarity will free up your emotional reserves for other important 20-something tasks, such as . . . finding a mate. Let's move on to that titillating topic.

PART 2

Our Love Lives

4

The Mating Frenzy

A couple of chapters back, I likened the job search to dating, since so many of the little seduction rituals and self-promotion tactics we use to attract a mate can be modified quite appropriately to convince potential employers that we're exactly what they need. Unfortunately, the analogy doesn't work in reverse: searching for a mate is nothing like looking for a job. That's because in our job hunt, we know what we're after (steady employment, challenging work) and, conveniently, the company we approach has equally clear objectives (hire a reliable worker for the long haul). With dating, every single player has a different agenda. Some, for instance, believe the sole purpose of dating is to let off a little hormonal steam when the occasion arises. Others have an entirely different goal: to find a marriageable mate who will permanently relieve them from single status.

Problem is, there's no way of knowing who wants what until we invest enough of ourselves in someone to find out, since it would be embarrassing and conspicuous to ask for a detailed motive behind every invitation out. Even more discouraging is when we think we've found someone who shares our dating agenda, but then the prime candidate does a complete about-face, convincing us that all the good mates are taken.

Dating in the 20s is sort of like race car driving, or what I imagine race car driving to be. With each new date, we follow the same track: postwork cocktails, Friday-night dinners, Saturday-morning brunches, and those hallmark weekend getaway trips. We go around and around in circles until we either (a) crash and burn because we ignored all the red flags warning us to slow down, or (b) learn how to start the course at a moderate pace, changing lanes when red flags dictate, and, eventually, if our strategic driving worked, cross the finish line. This achievement qualifies us for level two, the relationship track, which we'll discuss in the next chapter.

For now, let's focus on getting to the starting line, which can be difficult these days because our country lacks standard dating protocol and etiquette (unless you live in the South, where chivalry still guides the local dating scene). The whole concept of dating is in flux, causing everyone involved to become panicky when relating to the opposite sex, forcing us to consult magazines for current interpretations and advice. While I'd never suggest we go back to the gender-specific roles that made courtship not too bad a place to linger 50 years ago—it would be helpful if all the residents of Singleville could agree upon what "going out for a beer" *really* means and what "I'll call you" translates into in layman's English. This chapter sheds a little headlight on some of the common roadblocks that those of us who've been around this track before have learned to steer around.

GETTING TO THE STARTING LINE

The question of the decade among the singles crowd is: Where are all the good guys? Well, most of them are in their 30s waiting for us to notice them. (They're often less aggressive than their younger competition, so we may have to make the moves.) Admittedly, I'm biased about older guys because my own boyfriend is in his 30s, and he's way more mature and easygoing than any of the guys I dated before. Then again, I'm way more mature (though debatably more easygoing) than I've ever been in relationships past, which leads me to the first truth about dating: The older we get—regardless of our sex—the more relationship experience we have, making dating and mating more an exciting road trip than a frantic car race with flat tires and injuries. And that's coming from a girl who's had some pretty disastrous first attempts at submitting to that beast called love.

Thirty-something guys know all about our weird 20-something relationship fears and antics. In my experience, they have a little more patience and even a sense of humor about dealing with them all. Of course, the older a guy gets, the more likely he'll have been burned by some devilish ex-girlfriend, so there's the chance he'll have more baggage in the trunk. However, the knights of the baggage carriers have picked up a few relationship survival skills (the mental equivalent of those luggage carriers that flight attendants drag onto airplanes) to manage their load. Typically, these guys not only are aware of their luggage but also know how to store their hangups an adequate distance away from us. Along with relationship skills, these noble and slightly older men have often developed a realistic outlook on what relationships are all about. They understand the peaks and valleys that love must endure, so we don't have to explain it to them over and over again.

Of course, everyone matures at a different rate, so it'd be silly to write off guys our own age, but if you want to cut your losses, start scouting around for a man who's just a few years older. There's also a bonus: All their years of bachelorhood have taught them one skill that most of us lack: cooking. Many even take pride in impressing us with their culinary talent, which in my book earns huge points. Only one warning about older guys: They may be looking for a mate to settle down with immediately, and you may not be nearly ready to start thinking about long-term love. While your maturity levels might make a perfect match, your dating goals could grossly conflict. If you find yourself in such a quandary, go slowly, and at every turn, make sure you're both in the same lane about where your relationship is headed.

Age aside, the key to dating is *finding* a few good mates to get to know. Since there is no Good Guys Factory pumping out various models for us to pick and choose from on a Friday night (a girl can dream, can't she?), we must rely on other tactics. Here are some tips for judging the talent as you approach the starting line.

The Good Guys Always Appear When We Least Expect Them

I know you've heard that before, but it really is true. I met my current boyfriend on the street at a stoplight while walking to work one morning. The last thing I was looking for was romance, I already had a boyfriend at the time and was totally weary of strangers approaching me on the street, even if they *were* extremely handsome. But since he and I were both headed downtown and walking at the same pace (coincidence?), we struck up a conversation that continued until our routes diverged. Months later, we ran into each other again on our morning sojourn and made plans to meet for lunch. After a movie here, another lunch there, a painful (and unrelated) breakup with my boyfriend, and a couple more months of friendship, love began to squeeze its way into our little camaraderie, and we started dating.

Why this strange phenomenon occurs is one of the big mysteries of the human mating ritual, but Claudia, 29, of San Francisco, has a theory: "No one likes desperation. People are attracted to happiness and confidence—not neediness. If you're happy about yourself and not needing someone else to make you complete, there's a natural attractiveness to you." Besides, the minute we start making those checklists of the type of guy we want to date, we shoot ourselves in the foot. Not only is it highly unlikely that we'll find someone who has each and every quality we're looking for in a companion, but also when we fixate on finding that particular someone, we end up missing all the other amazing people out there who probably have even more attractive qualities than the ones we could think to scribble down on a mating wish-list while watching "Seinfeld" reruns. It's sort of like having an orgasm: If you fixate on getting one, you'll completely stress out, and your body will refuse. But if you just let go and relax and let life take its course, the pleasure has a better chance of sneaking in. And you'll laugh at that checklist you once thought could create the man of your dreams.

The Good Guys Like Doing What We Like to Do

If your idea of a perfect weekend day is an extreme mountain-bike ride through muddy trails along perilous cliffs, but the incredibly gorgeous guy who lives a floor above you would rather spend a sunny day slinking between sick and twisted cartoon flicks at the semiannual animation film festival, you may have trouble relating, much as you and your hormones may be willing to overlook that minor point. If you can't find a mutual medium through which you can interact and have fun (but, by all means, try to find one), dating this guy would probably turn into a frustrating and disastrous affair, like the kind you see on "Ricki Lake."

If your goal in dating is to find a mate who might be relationship-worthy, you're probably better off scouting around for someone who loves doing what you get your kicks from. Take it from those of us who have tried again and again to reform the unjustly sexy but sick and twisted men of the world: relationships don't survive on sexual attraction alone. Reserve those guys for sexual relief if you'd like, and narrow your pool of potential dates to those who share an earnest interest in the political views, intellectual disciplines, hobbies, sports, and entertainment mediums that make you who you are.

Joining clubs and groups with activities that you love doing will greatly narrow that pool. Even if these groups don't attract mates that you find attractive, they will introduce you to a new circle of friends who may have incredibly attractive roommates, coworkers, or guy friends who are also big in-line skating fanatics or photographers or whatever it is you love doing. This leads me to my next point.

The Good Guys Know Our Friends

While you're trying to trust that the universe will place a good potential mate in your path when you're least expecting it and otherwise preoccupying your time with activities you truly enjoy, it never hurts to get your friends involved in your quest for an interesting date. After all, meeting a guy through those we know and trust decreases the odds that underneath the charm lurks a psychopathic weirdo who creepily hangs out in front of your apartment to spy on you after one innocent coffee date. But more important, your friend knows both of you and probably wouldn't put her matchmaking credibility on the line if she didn't think the two of you shared the same values and interests, which are essential for any relationship to take off.

Don't limit yourself to setups from close friends only; enlist your friends' boyfriends and your coworkers for names and numbers as well. If you hit it off with a new acquaintance, don't be shy about asking her for blind dates too, advises Simone, 28. She says it worked for her: "I was once in a clothing store trying on clothes and started talking to the owner. We were joking around, and I said, 'Hey, do you know any guys you could set me up with? Ha, ha, ha!' She did, and I ended up going out with one of her friends."

If you are new to the area and have no connections, your first priority is to start making friends immediately; put the quest for a date on hold. If you don't have friends, you won't have a life of your own, and if you happen to meet a guy before you have a life, you're at risk of becoming dependent on him for fulfillment. This is an entirely bad move that we'll discuss in the next chapter. For now, concentrate on making a life for yourself. If you trust the wisdom and experience of those of us who've been there, the mate of your dreams will one day appear. You won't even know how he got there, because you'll be too involved in your own life.

The Good Guys Just Might Be the Guy Next Door

You'll never know unless you take a few chances, like talking to that friendly guy who says hi to you on the street. Safety, of course, is a huge issue, so when you meet someone new, keep your interactions entirely public—don't even catch a ride home with him—until you meet at least one of his friends, coworkers, or family members. That doesn't ensure that the stranger isn't a serial killer in disguise, but it will help give you peace of mind. It did for me when I was first getting to know my boyfriend.

The goal is to allow yourself extra time to build trust, which will be absent from strangers you meet, but don't lock yourself in your apartment because you're afraid of getting involved with the next Ted Bundy. Dating requires taking a few chances. "Go see a band with a really attractive female singer, suggests Trixie, 25, of San Francisco, who has no qualms about approaching guys and striking up a conversation. "All the guys there are really good looking, and they all go alone."

There's also always the bar scene, and for as many girls who warn against it, there are an equal number who have met really nice guys at bars and clubs. Mary, 25, of Washington, D.C., for instance, met her current boyfriend at a pool hall. "He was with a group from work, and we struck up a conversation. I was really attracted to his personality—he was very open and fun and had a good sense of humor—but he is nothing like the profile I usually went for. Later, we started playing pool, and he was my partner. After that, we met for dinner and had a fantastic mutual attraction." A year later, they are still dating.

When All Else Fails, There's Always the Internet

I can't boast of having experience with Internet personals, but I've been told by several women who have that the Internet is one surefire way to get in touch with available men who are also looking for dates. Whether these men are even remotely good matches for you is a different story. That, you can tell only by meeting the guy in the flesh to assess each other's physical vibe and real-time verbal skills. Several women who've met men on the Internet say that what they consider "attractive" changes when they're meeting men on-line; wit, intelligence, and humor are the digital equivalent of *babe!*

But, honestly, if you and your virtual flirt don't vibe in person, the two of you should strive for friendship or stick to electronic coquetry. My friends used to make fun of me because assessing a guy's vibe was my specialty, sometimes to my detriment. I'd often overlook such basic qualities as integrity and respect in the presence of a strong vibe. Still, sex appeal matters—it is the one thing that separates lovers from friends. And if you've found a strong connection on the Internet, but there's no vibe when you meet in the flesh, don't even try to cross the line, or you'll risk the friendship.

"I've done Internet dating on three separate occasions, and each time I've placed an ad, I've gotten 30 to 50 responses," says Stephanie, 26, of San Francisco. "But 99 percent of them were people I wouldn't want to get to know. You have to wade through a lot of wackos. Plus, you can't really get to know a person through E-mail messages; you don't know how long they sat there at work figuring out what to write. Or they may have had 10 of their friends helping them out. I've made some friends through placing ads—this one guy and I have kept in touch for about a year, bouncing work ideas off of each other through E-mail and phone calls—but in most cases, when I've met the person, there wasn't an attraction."

Still, if an electronic meeting indicates that there's a humorous and intellectual connection between you and someone else who's looking for romance, why not take the time to have coffee or a drink to see if the physical attraction is there, too? You won't have much to lose unless the guy's verbal skills are on a par with those of Koko the sign-language-savvy gorilla. My view is that if we can get books, music, airplane tickets, furniture, and even our groceries on the Internet, why not dates?

"On-line personals are just a way to get introduced to new people," says Melissa Weiner, 27, editor in chief of Swoon.com, a relationship website with free personals. "Every generation creates new venues for dating. Our grandparents met at church, our parents met at bars, we're meeting on the Internet. Twenty-somethings have been brought up on computers, so they are a natural extension for us to use in dating."

Just as with any stranger you meet at a bar, though, safety is paramount. Use the same precautions as you would if you met someone on the street. "The Internet highway is like hitchhiking," adds Swoon's on-line relationships expert Melissa Cochran, a.k.a. Jane Err. "It's not smart to hop into a stranger's car. If you read an ad that you like, insta-message the guy, and get the ball rolling. But meet in a public place for the first time. There's a wealth of guys on the Internet, and there are plenty of sites that are strictly for people who are looking for potential mates. Just play it safe."

LADIES, START YOUR ENGINES

I admire women who are ballsy enough to approach a guy with a strong vibe, probe for a few essential signs of compatibility, and then ask him out. Employing such bold maneuvers at the starting line puts us girls at a distinct advantage. "People get what they want by going after it. That's why it's important for you to become the chooser in the dating scene," says marriage and family therapist David Steele, L.M.F.T., president and founder of LifePartnerQuest, a relationship coaching service for singles and couples, in San Jose. This applies particularly if you're the type of gal who tends to get sucked into relationships before you even know what you want, because the guy who is after you is so adamantly into *you* that you forget to ask yourself if you like him back. When we become the pursuer, such dynamics are less likely to get the best of us, so to speak.

When you approach a guy, there are a few things you want to find out before you make the move and ask him out: Is he available? Does he like doing the same things that I like? Is he interested in me? As you're probing and liking what you hear, the direct approach to asking him out is always best. That way, there's no question about your intentions, and you won't get yourself into one of those sticky situations in which you don't know what your object of desire is thinking. Jan, 25, of San Francisco, who's one of those bold and ballsy women, sums it up like this: "It's all about getting the most amount of information about the guy in the least amount of time. You can be in a grocery store line or in the park skating: just talk to whomever you're interested in with confidence, sass, and wit. Find out if you both enjoy the same thing. If the guy's on in-line skates, say something like: 'Oh, I've always wanted to learn. Do you want to go together sometime?'"

Don't waste your valuable time trying to get a guy to ask you out; just make the suggestion yourself. That, of course, puts you at risk of being rejected—nothing any of us is too thrilled to experience—but consider the alternative: If the guy doesn't ask you out, you'll feel rejected anyway, and you'll torture yourself for not making the move. Vera, 26, of Denver, attests, "I'm a very direct person, so if I like someone, I'll say: 'I'd like to get to know you better. Would you like to go to dinner sometime?' "I've been turned down, and it was only hard the first time. Now I just think it's his loss!"

The Phone Thing

One of the most agonizing aspects of meeting someone new is waiting for "the call" after exchanging numbers. This is all the more grueling if we've made the first move and left a message with his roommate or voice mail and then we don't hear back. We wonder: Did he get the message? If he didn't, what if he thinks I'm not interested? Should I call again?

I'm going to be blunt, here. If he doesn't call, he's not interested. Let him go. If he were interested, he'd call you on his own, whether or not you called first. Right? We girls get way too caught up in trying to justify other people's behavior and make up excuses for people: He's insecure. Maybe he's shy. He's probably just busy. And that's a waste of our mental abilities. Even if he is insecure or shy or busy, you have to ask yourself if the guy is really worth dating if you're the one who's always initiating plans. That gets tedious.

Even worse than never hearing from a guy you just met is not hearing back from one after you've had a few dates. That is rejection, and it's a major ego blow, but there's not much you can do about it except stop fixating on the phone and direct your mating calls toward someone else. "Try not to think about it. Go to the gym. Make other plans. Go out with friends," advises Marie, 27, of New York. "You can't control whether a guy's going to call you, so if he tells you he'll call, blow it off. Pretend you didn't hear it."

There is one exception to my blunt conclusion above: He might *not* have gotten your message if you left it on the machine or with a human being; and he might not have your number. To avoid these precarious situations, never leave a message. Just call back again. That way, you can gauge whether he really wants to get to know you by the eagerness in his voice.

AND THE RACE BEGINS (THE FIRST DATE)

The best first dates are short (with the potential of becoming longer if the mood is right) and provide ample opportunity to assess whether the semistranger you're sharing a cocktail with shares similar values and interests and has a sense of humor, three indicators that will help you determine whether or not you want a second date. Contrary to popular mating-ritual practices, dinner is not the best first-date activity. Sitting at a table with someone you don't really know can be uncomfortable, and the conversation is always the same—what do you do?, where are you from?, how long have you lived here?, blah, blah, blah—and therefore has the potential of becoming dull and tedious. Sometimes within the first five minutes, you're blinking at the salt and pepper shakers, wondering why you thought this guy was cute in the darkly lit club where you exchanged numbers. Besides, wouldn't you rather see the guy in action? According to my sources, the best first dates are those in which you're doing *something*, so that you can see how the person interacts in a natural and spontaneous way.

"Going on a bike ride is a great first date," says Trixie, who is a fervent cyclist. "You're doing something physical, and you're not looking your best, so you don't have to get hung up on your appearance. Plus, you quickly get to see how the person interacts with you." The other advantage of having an activity involved—a baseball game, in-line skating, a concert—is that you can focus on the activity if you're having a horrible time, notes Diane, 27, of Chicago. If you don't want to commit as much time as a baseball game or a long bike ride may take, opt for the coffee or drink date. That's a particular favorite of Lynn, 25, of Portland, Oregon, because of the flexibility it offers, especially for blind dates: "Meet for a beer after work at a pub. If the date is going well, you can always order dinner."

Trixie offers one more piece of advice for first-timers: Have an escape route so that you can leave if the date is really bad. She was glad she had one: "I went out with this one guy for dinner, and it was horrible from the moment he picked me up. We had nothing in common. I kept thinking, 'Everything will be OK as soon as I get a glass of wine,' but it turned out that he was a recovering alcoholic, so I didn't feel I could order a drink. Luckily, I had organized a bunch of friends to meet me afterward to go see a band. So, he drove me home after dinner, and I ran! Backup plans are essential—even if your excuse is that you have to work."

LAPS TWO AND THREE

The few dates after the first are always hormonally challenging, depending on how much we like the guy and how much he makes it clear that he likes us back. Being female, most of us during this time will enact that gender-specific ritual of reading all sorts of things into our date's actions, moves, and gazes. It's an attempt to gauge what's going on and help us determine one very important thing: whether or not we want to get involved in a relationship with this guy, should he desire. Sometimes, that's not an easy thing to assess, such as when we're so deluded with the lust hormone (the consequence of very strong vibe frequencies beamed straight at all our reasoning powers, causing daft confusion) and so intoxicated by the idea of being in a relationship that we overlook a few character flaws. For these reasons, it's helpful to have a few diagnostic questions in the back of your head to pose during these early hazardous laps around the track:

Am I Having Fun Yet?

Humor is the glue of any relationship. Without it, you'll never get through the bad times, and the good times just won't seem that great. So, advises Naomi, 23, of San Francisco, if you're not laughing or having a titillating conversation, don't bother seeing the guy again. This may sound obvious, but sometimes we can become so myopically attracted to certain attributes a guy may have—good looks, sophistication, a noble profession—or we get so insecure about ever finding someone who *really* inspires us, that we forget this reality-check wisdom. Trust the experience of the pros who have looped this track many times: those with a good sense of humor are the real medal-winners, because when we're laughing (earnestly), we are being ourselves, which is the foundation for any relationship.

Would I Be Friends with Him?

It's just as important to ask yourself if you like this person as it is to rate how much fun you're having. Doing so forces you to review the guy's integrity, honesty, reliability, and values—all of which are easy to overlook in the heat of attraction and in the presence of a charmer. First and foremost, observe how much this guy wants to get to know you, your opinions, your feelings, your dreams, your friends and family life, your job, and even what you do every day between work and sleep. A guy who questions is a guy who finds you interesting.

If social interaction isn't a problem, observe other character traits, advises Lynn. For example "If someone cuts him off while he's driving, does he get all tense and talk about it for the rest of the night? If he doesn't drop it, that means he's pretty uptight and dwells on things. You have to ask yourself if you want to be with someone who might get that upset at you if you did something little. Also, pay attention to the way he talks about his past. Does he trash all his ex-girlfriends? There must have been *some* good relationships, but if he's still bitter about them all, think twice. You want to get the feeling that he can have good relationships."

Another window into the guy's character, how he treats others. If he's rude to the waiter, he'll likely treat you rudely too at some point, and even if he doesn't, he'll continually embarrass you in public with his unattractive manners. Or, if the waiter gives him more change than he's due, does he pocket it or give it back? Little things like that can tell you about a guy's integrity. While you're on character traits, think about this: Would you want your friends to meet him? If your inner radar flashes *No!*, slow the romance way down until you figure out why not, or end it abruptly if you already know. Otherwise, you'll end up disappointed or exhausted from trying to change him, which won't work. Save yourself the heartache and move on to finding a nicer mate.

As you're weighing these variables, consider being friends before submitting to any type of romance, suggests Melanie, 28, of Austin, who was friends with her boyfriend for two years before they started dating. "As friends, you can build trust with each other. And when you have trust, you don't put on protective armor that makes it hard to share yourself intimately with another person," she says. And in case you're wondering, you don't miss out on those exciting first few months of dating when you've been friends for a while. "Even though you know each other very well, the boyfriend-girlfriend relationship is still new for you, so it's just as passionate."

Is This Guy Happy?

Unlike dogs, whose state of bliss you can often judge by the sheen of their coats and the whiteness of their teeth, with men, you have to monitor the subject's behavior to assess the health of his mental state. (Although, come to think of it, if the guy's hair looks as if it hasn't been washed in weeks and his teeth are stained yellow from chain smoking and the dozen or so cups of coffee he chugs every day, that could be a good indication of his emotional well-being.) Naturally, it would not be wise to get involved with someone who is in the midst of an identity crisis or has weird mother issues he's not even aware of himself.

I once went on a date with a guy I had met at a club who spent the evening talking about his therapist and medical school student loan repayment schedule, which was propelling him into the black hole of depression. Why he thought I wanted to hear this is still beyond me, but I do tend to turn into a therapist around certain people, so I can't put the entire blame on him. Nevertheless, I'm pretty sure that his emotional purge over Ahi tuna left *me* more depressed than him. Whether I'd date him again was never a question, based on what happened next, which I still feel guilty about, so indulge me in my little confession.

After he dropped me off that night, he called from a pay phone to thank me for the evening. I motioned to my roommate (whom I was telling the melancholy details of our date when he called) that it was he, which inspired her to call me from our other house line. I clicked over, and after exchanging a few anxiety-induced hee-haws and gagging noises with her, clicked back to what I thought was his line, only to hear a dial tone, whereupon I realized that I had activated three-way calling instead of putting him on hold, giving him a full symphonic concert of our gagging repertoire and probably propelling him back a year's worth of therapy. I still feel bad about that. But what could I do? Anyway, the moral of the story (besides never make fun of someone who's holding on your other line, in case of phone-feature mishaps) is that it's important to take the happiness factor into serious consideration before you start dating someone new. Otherwise, your already fragile mental state will get more wear and tear than it deserves during this insanely hectic time of your life.

Before I go any further, let me make this brief clarification: By making happiness a requirement, I'm not talking about disqualifying guys who are in therapy or going through growing pains like the rest of us. After all, most of us would never get a date in our lives if guys judged *us* on our mental ups and downs! I'm talking about avoiding an emotional investment in the despondent or angry man who lacks motivation or goals, who sits around in his dark apartment all day blaming everything in his rotten life on his sordid childhood and landlord, in that order. These guys have got to work on themselves before they can love us. If you've got a soft spot for the emotionally trodden type, stay friends, suggest a self-help book, but do yourself a favor and look for romance elsewhere.

Do I Like His Friends?

You can tell a lot about a guy's character by the way he interacts with his friends. If the opportunity arises within the first few dates to meet them, take advantage of it. If the person was essentially a stranger when you met him, this experience will likely ease some of those worries that you might be dating the Unabomber's illegitimate son. Or, if his personality changes around his friends, as it sometimes can, you'll want to know that before you get too involved. If the guy has women friends or sisters whom he keeps in close touch with, give him a star: that is a good sign that he understands and respects our gender, which is always a plus.

If he doesn't have friends, turn on the alert sensors. This may sound harsh and even cruel, but it will save you a lot of heartache if you analyze why no one wants to hang out with him. Trust those of us who have dated these types before: There are *reasons* that loner-type guys don't have friends, and the reasons usually don't make him more attractive.

For instance, these guys often have commitment problems or lack basic social maintenance skills—such as reliability, or taking the initiative, or even honesty—which isn't exactly a selling point for romance. If the guy is new to the area, give him some slack, but find out how well he keeps in touch with older friends from high school or college; consider him OK if he speaks highly of them. If he doesn't have at least one good friend, he probably has some issues you might want to carefully consider—unless you're a loner too, in which case you might be a perfect pair.

Does He Past the Test?

Despite my previous rant about throwing away the checklist and staying open-minded to dating new and different people, there's one checklist-type tactic that many of us find quite useful when trying to decide if the person we're dating is relationship material: the "test." The test comes in all different varieties. Naomi uses the Scar Story Test: "I think people's scars are really interesting, so I always ask guys about theirs. The way a guy tells the story of how he got his scars tells me a lot about him—what he likes to do, how open he is in talking about his life, how personable he is. You also get to see how he responds back to you. I love talking about my scars, so if he's interested in finding out how I got mine, that's a good sign."

Gillian, 26, of San Francisco, employs the Vacation Test: "I've started asking guys I meet where they would go if they had two weeks' vacation to do anything they wanted. Their answers tell me about their dreams and whether their sense of adventure matches mine. I really liked this one guy until he told me his ideal vacation would be to go to a five-star resort and sit by a pool all day. I'd rather spend the two weeks on a safari in Africa. We'd never make a good match."

Lynn and her friends use the R.E.M. Test: "It's always a good sign if the guy likes R.E.M., or if he can at least appreciate that the band members are artists. My friends and I joke about it, but so far, the R.E.M. Indicator has proved pretty accurate in assessing whether the guy's a good match or not."

The Only "Rule" You Need to Know

After interviewing several women who read *The Rules*, that bestseller about dating (and who always prefaced their admission with a joke or some other disclaimer), I crept down to the local library and discreetly checked out a copy—lest someone I know might suspect I need that kind of how-to-hook-a-man advice—to try to understand the mysterious power this little book has had over so many women. After a few pages, I had an epiphany: this was a joke book. A gag gift book. A tongue-in-cheek attempt to offer women a brainless chuckle or two about the confounding reality of today's dating scene. But somewhere along the way, maybe even to the authors' dismay, some women started taking *The Rules* seriously.

I think one of the reasons why that book has become so popular is that it offers an answer to a problem we're all familiar with—dating etiquette ambiguity: the who-calls-whom dilemma, the who-initiates-the-date agony, and the who-pays-for-dinner uncertainty. Most of us who cackle at that book believe that the answer is not to engage in silly and manipulative behavior that's downright devastating to our vibrant personalities, but, instead, to find men who love us for our quirks and perks equally. So, instead of doing all those bizarre little rituals—talk no more than 10 minutes on the phone, never accept a Saturday-night date past Wednesday, dump a guy if he doesn't give you a romantic gift on your birthday—consider this one simple alternative rule for dating: Geek out! If you can't be goofy around a guy, he's not worth your time, and he's probably not fun to be with.

Do I Like Myself Around Him?

How you feel is, by far, the most important question to ask yourself when you start assessing the relationship potential of a guy you meet. If your personality changes around him (if you're not sure, ask your friends) or if you can't be your normal goofy, wacky, jokey, lovable, sexually aggressive, outspoken, opinionated, adventurous, fill-in-the-blank self, he's probably not the right man for you.

RED FLAG ALERT

During those first few dates, when sexual attraction may be the most salient factor driving your consciousness, it's easy to ignore the red flags that are often waving frantically in our faces. They're trying to alert us to potentially questionable behavior exhibited by the object of our desire. Sometimes, we're so enamored by the possibility of dating the babe who's paying so much attention to us that we don't even see the flags. I've done this look-the-other-way-and-they-don't-exist mind trip on several occasions, and I've always regretted it. So, to help you save a little gas around the race track and avoid some serious hazards, I (along with all the other 20-somethings I spoke on with the matter) have come up with seven fairly common warning signs that it's time to slow down and proceed with caution:

1. **Chronic flattery.** Compliments are always welcome, but if a guy you meet starts flattering you about things he couldn't possibly know, he is not to be trusted, warns Monique, 27, of New York. For instance, if he tells you that you're an incredible writer, when you're pretty sure he's never read a word you've written, or if he tells you that he's never met a woman like you after two minutes of small talk in the checkout line at the grocery store, he's probably throwing you a line, hoping for a nibble. Our advice: Nibble elsewhere!

2. **An adhesive personality.** Beware of the guy who wants to spend 24 hours a day with you upon first glance. If you're a romantic like me, you're liable to misinterpret this behavior as an adorable sign of his affection and love. Come back to reality. Guys who are like this often have distorted conceptions (such as fears that you'll disappear if you're not kept in sight) or are inherently controlling and want to dominate your life. Even though it may seem cute that he wants to see you all the time, steer carefully. If he's not willing to give you space when you need it, especially before you really even

know him, you'll be smothered in a relationship, and at the rate he's accelerating, you'll be there in no time if you don't ease on the brakes.

3. **Unresolved oedipal issues.** If a guy tells his mother *everything*, do not get involved with him, advises Lynn, because he probably will discuss personal things about you with her, including your sex life if your relationship progresses. That is just plain creepy and weird.

4. **Unexplainable nervousness (on your part).** Being extremely attracted to someone can plow your judgment. If the aphrodisiac of sexual attraction invades your common sense, take a five-minute time-out and remove yourself from the source. Then do a head-to-toe body check to see if there's any part of you that's freaking out. If your entire body is jittery and nervous, this guy may be bad news, but if you've only got butterflies, you probably are just excited and should proceed with enthusiastic caution.

5. **Skeptical warnings from friends.** For the same hormonal reasons mentioned earlier, it can be easier than you think to get in the fast lane with a jerk, especially if you suffer from low self-esteem. Luckily, in these situations, our friends can be more objective about the guys we're dating. So, if your friends believe there's something extremely wrong with the object of your infatuation, *listen to them*, especially if they're telling you that your personality changes in a bad way around the guy. If you trust them and respect their judgment, they're probably right, and you should proceed with *their* awareness in the forefront of your mind.

6. **Boundary disregard.** Some of those adhesive guys (see #2) are guilty of not respecting our needing-to-be-alone boundaries, but even more dangerous are those who disregard our physical boundaries. Any guy who puts on the moves against your will *must* be kept at a distance. Owing to our relative lack of dating experience, and, therefore, lack of practice at handling unwanted advances and avoiding dangerous situations that could lead to date rape, we 20-somethings have to be all the more wary of guys who don't respect our boundaries. If someone oversteps yours, firmly state that you are

not comfortable with his hand on your knee, his arm around your waist, his trying to take off your shirt, or with whatever line he is attempting to cross. Then take note of his reaction. If he makes fun of you, tries to blow off what you're saying, or ignores you altogether, get away from him immediately, and don't return his calls. He is a bona fide asshole. And assholes don't get second chances.

7. **Controlling tendencies.** Not only is it a drag to be around someone who's controlling, but also, this personality trait can be the forerunner to verbal or physical abuse, warns clinical counselor Dee Marx-Kelly, M.F.C.C., of San Jose. Steer clear the minute you meet a guy who tries to control your behavior, including how you act, what you do, who you hang out with, and how you spend your free time. These guys are nothing but trouble.

SAFETY HAZARDS

One danger to look out for as you loop the track in search for a mate is date rape. This crime is extremely prevalent in our age-group, particularly in our early 20s on college campuses. Date rape, by definition, is sexual assault due to physical force or the threat of force by someone we know. Experts say we're more vulnerable to date rape on college campuses, because we tend to be more trusting of our fellow students than, say, a stranger we meet through the Internet. Trust puts us more at risk.

There are also several date rape drugs making the college rounds, as well as circulating among bars. Rohypnol, or "roofies;" GHB, or "easy lay"; and ketamine hydrochloride, or "Special K" are three such drugs that can be dissolved in drinks. They produce tranquilizing effects that lower inhibitions, act as a muscle relaxant, and, in some cases, cause amnesia, preventing the victim from knowing what happened.

To protect yourself from date rape, always watch your drink at parties and bars, and consider establishing a buddy system with your friends, as Mary did in college: "My girlfriends and I would always buddy up with a partner when we went to fraternity parties, where guys keep handing you more and more glasses of beer. We'd help each other out when one of us got in a bad situation. I was at a party once where my friend disappeared with the guy she was talking to. I was worried, so I found the school directory and looked up his address, then I went to his apartment and picked her up." Since alcohol itself can lower our ability to handle dangerous situations, it's always wise to limit your intake when you're out with someone new. Sticking to public places, as with Internet-spawned dates, is also a smart move.

Keep in mind, date rape is never the victim's fault. If you're sexually assaulted, don't blame yourself for drinking too much, for going into that guy's room, or for messing around with someone you had no intention of sleeping with. Do, however, get counseling and professional and legal guidance immediately through your local rape hot line or counseling center.

STAYING ON TRACK

If you take only one thing away from this chapter, I hope it's this: Don't be in such a hurry to qualify for the relationship course. Dating as many people as you can is one of the best things you can do for yourself in the 20s. If you've always been picky about the person you go out with, complete with the Checklist of ideal attributes down to eye color and number of months lived abroad, heed the wisdom of Anna, 27, of Seattle. She advocates dating around while you're still single and you have the freedom to explore who's out there. "I went through a couple of years where every two weeks, I'd date someone new: from the cook at the restaurant where I was moonlighting—he was gorgeous!—to the geek who had made a million dollars at Microsoft but who was emotionally retarded," she says. "I wasn't picky, and it was so much fun. If you take dating too seriously, you miss out on meeting a lot of interesting people." You also miss out on learning what you like and don't like in a mate.

If, while sowing your wild oats, you happen to meet someone you really like but aren't ready to dive into a relationship, accept that the timing is off and hope that when you are ready to be part of a couple, he'll still be interested. If you tie yourself down to one man before you're ready, you'll likely be resentful, which won't do that relationship any good. "I'm always honest with guys and usually tell them after we've gone out a couple of times that I'm hanging out with other guys too," says Lauren, 23, of Santa Barbara. "Until I meet someone I'm happy with, I'll always date around."

THE FINAL LAP: ARE WE DATING YET?

You did drinks after work. Eventually, you progressed to dinner. You've even fooled around a bit. But the one thing you haven't quite determined is where all this amorous ambiguity is headed. Maybe you don't really want to know, which is perhaps why the oft anxiety-provoking subject of relationship status hasn't yet surfaced. Maybe your "friend" would also prefer not to define what's become a weekly—or even more frequent—rendezvous. But possibly, you're both just too chicken to pose the loaded question: "So . . . what's going on with us?"

I could name a million reasons why not to bring up this touchy subject, some of which I, myself, have used in the past: "If he wants to know, *he* can ask"; or "I don't want to appear the nagging girlfriend"; and my favorite, "I don't even know what *I* want." But sooner or later, there comes a point when one of you starts feeling anxious about the lack of relational definition, and "the talk" becomes inevitable. Ideally, this should precede emotional and physical attachment, but we girls are only human. Therefore, such discussions more often than not come after the fact, which makes them all the more awkward. If the topic has escalated in your mind to all-consuming proportions, there's probably one of three things going on:

Your "Friend" Honestly Doesn't Know What He Wants

This is totally fair if the guy is up front about his confusion, as Amanda, 24, of San Francisco recently experienced: "I get into a lot of those semi-relationships where I'll go out all the time with a guy but not really know if he just wants to be friends. I have a hard time stepping up and saying, 'What's going on here?' Or I'll tell myself, 'Next time something will happen; I'm sure I'll know what's going on then.' The last guy I saw was honest and open. He told me that he was really interested in me but didn't want to make a move before he was sure how he felt about me." Such honesty makes the unknown status more tolerable. If the guy, however, is confused *and* lacks verbal skills to express his confusion, the situation becomes insufferable.

Take Kelly, 28, of Brooklyn: "A professor of mine set me up with this guy who had just moved to New York. He was really cute, and it turned out that we had a lot in common and even knew some of the same people. He started calling me to go out as a friend. Gradually, I began staying over at his place on nights we'd go out, because we'd stay out really late, and taking the train back home at four in the morning was dangerous. This went on for four or five months, where we'd be sleeping in the same bed, but we never kissed. Neither of us would make the first move. I was totally confused about the status of our relationship. Finally, I got brave and asked him what was going on. We talked, and both of us said that we liked each other, so we decided to start dating. But the second time we made plans to get together after that, he stood me up. He told me later, 'I guess I didn't feel that way about you.' A couple months after that, he moved away." This is a good example of why it's usually better to clear the air sooner rather than later, so you can get on with your life rather than ruminate over the real meaning behind the currently status-ambiguous friend's suggestive smile and comments.

The Guy Has a Girlfriend and Is Too Socially Inept to Mention Her While Leading You On

Kelly has also driven a few laps with the socially inept type: "I went out with another guy for six Saturday nights in a row. It seemed as if we were dating. Then one day, he called and asked me over, and the first thing he said when I walked in was, 'Look at this picture of my girlfriend.' I didn't know what to say—I was shocked! We went out for drinks, and then I split. Later, I called him up and asked him what was *up* with that."

We know what was up, don't we? Social ineptness writ large—lack of communication skills, coupled with the male desire for two women at once, but suddenly overwhelmed by a wave of guilt (or by an external force, like said girlfriend suddenly deciding to move to the area, foiling his secret social life with you). It's something many of us will taste to some degree during our 20s. We may even have been guilty of it ourselves, when we were the ones not sure of wanting whatever it was we were slipping into and not really making our ambiguity clear early on. If you're on the unfortunate receiving end, the best thing to do in these situations is admit that you picked a loser. Then make a break to the nearest party, where hopefully you'll meet a guy who is clear about his intentions with you from the outset.

The Guy Senses That You Don't Want a Relationship and Believes He Can Avoid Rejection by Avoiding the Subject of Status Altogether

If you're ambivalent about the relationship, but your mate is passionately in love, give him a break. Many men, overwhelmed by love-induced testosterone urges, may assume that you are not dating others unless you tell them up front that you are. They may choose to avoid the subject and interpret their dates with you as a "relationship" whether one is verbalized or not. If you are guilty of avoiding the topic because you don't want a relationship but have given obvious overtures that you're willing to head in that direction, do the honorable thing and lay out what you want with this guy, risking the fact that he may not want the same thing and leave.

I'm a firm believer in the old saying, What goes around comes around. If you burn a nice guy, he or someone else will most certainly burn you back. Besides, open communication is one of the core lessons we 20-somethings need to learn about love, so take advantage of practice sessions whenever you can. Eventually, you'll find a guy whose stars are aligned with your own. And before you know it, you will have crossed the qualifying finish line in the car race that dating is, and a relationship will be staring you in the face, breeding all sorts of exhilarating new feelings and anxieties. Naturally, I've got a lot to say on that.

5

Adventures in Couplehood

*O*ne could argue that I'm not the most qualified girl to give advice about relationships. I'm just now, at age 29, feeling as if I've got a grip on the whole concept of what a healthy, happy, challenging relationship entails. And that's after years of failed attempts and hideous moments with past boyfriends. I wasn't at all prepared for the maelstrom of emotions and complications that infiltrate most relationships in the 20s. I went to a woman's college, so men were an infrequent and exotic curriculum for me during that formidable passage from teen to 20-something, and looking back at some of the amateurish ways in which I dealt with certain relational incidences during my first few adult experimentations with couplehood, I was clearly a few years behind. I won't bore you with the details. (Besides, I'd rather not publicly admit them!) One thing's for sure: if you think dating is exhausting and frustrating, just wait until you get involved in a romance that has potential for long-term commitment. All I can say is, grab a handful of Prozac and get ready for the emotional deluge of your life.

Ok, I'm exaggerating. Relationships are *awesome* once we get over the initial infatuation and freak-out phases, but most of the time, they're also really hard to adapt to because of all the work they entail and the coordination they require with everything else going on in our lives.

Plus, because the love is often so loaded with the potential of evolving into lifelong commitment, all the stakes are much higher (in our overly analytical minds). In this chapter, I hope to help prepare you for what's ahead as you immerse yourself in your first few adventures.

First, the four big lessons of love followed by further insights to aid your psyche and sanity as you explore the crannies of adult amour.

LESSON #1: SELF-PRESERVATION

We all had friends in high school or college who became so preoccupied with a new romance that they put the rest of their lives (including us) on hold. Perhaps we were guilty of doing that as well. You'd think our gender would learn our lesson by the time we hit 20, but that isn't always the case. In fact, because so many of us for the first time really *want* a long-term commitment that could lead to marriage and family (these feelings start pouring in around age 27 or 28, even if you never believed they would), we're often even more at risk of letting the rest of our lives (including, in many cases, our own identities) go by the wayside. The likelihood is even greater during those first few hormonally driven months of spanking-new love.

The identity slide starts innocently enough: We slack off at the gym, we put the job search on hold for a while, we put off making plans with our friends to keep our weekends open for dates with our new favorite playmate. Or we drive ourselves nutty trying to do everything we did before *and* forge an intimate bond with our new lover: we have those after-work drinks with friends; make a quick stop at the gym for a trot on the mill; run home and throw in a load of laundry while paying bills, returning calls, and watering the plants; then grab something to wear for the next day (in case we decide to sleep over, which we probably will) and head off to meet our lover for a late dinner at his place. If we continue on either track, we end up in the same mental breakdown zone, suffering exhaustion-induced depression and a borderline identity crisis because we no longer have time to think about ourselves and our dreams.

To avoid breakdown trauma, handle the new conflict—and adding an intimate relationship to your life does create conflict with establishing an independent identity, which is what the 20s are all about—by setting a few boundaries. Decide how often you want to rendezvous with your new mate, giving yourself a night alone when you need one (you'll need at *least* one night a week all to yourself); maintain your friendships; and keep your dreams and goals as high a priority as falling in love. Maintaining your identity within a relationship is essential to making love last; if you keep yourself a priority, you'll do pretty well.

In fact, Leslie Parrott, codirector of the Center for Relationship Development at Seattle Pacific University and professor of a course she helped designed called Relationships 101, says that having a strong sense of self is the key to intimacy. You can't share yourself fully with someone else unless you know who you are and what you believe in. "Many people believe that a relationship is a shortcut for personal maturity, but that's not the case," she explains. "If you're trying to build intimacy with someone before you've become whole on your own, your relationship will be based on trying to complete yourself. Everyone talks about that line 'You complete me' from the movie *Jerry Maguire*. The idea is romantic and all, but you just can't find completion from someone else." In other words, you're not ready for a relationship until you've taken control of your own purpose in life. If you don't have a life vision, you need to get one.

LESSON #2: COMMUNICATION

Not to drag our parents into our relationships where they clearly don't belong, but when it comes to the topic of communicating with our mates, we must, because we learn our primary communication skills from them.

Perhaps you grew up in a family that communicated through a blizzard of guilt-inducing accusations followed by no-room-for-discussion commands like "Go to your room!" Or, in the extreme opposite case, perhaps your family never verbalized anger, affection, or minor upsets until one member blew a fuse and stormed out of the house for several hours, only to return as though nothing had happened.

Given such history, it will be harder to learn how to express yourself around your current mate without doing the same, simply because you don't know how to communicate otherwise. In these cases (and few of us had perfect models in the verbalization department), we have to learn good communication skills through experimentation with adult friends and lovers, but more so with lovers, because they rattle our emotions far more fervently than our friends usually do.

To complicate matters, our youthful inexperience in serious romance dictates that many of us don't really know what we think, believe in, or even want from the relationship ourselves. This lack of a clue naturally makes it difficult to express our thoughts and opinions to our partners. That's why the first goal in communication is to know yourself, which goes back to my first point and the one underlying task of all our 20-something lessons in love: work on that identity of yours. Know who you are and what you believe in. You can't share yourself with someone else (not to mention engage in serious and meaningful discussions) until you're in touch with your own beliefs and convictions. Then, all you need is practice.

One of the hardest communication skills for us to master is the ability to freely and openly express our emotions to our mates. Doing so makes us vulnerable to all sorts of undesirable things—rejection, criticism, the prospect of being judged—all of which can do nasty things to our already fragile egos. However, to get closer to our mates, we must put ourselves on the line, scary as that may be. Jumping in and experimenting in new ways of communication is the only way we'll learn how to open up. If you have a mate who's adept at drawing out your emotions and thoughts, this will help.

"One of the first things that attracted me to my boyfriend was that he wanted to know how I was feeling all the time," says Nina, 26, of Miami. "No one had ever been that way with me before. When I get angry, my tendencies are to blow off my feelings and just say, 'Whatever!' My boyfriend was the first person I've ever known to insist that we talk about things that bothered me." One caution: While such boyfriends are great for helping us open up, it's not wise to become dependent on them, because most of them willingly play Anne Sullivan to our Helen Keller tendencies only for so long before becoming thoroughly bored, annoyed, or both. Still, these guys are great for getting us going, so try to find one if you can.

Also, keep in mind that even with communicatively adept men, perfecting verbal skills takes time. It took Nina about a year before she could spit out exactly what she was thinking with her mate. Time and a string of successful experiences give us added reassurance that communicating what we feel will not scare our mates away or cause us to spontaneously combust as feared, perhaps due to cartoon overexposure during childhood. After all, if the relationship is so unstable that it can't withstand a little free expression or conflicting opinions, do you really want to be in it? I thought not.

Concentrate on initiating conversation that doesn't lead to shutting down or avoidance, which is one of the toughest battles couples must face, says relationships expert Leslie Parrott. She suggests following what she calls the "x, y, z formula" as a conversational starter, which helps keep both partners engaged: "In situation x, when you do y, I feel z." Practice by bringing up subjects that aren't critical, such as how far in advance you'd like to make plans for the weekend, or how soon he needs to call if he's going to be late. Then, when you're comfortable expressing views that are slightly difficult, dive into the bigger concerns.

Since communication takes two, the next step toward becoming verbally savvy is learning how to listen to your partner. Diane Sollee, founder of the Coalition for Marriage, Family and Couples Education, an organization that teaches couples skills for a successful marriage, often recommends that couples learn what she calls the speaker-listener technique: "The speaker is responsible for knowing who she is and what she believes in, as well as explaining her position to her partner. Her partner's job is to acknowledge that he understands every nuance of what she is saying. He may not agree with her opinions, but he must know them so well that three days later he could present her point of view exactly back to her. And vice versa. When couples communicate this way, they feel so understood." That's because most of us tend to miss so much and make so many assumptions when we're talking about heated, emotionally heavy subjects.

Another possible block to mutual understanding is that men and women have different styles of communicating, which you know if you're familiar with Deborah Tannen's bestseller, *You Just Don't Understand*. "Women's approach to communication is to build a bond or connection. Men's style is to transfer information. Understanding this may enable you to turn talk into a conversation with both head and heart," says Parrott. A case in point is Naomi, 23, of San Francisco: "I like to discuss things in the open, but my last boyfriend tended to ignore problems or completely not listen to me when I wanted to talk things out. I was the one who was always bringing things up—not because he didn't care, but because that's just the way he was."

In such cases, or when the coin is flipped and we're the one having trouble expressing our thoughts, our task is to find a compromise for dealing with each other's communication style. Here's how Audrey, 26, of Chicago, handles it: "I like getting things out in the open, but my husband prefers taking everything in and thinking about things before talking, so we came up with a compromise. Sometimes we talk about things immediately, and sometimes I have to wait for him to think things over." Compromise is the heart, in fact, of the third big lesson of 20-something love.

LESSON #3: CONFLICT RESOLUTION

If you are practicing the aforementioned lessons—paying close attention to yourself and expressing your opinions and beliefs, and accurately regurgitating your partner's point of view back to him for as many as three days after he's expressed it—you will indubitably, unavoidably, incorrigibly come face to face with conflict over *something*. It may be how often you see each other, where to spend your coveted vacation days (assuming you can coordinate work schedules to get the same time off together), whose turn it is to plan a fun night out, how frequently you have sex, or when you'll get engaged. No matter what degree of conflict exists, there's one important concept to accept, as counterintuitive as it may seem: Conflict is good for a relationship.

Think of conflict as a hearty round of kick boxing: you've got to practice your punches and kicks (we're talking figuratively here) to remain strong, grow, and challenge each other. Unfortunately, many of us don't realize this until it's too late, and instead of trying to work around the issues, we either take the approach of fighting to win disagreements or avoid the problems altogether. First let's discuss the more detrimental approach to conflict, avoiding it altogether.

Pretending that conflict doesn't exist is not the way to approach problems, no matter how big or small. In fact, according to Diane Sollee, avoidance (which most often takes the form of emotional or mental withdrawal) is the number one predictor of divorce, assuming that your relationship progresses to marriage. That's because dismissing or ignoring problems ensures that neither you nor your partner will develop good communication skills for dealing with conflict that might grow and eventually rock your relationship in the future. When you avoid matters that, if discussed, might result in fights, fears, or other emotional trauma, the relationship will eventually stagnate or collapse. It lacks the structure of understanding and compromise that enables healthy relationships to weather all types of storms.

If your response to conflict is to agree on everything your partner believes, you will develop the horrible disease of being afraid to have an opinion. This not only does bad things to your mental health but also does substantial damage to your relationship; you will eventually bore or outgrow your partner (or vice versa if he's the one who always concedes).

To eschew such avoidance tactics, you have to learn better ways of communicating. Let your partner know where you stand on all the important values and morals and decisions you make. If you have trouble communicating on the spot, or your body shuts down whenever discussions take place, spend some time preparing what you'll say before you open the floor with your mate, especially if you predict opposing views. Trixie, 25, of San Francisco, is an extreme example; she falls asleep whenever a boyfriend starts to argue with her: "My body totally shuts down, so writing things out helps me collect my thoughts on things that are annoying me or things that I like," she says. "When I can see it on paper, it helps me know where I stand."

Likewise, make sure you know your partner's stand on similar issues. When your points of view change—and they will—keep on talking. "When problems arise, you need to speak up right then and there and say, 'Look, you're doing something that bothers me.' Never keep anything inside," advises Mary, 25, of Washington, D.C. She employed such frankness with success when her boyfriend began urging her to attend a self-improvement seminar. "I told him that I really appreciated what he was saying but that he was making me uncomfortable by pushing the seminar on me," she says. "We discussed why, and he said he'd drop it for now."

The second conflict-resolution tactic that gets many of us in trouble is taking the common view of "fighting to win," according to clinical counselor Dee Marx-Kelly. "Fighting to win sets up a tug-of-war between the two people involved, which ultimately leads to resentment," she says. "The goal in working out problems is not to fight to win, but to fight to resolve issues, so that both sides come out winning and happy. This requires problem-solving skills in communication that most of us haven't learned by our 20s. If you don't learn these skills, you'll never learn how to argue in a conceptual way." The result: conflict escalates to cursing or sends the conversation into a downward spiral, causing withdrawal. Back to square one.

Another reason why fighting to win doesn't work is that the tactic is based on the false assumption that you will be able to change your partner's opinion, actions, or whatever he's doing that's making you nutty. This is a fallacy; you can't change your mate. While you may believe (or really, really wish) that if you pursue your improvement program hard enough, you can alleviate conflict on the rise, that's just not the case. Don't fool yourself. "We're taught to believe that love conquers all, that you can take the diamond in the rough and polish the person, or that if you give him enough of the 'right kind of love,' he'll change," says Marx-Kelly. "But that's a mother's instinct, and it doesn't work. You can't change a person, and you can't motivate him to change." That's why fighting to win never works.

Problem-solving tactics that *will* help navigate conflict involve figuring out ways to get past the issues your relationship is particularly vulnerable to. The reality is that many conflicts are plain irresolvable, even within healthy, happy couples. The best method for learning how to live with the conflict is, once again, communication. You start with acknowledging each other's opinion, then work out mutually acceptable ways of dancing around the issue, keeping the dance floor eternally open.

Conflict-resolution skills are so important because even if you have very little conflict now in your romance, you likely will have your share later on. You and your partner may move in together, share finances, and have increasingly busy work schedules, as well as a kid or two, mortgage angst, and other huge stresses that your fairly predictable life of today can't even fathom. So, don't blow off those little conflicts, start the discussions right away—if anything, just for the practice.

LESSON #4: ROMANCE MAINTENANCE

With all the lessons we must learn, it's easy to get caught up in the trauma induced by becoming intimate with someone instead of nurturing all the fun and passion that brought you together in the first place. This is true more so in the 20s than other decades because we have so little experience of what relationships involve, and so little idea of what we want. Once we're in solid relationships—many women find their partnerships beginning to resemble friendship more than the hot, fiery, passionate affairs that they had in the beginning.

I have a theory as to why the fire sometimes dims. It has to do with a subconscious sibling thing that seeps into our long-term relationships. Before you scream, "Sick, incestuous thought!" and hurl this book across the room, hear me out. If you have been living together or have otherwise merged your life intricately with your mate's, you know your partner probably as well as you knew your sibling growing up, assuming you're not an only child. That, according to my theory, confuses your brain's ability to imagine a passionate, fiery relationship with this person. I've heard that the same sort of thing happens after we get pregnant and become mothers: our partners often have trouble seeing us as the same sexually enticing women they fell in love with.

All is not hopeless, though. Romance ebbs when we're stressed or unhappy at work and flows when we're relaxed, planning our future with our partners, excited about things going on in our lives, or are on vacation. The trick is to not withdraw during low tide. Figure out ways of

Blow Off the Little Things

Resolving disagreements is one thing, but there comes a point where we have to just sit back and let the little stuff go. When every minor offense starts to ride on your nerves, that's a neon sign that you're not managing the bigger matters. But if the annoyances cause just an occasional tiff, one of the best remedies is humor. Two ideas on how to keep it light:

"When you're fighting about things, do something stupid," suggests one woman whose boyfriend sometimes farts during fights to break the tension. "Sometimes it's important not to take life too seriously," she says. "Instead, just ask each other if whatever's going on is worth fighting about."

"My boyfriend watches wrestling with his friends, and there's this one move called the dust spin, where one guy picks the other up over his shoulder and spins him around in a circle. Whenever I make my boyfriend angry, like when I'm late, he takes me outside, and I get the dust spin," says Miranda, 24, of Nashville.

relating to each other sexually during those times so that the romance remains on a slow burner until the next flow gets those flames sparking.

Jane, 25, of Chicago, has reestablished going out on dates with her boyfriend, whom she's dated for several years: "Once a week, we take swing dance lessons. Then one night each week, I'll cook for him or he'll cook for me." Nina and her boyfriend sometimes reenact significant dates from the past—such as the night they first kissed—to keep their romance afloat. Marie, 27, of New York City, who has been with the same boyfriend since college, says the romance upkeep works best when both partners take an active part: "We've been through periods where the relationship is stale. We're always both so busy, so we have to plan times to get together and be inventive and creative. One thing that helps is giving each other little presents; my boyfriend sometimes brings home flowers, or I'll bring him home a brownie. What's nice is knowing that the person is thinking about you."

Maintaining the heat beneath the sheets is another priority, which we'll get to in Chapter 7, "The Unpredictable Female Orgasm."

First, I have a few additional thoughts on relationships.

LONG-DISTANCE DATING

Face it, we are mobile creatures. Jobs, graduate programs, and wanderlust lure us away from our mates to titillating opportunities around the country and globe, adding an additional dilemma for those of us who are sipping the cocktail of couplehood. Knowing that this is a rare time in our lives when we lack major financial responsibilities such as a mortgage, or familial obligations such as babies, many of us feel maniacally determined to explore every city, educational opportunity, job, or chance to live abroad—say, leading cycle tours along the Nile—before life slows down in our 30s. More and more relationships, as a result, are being forced to adapt.

Never having long-distance dated and not knowing many people who had, I'd always been quick to write off relationships with geographical obstacles as a sign of intimacy avoidance. But after interviewing many women for this book who've not only maintained distant romances but also grown from them, I've done a complete about face on the matter. Here's one example why: "My boyfriend and I dated for eight years before we got married, and five of those were in separate cities a couple hundred miles apart," says Audrey. "The distance was actually one of the key reasons our relationship survived, because being apart forced us to make our own friends, do our own things, and learn to be alone. We still talked every day—sometimes just to say hi for a couple of minutes, other times for longer conversations, especially if we had problems to talk out—and we'd see each other every three or four weeks, but, ultimately, the distance is what allowed us both a chance to grow up and be independent."

While there's definitely something to be said for these phone-fed romances, especially when we've found love before we find ourselves, it's important not to let such relationships (and the phone maintenance they require) take over your life. "Don't not give yourself a life just because you're dating someone long-distance," warns veteran long-distancer Marie. Due to work, she has had periods of long-distance love with her current boyfriend, whom she now lives with. "Staying in your room is no way to live. You still need to really get to know yourself and have fun. Go out with friend and coworkers." After all, if your long-distance love has you parked in front of the TV, phone glued to ear, TV dinner in the microwave, every night from 8 P.M. to midnight, then you're not growing any more than you would if the two of you lived together and never left your apartment except to pick up and return videos.

Phone talk, in moderation, along with regular visits, is what makes these relationships work. Use your time together wisely. "When you do see each other, try to plan ahead," advises Marie. "Make special plans, and get all the little errands done during the week so that you don't have to do them when your boyfriend is visiting. If you have to, work a little harder for a few weeks before he comes so that you won't have to work on the weekends, or so you can take time off." Also, advises Melissa, 28, of Houston, who never lived in the same city as her boyfriend before they got married (but lived close enough that they could see each other every weekend), don't turn into an exclusive couple when you do get together. "We made an effort to incorporate each other's lives when we saw each other on the weekends," she says. For example, "We hung out with each other's friends; we got to know each other's roommates; if we wanted to go out to dinner alone, we'd do that, but then meet up with friends after." A distant romance won't do you any good if it adds distance to your friendships.

WHEN IT'S TIME TO DUMP A GUY

As we venture into relationship territory, the learning curve includes involvements with a few mates who, for whatever reason, are terrible matches. We need these experiences to know what we don't want, so they're not always terrible mistakes, as much as they may feel like it at the time. We can, sometimes, recognize the ill-fated attempt at couplehood right away and put the affair to an end before too many of our emotions are traumatized. Other times, we second-guess ourselves—convincing ourselves that we might have commitment problems, intimacy issues, or relationship baggage that we must work through—and end up staying in a relationship longer than we should. Figuring out when it's time to move on is always tricky. However, those of us who've been in a few relationships have learned a few telltale signs that a clean break just might be in order.

"If *everything* is a struggle, and the relationship is more damaging than good, it's clearly not working. I look at the amount of time we're happy and building each other up—that needs to be at least 85 percent," says Claudia, 29, of San Francisco. Another indicator that it's time to initiate the old heave-ho, adds Mary, 25, of Washington, D.C., is when you realize that you're spending more time analyzing the relationship and doubting it than believing it's headed in the right direction. Both partners also need to be making a mutual effort. If you're the one who's doing all of the relationship work, or if you give more than you receive, you won't be able to grow, since a relationship involves two.

One more point of logic: If every little thing about your mate annoys you—from his nasal voice to the smell of his armpits—you've got to ask yourself why you're with him. When you're really in love, little things like this become endearing, not gross.

Lynn, 25, of Portland, Oregon, uses her journal to help keep track of where her relationships are going. "Many times, all the little things that annoy me don't seem so bad at the moment, but if I look back through my journal and read how much my boyfriend and I have been fighting or how often he said he'd call but didn't, I can get perspective." The journal assessment can also serve as a comfort of sorts if your boyfriend dumps you, she says. "You can go back and read how unhappy you were, which helps you feel better about the relationship being over."

A second omen that it's time to call the relationship quits is finding that you're unable to be yourself within the relationship. This goes back to the first lesson of love, and it may have nothing to do with the guy: you just might not be ready to balance your life with someone else right now, and that's a perfectly acceptable reason to break up with someone. "I dated one guy who totally fit the profile of who I wanted to be with, but I couldn't commit to him, so I thought there must be something wrong with me," says Mary. "He sat me down and told me, 'I can't be your yo-yo; if you can't say you want to be with me now, we can't be together.' It took that for me to realize that I didn't want the relationship. It's difficult to admit that you're not ready, but get comfortable with it. Don't be in a hurry to find the person you want to spend your life with."

Sometimes, though, it's the guys who are making it hard for us to maintain our identities, by invading the boundaries we so adamantly try to set up. "My last boyfriend called me once on a Sunday night and asked if I wanted to come over, but I told him I wanted to be alone. He responded by saying: 'Ok, I'll come over.' I told him no, and he never returned my calls after that," says Anna. " I know that wasn't about me; that guy totally disrespected my boundaries, so it was a good thing to happen." If your boyfriend does something unacceptable, such as asking you not to hang out with your girlfriends anymore or pressuring you to be someone you're not, dump the jerk. No guy is worth losing yourself or dissolving the boundaries that you desperately need during this formidable time of life.

If your boyfriend is consistently inconsiderate or betrays a trust, you can infer that he doesn't respect you, which is one more reason to dump a guy. "I had let little things go with one guy I dated, such as his not calling, leaving me waiting around. I was definitely compromising myself and not spending time with my friends," says Simone, 28, of New Orleans. "What finally did it was when he didn't show up to my birthday dinner that some friends had planned. Instead, he showed up at 1 A.M. at the club we went to afterward. I stopped dating him the next day."

A relationship also has no room for betrayal, which can take many forms, including lying, cheating, and disclosing intimate details about you behind your back to mutual friends. If your partner is betraying you, he either has no respect for you or has some major relationship issues he needs to work on before committing to you. Don't blow off betrayal, and don't wait around for your partner to change unless he's making an honest effort through therapy or counseling, which he obviously needs. By the same token, if *your* eyes start wandering, do the honest and honorable thing, and renegotiate the monogamous policy with your mate before you do something—such as start seeing other guys—that's going to give you regrets for the rest of your life.

Another vital sign that it's time to end a relationship is your inability to envision yourself and your mate together, in love, for the long haul because you have conflicting values or opposite dreams, or simply aren't in love. Why settle for someone who's not right for you when you're so young? Clinging to a stagnant relationship will prevent you from exploring who else is out there and finding someone who really *does* make you dizzy every time you think about him. "If you don't see a future with someone, staying with the person wastes time," says Jane. "It's better to be on your own than dating someone who you know isn't right for you." Likewise, if your mate can't see you in his future (and he tells you this) it's time to let the relationship go, tough and depressing as that may be.

Most important, if a guy ever uses physical force to make a point or becomes verbally abusive, get out of the relationship immediately, warns Naomi, whose first boyfriend, after two years of dating, became physically violent. She relates: "The abuse began around the time I started becoming more independent from him. That's when he freaked out. We'd be arguing, and he'd punch my arm or shake me. Then he'd get mad at me for no reason. Once, I told him I loved him, and he slapped me. We were at his dorm, and his friends came out and held him back. That's when I drew the line. I saw a counselor and got a restraining order."

If you find yourself in an abusive or potentially abusive situation, you must realize two facts: you did nothing to provoke the attack, and there's nothing you can do to help your partner. "As soon as someone starts telling you that you're stupid or calls you names, that needs to be dealt with. Nobody deserves to be yelled at," says Naomi. "An abusive person can't change without help. He needs to get counseling, or the abuse will only get worse. You, alone, can't help him through that."

Along those same lines, if a guy ever makes you feel bad about your body or tries to coerce you into doing something sexually you're not comfortable with, drop him.

There are so many amazing men out there: why settle for one who smothers your esteem or, worse, threatens your safety? That's not love. And there's no acceptable excuse. Besides, if a guy flies off the handle about something, do you really want that kind of behavior around your kids if the relationship were to progress?

Breaking up, no matter how you slice it, is never easy. But there are good and bad ways of approaching the discussion to end all discussions. "When you're ready to end the relationship, talk it through, so that you're both clear on why you're breaking up," advises relationships expert Leslie Parrott. "Don't put it off; you want a clean break, not many minibreakups." As you gather up your courage to end an ill-fated twosome, prepare for the hurt that is bound to follow—even if the hurt comes solely from knowing that you've hurt your partner. Those are some of the toughest splits to carry through. Then stick to your plan, and try to look at your decision as a chance for you to take control of your life and change it for the better, because that's exactly what breakups are.

GETTING OVER A BREAKUP

First, the reality of breaking up: You will feel morose and dejected. You will feel lonely. Your self-esteem will likely plummet to an all-time low. But along with the negative aspects of ending a relationship, also accept this important truth (even if you find it impossible to believe at the time): You *will* eventually get over your loss, and you *will* find passion again with someone even better. That's because when you walk away from a relationship, you gain an ounce more of understanding of that amorphous thing called love. From this romantic clarity, you will gradually become enlightened to the type of mate who just might suit you best for the long haul.

Naturally, a breakup is easier when you're the one who's doing the dumping, because you can avoid feeling like a total reject. But even when you're instigating the dissolution, you may feel a bit unsure about your decision and lost about what to do with all the time you suddenly have on your hands. You may even have to consciously fight a few ugly pessimistic thoughts that there's no one in the world's pool of available mates who could possibly make a good match for you.

No breakup is seamless, of course, but there are a few tricks to getting through those first few torturous months, as follows.

Scream, Cry, and Let the Agony Roll

It doesn't take much to intellectually accept that a relationship is over. First we have the breakup talk. Then we tell our friends (and any guy we might be interested in) that we're single again. Next we immerse ourselves in the swinging singles' lifestyle—going out every night, hooking up with random guys, throwing ourselves into our jobs, making the gym and local bar our homes-away-from-home. What's a bit harder to accomplish is getting our emotional state to acknowledge the breakup, too.

The only way to do that is to really grieve our loss. Until we allow our emotions to fully accept that a relationship is over, we won't be able to fall in love again, because those emotions will, in a sense, still be preoccupied with our past loves. Also, warns one 28-year-old who knows, if you don't mourn the end of a relationship, your buried grief will likely resurface in the future when you're probably least expecting it and most certainly not wanting to deal with it. "When my husband and I got divorced, I tried to swallow all the hurt," she says. "But all those feelings came flooding back when I met my new boyfriend's family. I started feeling latent mourning."

One barrier that sometimes prevents us from truly purging our emotions is that whole analyzing thing we girls are so apt to do. We wonder: Why did he act that way? What would have happened if I had done this? How might things have turned out if only I had blah, blah, blah . . . ? Analyzing and blaming, which often accompanies the analyzing, are great tactics for distracting us from what we feel, because doing so intellectualizes and rationalizes—if it does not completely smother—our pain.

There's a time and place for examining what went wrong—and there's quite a bit to learn from a failed romance—but don't try to figure out the nuances of the breakup when your esteem is lower than low and your emotions are so desperate for attention. You'll get only an abstract picture of what went on, and the longer you put off your grief, the longer it will take to fully accept that the relationship is no more.

"You can't focus on what went wrong until you're back to yourself," says Vera, 26, of Denver. "When I was getting over my last relationship, I couldn't figure out anything until I got back to where I was myself. Only then could I begin to take responsibility for my share of the problems. Once your esteem has leveled out, you need to evaluate why the relationship wasn't good so you won't make the same choices next time."

So, stop the rumination, and get angry and depressed right away. "It's important to wallow in misery and mourn the breakup," agrees Claudia. "You have to let those emotions out. Try to get as low as you can. You'll eventually get tired of feeling so depressed all the time and come back up. But if you stay in the middle level, you'll never get rid of those feelings." Rebecca, 23, of Chicago, who had an exceptionally painful split with one of her past boyfriends, wishes she had allowed herself more time to mourn: "I had just moved across the country to go to law school, and the guy I was seeing didn't call me for three weeks. Finally, I had to call his mom to get his new number. He never called me after that, so there was no closure. I squelched my pain. If I'd given myself as little as one day to cry and look at old pictures, that would have helped me get over him more quickly."

The final act of grieving is moving toward acceptance that the relationship is finished, knowing that you can't do anything to repair or undo damage done—the kinds of steps you probably took before the breakup. Acceptance may involve letting go of a dream you had for what the relationship might have been. "Only one breakup has really upset me in the past," says Miranda. "What was most disturbing was the vision I was losing of who my boyfriend potentially could be rather than who he really was."

To help move toward acceptance, light a candle and chant a spell—it's meditative, suggests Melissa Cochran, who pens the Jane Err advice column for Swoon.com. Rituals always help reduce anxiety. So, burn a few letters and pictures (store the ashes in an urn); bury a present you once received from your lover, or give it to charity; do whatever it takes to help your mind finalize the end of your romance. Then bottle up the good aspects of your relationship, and preserve those memories for recall later on.

Rally the Troops

"What helped me get over my breakup was going out and doing things," says Rebecca. "I got involved in lots of activities: I joined clubs, did law journal, tried to meet guys. I also learned that in future relationships, I will never give so much of myself to one person." This takes us back to that first lesson I mentioned (as do so many of the nuggets in this chapter): If you ignore yourself while you're in a relationship and it ends, you're left with nothing but the shell of your former self. Any alternative is better than ending up feeling empty. Our "filling" is the one thing we really own in this world; don't sacrifice it to someone else. Unfortunately, most of us learn this the hard way, through a nasty breakup. So, when the emptiness appears, make immediate attempts to refuel your soul with activities, friends, and self-confidence.

"When my ex-boyfriend broke up with me, my family told me, 'You knew this was coming; this was your worst fear. Isn't it a relief it's over?' Well," recalls Molly, 27, of Philadelphia, "my worst fear *had* come true. So, in a sense, I had nothing left to fear, but I still felt as if my world had dropped out. The first month, I made sure that I had something planned every weekend. One weekend I spent with a friend who let me take out the photo album and cry. Another weekend I spent with my parents and sister. During the week, I worked my ass off, some nights until 10 P.M. Then, work friends invited me out for drinks, and that opened up a whole new world to me. I surrounded myself with new friends for the first few months. I dated a lot but stayed single for almost a year, and I gained a lot of self-respect. Dating suddenly wasn't about getting someone's approval: it was about learning to like myself."

Not only are friends great for drawing us out of our breakup mourning when we need relief from all those depressing thoughts, but also they're the best form of support. "When I was once going through a breakup, my friends taped a big note to my phone: 'Before you call him, call one of us,' " says Claudia. Likewise, "If it weren't for my friends," says Hannah, 24, of Los Angeles, "I'd probably have second-guessed myself and given my ex-boyfriend a third chance." "They pushed me to stand up for myself, reminding me that I wasn't doing anything wrong by breaking up." Friends also came to the rescue when Mary and her my ex-boyfriend broke up. Says Mary: "I have three very good friends, whom I call my Holy Trinity. They all provided different kinds of support. It didn't matter how many times I called them to talk about it, they'd always tell me, 'I know it sucks, but it will be over. Tomorrow will be a little easier than today.' "

As you reconnect with old friends and make new ones, also make a concerted effort to build up your esteem, because it will probably have dropped to low levels, regardless of who did the breaking up. A failed romance, no matter how bad it was, can still make you feel like a failure. "Try to focus on something that's going to benefit you, like work, going out with friends, or even reading a book," suggests Vera. "Realize it's going to be hard, no matter how you deal with it."

Make a Clean Break

Many of us are familiar with that breaking-up-getting-back-together dance: The relationship ends. A few weeks later, you call just to say "hi." You meet for dinner to "talk." You confess to each other that you miss the good times. But can it work? Maybe. You'll both try to change. Again. Next thing you know, you're groping each other madly over the table at the bar, unleashing all that sexual energy you've both caged since the breakup. Meanwhile, you're feeling nothing but the daunting prospect of another failed attempt to love each other the way you both need.

There's also the let's-try-to-be-friends dance, which rarely turns out to be a friendly twirl around the dance floor, especially when one of you starts dating someone new. Besides, if you do the on-again, off-again relationship thing, your friends will stop caring each time you break up, because they'll believe it's only temporary. Without their support, it will be harder for you to call it quits for real when you get to the point that you can no longer endure the going-nowhere romance.

If you both made an honest effort to make the relationship work while you were still together, don't put yourself through the misery of trying to force an ill-fated love affair to be anything more than that. You may know in your gut that your desires to be together again are prompted by loneliness; in these cases, you must just walk away. Don't even call or try to see what's up with him. Lynn offers this sage advice: "Do not call him until you no longer *want* to. That's when you know you're over him. Even if the breakup was amicable, it's much healthier putting on the freeze. Doing so speeds up the process of getting over someone."

Take Your Time with the Rebound Guy

The quickest way to boost esteem following a breakup—especially if you've been dumped—is sometimes through affection and attention from a new guy. Post-breakup flings are fun, distracting, and great for the ego (at least temporarily), but take your time before getting into another serious relationship. If you don't, you won't have a chance to fully grieve your loss, and you'll never learn how to build esteem on your own. The first guy you meet after your breakup may indeed be your soul mate, but if he is, he'll give you all the time and space you need to recover from your recent loss to figure that out. If he doesn't, then he doesn't really respect you. Remember that, and work on rebuilding your core before immersing yourself in a new relationship. You'll be so much happier and more confident in the end for doing that. And your next boyfriend will love you all the more for respecting yourself enough to do so.

Don't Become Jaded

Of course, it's hard not to be bitter about relationships in general following a breakup—again, especially if you were the dumpee—but don't fall into the trap of thinking there's no one out there for you. "There are hundreds of guys out there who are probably good matches for you; it's just a matter of running into each other when both of you are ready to be in serious relationships," says Mary. Adds Lauren 23, of Santa Barbara, "If you've been hurt, there's a tendency to close off to someone the next time, but let your heart be free when you date." Also, remind yourself of some of the healthy relationships you've had in the past. If there aren't many of those, find role models of good relationships among your siblings or peers to remind yourself that all's not hopeless. "Look at friends who are in wonderful relationships, and talk to their boyfriends about your breakup," suggests Marie. "They'll probably have some good guy insight."

ON TAKING MINIBREAKS

Breaks can be wonderful little tactics for reassessing a relationship, particularly if you're the type of relationship partaker who spends every waking minute with your mate. Breaks may give you the space you need to reorganize how much time you're happy spending with your boyfriend, as well as how much you really love him—or don't. Breaks may be exceptionally insightful for those who continue to date their first loves from high school or college during their 20s (and in case you're wondering, those who do, I'm told, go through the same relationship battles as the rest of us, except the crossfire just happens to be with the same person). "Taking breaks taught me that there are a lot of jerks out there," says one 29-year-old woman, who married her high school sweetheart 5 years ago. "A lot of guys may seem really great, but when you get to know them, they're not so nice deep down."

If you and your partner opt for a break, be sure to define what a 'break" means. If it means dating other people, make sure you both realize the possible outcome of this daring move—that one of you might meet someone else and fall in love. Also clarify whether the dating allows the possibility of a sexual relationship to develop and, if one does, how that might affect any plans of getting back together after the break. If the hiatus is simply to give you time and space alone, use that time to figure out how to allow yourself the space you need within the relationship, without taking formal breaks, because needing breaks from one another is often a blaring signal that you're ignoring your own needs day-to-day. One compromise solution to contemplate: reserve several nights a week for yourself and your friends instead of seeing your significant other every single night.

Wanting a break or becoming a serial break-taker could also indicate that you're bored with the relationship or hesitant, for various reasons, to wade deeper into the romance you're pursuing. If either of those is the case, a break isn't going to help. Making changes in the relationship with your partner is the only thing that will. Sit down and discuss several solutions for improving your relationship, suggests Marie, who has had several breaks from her long-standing college boyfriend. In her experience, "You may just need to make more of an effort to keep your relationship exciting: plan more things to do together, take vacations, get back into your sex life." Her conclusion: "Whatever you do, be as honest with each other as possible."

MOVING IN WITH MR. MAYBE

As soon as you even remotely begin to think about moving in with your mate, the first comments you'll probably hear from girlfriends (or parents, if you let them in on the details of your love life) are those grave statistics that came out several years ago suggesting that couples who cohabitate before they marry are more likely to end up divorced later on. And if you're anything like me—my boyfriend and I have been cohabitating for about a year and a half now—hearing about these studies will probably make you more neurotic and insecure about your decision. But it's OK to ignore these studies. Here's why.

Most of those reports were conducted about a decade ago, when living together was considered less acceptable than it is today, says Susan Brown, Ph.D., professor of sociology at Bowling Green University, who has written on the subject. Because living together was less common even a few years ago, the couples surveyed likely had more liberal attitudes about marriage than those of their peers, which means that they were probably also more willing to opt for divorce if marriage didn't work out. If the same studies were conducted today, the results would probably be different, since living together is in vogue, even among those who don't consider divorce an option (about 55 percent of couples live together before getting married, according to Brown).

So, you see, the act of living together in itself has no influence on marital success; how much a couple shares a willingness to do whatever it takes to make marriage work, however, does. In fact, because many of us value marriage so much, the main reason we want to live together with our partners in the first place is to make 120 percent sure that the partner we've chosen is who we want to marry. Living together is a good test.

For what my own happily cohabiting opinion is worth, I think living together is an especially wise move if you're a nervous wreck whenever you think about settling down with someone for the long haul, as I have been in the past, having witnessed several divorces in my family. Not only has living together given me some pretty convincing evidence that I can share my life with my boyfriend and still maintain my independence (my biggest worry), but it also has taught me how much I love living with him, not to mention how compatible we are at sharing expenses, tempering bad moods, and divvying up such unromantic tasks as cleaning the bathroom. If we hadn't lived together, I think it would have taken me a lot longer to grow confident that my boyfriend is the man for me. And if he ever gets inspired to pop the question, he can rest assured that I'm absolutely 120 percent ready to get hitched. No more questions in my mind. No siree! I'm ready.

By the way, you are likely well versed in the adage, Why buy the cow when you can get the milk for free? which, in all its vulgarity, implies that a man won't want to marry someone if he can get sexual gratification and all the practical perks of being married without legal commitment. There are two reasons why I loathe this saying. One, it compares us girls to cows, which is not only visually disturbing but also just plain rude. And two, it assumes that all we want out of the deal is a guarantee to be bought and milked forever after. On the contrary, most women I know who are living with their mates aren't looking for a guarantee. They're looking for evidence of compatibility: how the cow-milkman team works out such challenges as having unwashed milk pails soaking in the sink for days, an occasional not-in-the-mood udder, and other such stresses that frequent the farm.

That said, I feel it is my duty to express one caveat about taking the big step forward: Do not move in with your mate out of financial necessity or because circumstances make sharing a flat easier. Living together for any reason other than wanting to take the relationship one step further will strain the relationship, usually before it has built up enough love muscle to manhandle the delicate task of merging the roles of roommate and lover. Even if you're spending five nights a week at your boyfriend's house, lugging half your wardrobe across town every day (but you still never seem to have the right outfit at the right apartment when you need it), all the while feeling thoroughly disgusted at the beginning of every month when you write that rent check for the apartment where you spend only one or two nights a week, don't assume that playing house will make life easier. If the relationship is not ready for the intensity that living together demands—and we're talking full disclosure on every aspect of your life, from any financial skeletons associated with your credit history to any embarrassing grooming habits, like wearing zit cream to bed at night, that you've managed to keep hidden from your mate so far—your life will become even more stressful. Moving in with your mate is one decision not to be made lightly.

Before you decide to live together, there are several subjects that you and your partner should discuss. And if you're too scared to broach these topics just yet, consider your fear a sign that the relationship needs a little more time on the vine. Most important, discuss your expectations for living together, advises Claudia, who has lived with two of her past boyfriends—once out of convenience, and the other time to test out marriage. If one of you considers the arrangement a stepping-stone to the altar, and the other finds it merely a good way to save money for that solo trip around the world next year, one of you is eventually going to get hurt. So, make sure you both agree on why you're taking this big leap.

Then discuss a few practical issues, such as how you'll divide finances and chores. "I lived with the first guy in a co-op, so we kept all our expenses separate, but the second guy and I split rent, groceries, and bills based on a percentage of how much each of us made," says Claudia. There's also the splitting everything 50-50 method, favored by many women and their cohabitating mates.

Also make sure that you discuss a few house rules, such as when you should call if you're going to be later than you said. As much as the calling-to-check-in act may trigger old rebellious feelings from high school, when we were forced to report to Mom and Dad on every little change in plan we made (which we never did anyway), you will appreciate the gesture when you're on the receiving end. You'll appreciate it all the more if your mate drives a motorcycle that not only has a questionable headlight and no horn but also has the habit of breaking down in the seediest parts of town. My boyfriend and I have never had a rule per se, but after staying out late once with my girlfriends and not calling, then getting the cold shoulder followed by an hourlong discussion at four in the morning about being considerate, I learned that it pays to take the 10 extra minutes and find the one working pay phone in the loud, obnoxious dance club and check in when you say you will. After all, you'd be worried, too.

You have one last thing now to think about (though you probably don't want to). Since moving in together is often a trial run for long-term commitment, there's always a chance that the trial will prove disastrous, and the relationship end. When you're living together, sharing everything from physical space to the photo album, these dissolutions are the most devastating. "It is like a divorce," says Claudia, which is why it's imperative during this trial-run period to maintain your financial independence and your friendships. If something (God forbid) goes wrong, you know that you'll be able to take care of yourself.

Now, some women would argue that the potential of such breakups is precisely the reason why you should never move in with someone without an engagement ring on your finger or a wedding date on the calendar. This precaution would presumably ensure that your mate is willing to work out all problems, whatever the cost. I tend to disagree, because living together puts new stresses on your relationship that would eventually emerge once you were married, such as finances, conflicting schedules, and naive expectations on how cohabitating changes a relationship. And aren't you curious to know whether you'd be able to work the stresses and strains out before you get the law or in-laws involved?

Living together can also enlighten you to certain aspects of your mate that you might not have seen when you were just dating. Claudia can elaborate on that one: "I learned so many things about the second guy I lived with that I wouldn't have known if we hadn't lived together. For instance, I never noticed how much he drank and smoked pot, but when we moved in together, I realized it was every day. Turns out, he was a drug addict and an alcoholic." Living with someone is the only way you'll see his true colors, adds Vera, who recently broke up with her live-in boyfriend. "Dating is about being in harmony, and it's easy to put on a façade: you say the right things, you don't fight, you cuddle, and you show your partner only what you want him to see. After 48 hours together, you can go away and be by yourself. But if you live with someone and have a terrible day or get into a fight, you can't send that person away. It's important to realize that when you move in together, your whole routine will change. When you're mad, you *will* take it out on your mate, and your mate will take a bad day out on you. This has been a big learning experience for me."

To avoid any potential feelings of moving in on each other's territory, once you decide to live together, try to find a new apartment, rather than having one of you move in with the other. That will also give you both an opportunity to clean out your closets, which, keep in mind, will most likely have to be shared in your new place. So, for space reasons, it's a good time sort through those boxes and boxes of high school memorabilia that your mom sent you when she was cleaning out your room back home, and throw away the stuff you never want to see again.

Then, once you move in together, realize that it may take some time to get your individual grooves back in sync while you're adjusting to a new lifestyle. Relax, many of us who've done it wouldn't have it any other way.

SWAPPING VOWS

If you foresee matrimony in the near future, this section has useful information for you. If marriage is a decade or so away, skip ahead to the next chapter, but come back when you meet Mr. Maybe. If you are already in a serious relationship and have started planning the honeymoon (even if only in your own private thoughts), listen up. After interviewing close to 100 women in their 20s—single, wed, and divorced—as well as experts on the subject of love, I've come to the conclusion that our gender should not marry before age 25 or so, when the great metamorphosis into women is complete.

Now, I know that there are plenty of 21- or 22-year-old girls out there who married their college or high school boyfriends and, by virtue of their own marital success, can trash my theory. But most of us aren't emotionally mature enough to make such a serious decision as naming the person with whom we want to spend the rest of our lives, let alone the father of our children. We probably don't even know for sure if we want kids. We're still debating what we want to do with our lives and where our career-in-the-works might take us one day.

What's more, our youthfulness alone pretty much guarantees that we don't have much real-life experience with relationships. This status makes it virtually impossible for us to even know what qualities we most desire in a lifelong spouse. With so much ambiguity cluttering up our impressionable minds, now's not an opportune time to make life-altering decisions.

Leslie Parrott, coauthor of *Saving Your Marriage Before It Starts*, encourages those of us pondering a life of matrimony to also ponder two attributes before swapping vows: personal readiness and relational readiness. Personal readiness is based on three principles: how well we know and like ourselves, how mature we are, and how independent we are from Mom and Dad. If we have so-called unresolved issues with the folks and base our decisions on the sole premise of either pleasing them or pissing them off, then we're not in control of our lives. We will probably experience matrimonial disaster when our future husbands discover that they married not only us but our folks back home and their dirty laundry, too. Of course, our chosen mate must also know himself equally well; so consider those aspects about your partner, and talk long and seriously about your plans.

Relational readiness, says Parrott, can be assessed by examining the history of your courtship. Longevity is the determinant, she says: "The longer you date, the more ready you are for marriage. Couples who date two or more years score higher on marital satisfaction tests." Time offers some of the same benefits as living together, in the sense that it's a lot harder to hide things about yourself over an extended period, as it is when you share a tiny apartment. So, the longer you date, the more likely you'll fully reveal all aspects of your desirable (and occasionally not so desirable) quirks to your partner, as he will to you. That way, you know *exactly* who you are marrying.

As you start the engagement talks, be sure to launch an open and ongoing discussion of some of the basic concerns that face all couples for as long as they plan on being couples. These include future child-care opinions and rearing ideologies, retirement planning and other financial savings-versus-spending debates, career growth, delegation of chores, libido fluctuations, in-law maintenance, leisure-time pursuits, and day-to-day living tasks.

Such talks defy our culture's romantic mythology of getting hitched purely on the basis of whether or not the glass shoe fits. "The first year of dating can be pretty easy, anyone can put on a facade for a year," says Jane, "but to really get to know a person, you need to go through money ordeals and other kinds of stress." If, during those normal ups and downs, your relationship maintains a relatively stable ride (resembling more of a kiddy coaster than the loop-d-loop), that's another predictor that you and your mate are in good shape for the altar, says Parrott.

And finally, if you and your partner share similar goals, interests, habits, and energy levels, life will obviously be easier for you starting out than it will be for couples who have completely different ideas about how to live life. But read on.

Compatibility, despite popular opinion, is not the most telling sign of a solid relationship, warns marriage and relationships expert Diane Sollee. Her website, www.smartmarriages.com, offers a directory of marriage education workshops around the country. She points out, "The person you marry will not be the same person 10 years later. People go through dramatic changes, even basic values about money, family, and religion change." We change as soon as we get a promotion. Or have a baby. Or win the lottery. Or (God forbid!) fall off a horse and become paralyzed from the neck down. And, going back to my original point about staying single until at least 25, one of the most active periods of change in our lives is during our 20s, when we're testing out so many different identities.

"How well a couple deals with disagreements and change is the main test of how prepared the relationship is to handle some of the challenges of marriage," Sollee says. "All couples in good, sexy marriages have about 10 irreconcilable differences, but they don't get alarmed by this. They have skills for cordoning off opposing views, keeping some areas contained, staying open to ongoing discussions about their differences for the rest of their lives." This is why communication and conflict resolution are important skills to practice and perfect with our mates before we even consider marriage. So, go back and reread those tips if you skipped over them. Since most of us don't develop these skills on our own—trial and error is really the only way to learn, unless you had exceptional parents as role models—premarital counseling workshops or couples therapy might not be a bad idea before taking the nuptial leap. Not only do these courses give couples a reality check for what marriage is all about, but they also teach vital marriage maintenance skills for communicating and managing differences.

The annoying aspect of taking your sweet time to decide if your partner is truly the lifelong mate for you is that the longer you wait, the more social pressure you will get for setting a date to tie the knot. This pressure becomes acute after you've dated your boyfriend for two years, moved in together, and started going to all your friends' weddings, where the bouquet is inevitably hurled toward you. The community pressure comes in all forms. It may be subtle overtures from acquaintances and colleagues: "So, *how* long have you been dating now? Hmmm." Or it may be direct interrogation, if not from family (mine innately knows that the subject is off-limits), then from friends: "So, when *is* he going to ask you to marry him?"

No matter how secure you are in the relationship and your decision to take love slowly, these social prods will likely make you panicky, forcing you to eventually bring up the topic yourself, despite your resolve never to do so. (Why guys collectively refuse to bring up marriage first is one of the most puzzling of all human mating rituals; perhaps they just can't hear the deafening tick of our biological clocks—which often starts faintly during our late 20s—and are waiting for us to sound the alarm.)

6

You Sexy Thing

*N*ame one thing more electrifying than a spontaneous roll in the hay and I'll eat it, since the only possible answer is chocolate. (My apologies to any guy who might be thumbing through this book and find this notion offensive, but, really, chocolate is sometimes the only thing that's going to do it for us girls. Make a note of that.) Sex in the 20s is what I imagine Paris in the spring to be like, since my one and only trip to France was in October, and my vision of a Parisian spring is therefore entirely based on impressionistic images of buds and blossoms so vibrant that your eyes dilate, which just about describes our burgeoning sexuality during this decade of prime-time female fertility.

It's no mistake on Mother Nature's behalf that we women delve into our sexuality right around the time our ovaries begin producing eggs like there's no tomorrow. However, the timing does tend to complicate matters, since so many of us are putting baby making on hold until we get our careers good and going, not to mention find a proper child-rearing mate! Birth control is essential to exploring sex, the most publicized venue of sexual expression, and we'll talk shop later. But first, on to other pressing matters.

One of the notable differences about our sexuality during the 20s, as opposed to our early hormonally crazed introduction to passion and desire brought to us courtesy of adolescence, is that we no longer have to sneak behind our parents' backs to explore the forbidden act (unless, of course, you had unusually enlightened parents). Along with this sudden freedom, another unique and curious force is at work: we have finally and undeniably cleared the jailbait years and entered what our society considers the pinnacle of female sexuality.

We are young, and youth is sexy. We are ever so curious about sex and often more than eager to explore. And we are the object of everyone's desire. Younger guys consider us far sexier and more sophisticated than their adolescent peers; older guys think we're hot young babes (because we *are*); and guys our own age usually don't have a chance with older women, so we are their only option.

All of these factors add up to one thing: delirium. While we may be at the height of our sexual experimentation, we lack experience to make the best decisions. That's why sex in the 20s can be yet another tricky and chaotic variable to add to the mix of anarchy that already exists in our transitional lives. Have no fear; we all somehow manage to make it through the pandemonium—not without the enthusiastic zest of a female warrior, I might add.

LET THE CANNONBALLS FLY!

Getting in touch with our sexuality is a bit like waging an internal sexual revolution: First, we must learn how our machinery works, if we haven't already figured out what turns us on. Second, we must don proper armor to fend off such casualties as pregnancy and disease. Then, we can begin to explore our position (What does sex mean to me? Am I attracted to men? Women? Both?) and engage in some experimental and strategic drills to help establish our boundaries. And finally, we must face the enemy (our inhibitions) and battle our way to victory, so that at the end of our revolution, we're not only comfortable with our sexuality but also confident enough to share it intimately with someone we truly love and respect (as opposed to someone we just want to . . . well, you get the point). Let's go over the battle plan.

Learn Your Machinery and Armor

We'll talk more about our wily and often unpredictable female machinery in the next chapter. For now, just know that learning how our bodies work—what turns us on and what doesn't—is the overriding maneuver for getting in touch with our sexuality, so to speak.

Masturbation is one of the most important drills to practice. If you don't know how to switch on those erotic zones, you will become reliant upon someone else for a little sexual relief, and chances are, that someone else just might not know how to get you going, either. That can lead to sexual frustration, which is counterproductive to our mission. So, begin your revolution by inspecting your machinery and learning exactly how it works.

Likewise, when you are ready to engage in a little one-on-one, protecting yourself from disease and pregnancy is an equally important strategic move. Acquiring a sexually transmitted disease or finding yourself with an unwanted pregnancy can do damaging things to your sexual confidence, not to mention stir up a lot of other emotionally difficult issues and decisions. Again, we'll talk specifics later. In the meantime, remember to take your armor seriously, young soldierette. Then carry on with your mission.

Explore Your Position

You may ask, What's to explore? Well, many of us have a lot of soul-searching to do when it comes to getting in touch with our sexual identity, and the 20s are when most of us do that, simply because we're likely to have more opportunities than ever to form new opinions about sex. One of the issues that often come up is deciding what sex (and related activities) means to us. For example, your view might be that sex is a fun and frivolous way to release tension from the rigors of being an overworked, underpaid 20-something and that it can and should be shared wherever and with whomever one chooses. Or you might revere sex as holy and spiritual and something to be shared only with your soul mate. You might just as likely consider intercourse on a whole different plane from oral sex or touching, reserving the latter for casual flings, as does a certain president we all know (sorry, I couldn't resist), and the former for more serious affairs.

None of these views is better than the other; they're all just different. And differing opinions are what makes the whole subject so titillating (and confusing). I would just like to lay out this one thought, though: You do not need to have intercourse to get in touch with your sexual identity. That, ladies, is for you to decide and not for me to advise. If you are still a virgin, it's important to consider what you want out of sex before you cave in to the overriding pressure to succumb to passion, a phenomenon that will surround you throughout this first decade of adulthood. "If a woman believes she should have sex only when she's in love or in a committed relationship, she should not engage in casual sex," says 20-something sex educator Sari Locker, author of *The Complete Idiot's Guide to Amazing Sex.* "She should also think about how long she wants to wait, and assess her partners carefully to determine if they share her values."

Our friends, our environment, new relationships, recent experiences, exposure to X-rated movies, and the holy scriptures can all play a role in forming our opinions about the delicate matter of sex. Our task is to wade through all these influences, then come up with a personal party line, bearing in mind that this position will probably change— sometimes several times over—during our debut into adulthood. Katharine, 28, of Los Angeles, for instance, experienced a change of values after she fell in love for the first time. "After I graduated from college, I went through a period where I was having a lot of sex, mainly just to explore, because I hadn't had sex in college," she recalls. "But after my first long relationship, I've come to view sex very differently. Now I associate sex with love. After making love with someone I really value and feel close to, I can't imagine having sex with someone I don't care about."

The second area many of us must begin to nail down relates to the object of our attraction—is it men, women, or both? Now, some girls never have to question their sexual orientation. They've known since puberty that they were, without a second thought, heterosexual or lesbian or bisexual. But because our orientations can expand, mutate, or do an about face when we move to a new community with ample resources and support for lesbians and bisexuals, or when we make friends with people who accept or even encourage exploring our preferences, new feelings can easily emerge. If they do, pay close attention to them, because they probably won't spontaneously disappear if you ignore them.

According to Paula Rust, associate professor of sociology at the State University of New York, in Geneseo, who has done research on lesbian, bisexual, and gay identities, the 20s are a prolific time to discover where our sexual orientation lies. In fact, most women who come out are in their early 20s. "It's healthy to explore any feelings you may have about being a lesbian or bisexual," she says. "It's better to face them when you're young rather than later on, when you may have lifetime commitments, such as marriage or children, to think about." Besides, don't you want to know?

Melanie, 28, of Austin, was curious, so she began dating a woman she was attracted to in order to find out where she stood. "It was fun to have a sexual experience with another woman, but it made me know, beyond a doubt, that I'm heterosexual," she says. Vanessa, 23, of San Francisco didn't have quite the same revelation when she began to explore her attraction to women: "I started to wonder if I was straight or bi at the beginning of my sophomore year in college. During the summer, I worked at a camp, and there were three of us there—me, another woman, and a guy—who were OK with homosexuality. We were at a party one night, and the woman came over to me and said that she wanted to kiss me, so we went outside and made out. I wanted to get the questioning out of my system, but I chalked that experience up to 'that didn't tell my anything.' In fact, I was annoyed with myself because it felt the same as if I had hooked up with a guy I wasn't attracted to. I shouldn't have experimented with her, but I don't have a huge amount of remorse. Now I'd like to see how I feel with a woman I'm really attracted to."

Questioning your sexual orientation and then taking that scary step forward to experiment requires the guts of a war hero; those willing to enter the minefield of emotions deserve a medal of honor. Here's how it went with Sloane, 21, of Syracuse, New York: "I was always open to dating women but felt that I had to be a certifiable dyke to experiment. It wasn't until one of my closest girlfriends told me that she had feelings for me that I felt no qualms about seeing what it was like. I was shocked at how natural making love to a woman felt—it was as if she was going straight to the core of me. I recently came out with my mom, and her reaction was, 'Don't you think I know?' Then she bought me a Beanie Baby."

Of course, not all parents are as accepting as Sloane's, but no law says you must divulge details of your sex life to your parents. In fact, many women and experts advise keeping your sex life far away from conversations with your folks, if only to facilitate your separation from them.

Exploring your sexual preferences can stir up a lot of difficult feelings; deciding to tell your parents that you've started playing for the other team can be even more challenging, and then some if you grew up in a family that discouraged or demoralized homosexuality or bisexuality. But keep in mind that you have a choice: you can live your life being true to yourself or spend your days denying your sexuality. Either decision conjures up unwanted emotions, but going where your hormones point will make you happier in the long run.

So, find a good support group through the Internet or community services, and take a stand (or begin to explore what your stand may be). This may be one of the hardest battles you'll face in the 20s, but better to bite the bullet now. Life is way too short, and getting in touch with your sexuality is way too wonderful to delay your victory. Now let's move onward!

Stake Your Boundaries

Once we know where we stand on the foregoing strategic issues, we can move on to one of our primary objectives in our sexual campaign: to determine our boundaries in the bedroom. In other words, we decide to what extent we'd like to share our sexuality with someone else. Then we clearly communicate our perimeters to our partners to avoid surprise attacks or unwanted assaults before, during, or after a sensual engagement. Accomplishing this builds the confidence we need to be in full control of our sexual identity, but it's also one of the toughest revolutionary tactics to learn, more so if you're the kind of girl who has trouble saying, "I'm not cool with that."

Knowing how you feel about casual sex, what you want out of the experience, and to what extent you're willing to try new things will give you some idea of where your boundaries lie. Communicating them to a new partner, however, can sometimes feel as unromantic as a two-hour session of strategic planning. But to fully enjoy sex, such limitations must be spoken. Otherwise, the whole time, you will just worry and fret that your boundaries might get crossed before you know it. Your partner, too, may be totally confused and probably not very smooth because of the anxiety that goes along with uncertainty. Or your bedmate may take the opposite, "all's-fair-in-love-and-war" approach and assume that because you didn't state your limits before the kissing and caressing started, you have none. In worst cases, such assumptions can lead to horrible war causalities, the most prevalent among us young 20-somethings being date rape.

This is why boundaries must be stated long before the heavy breathing starts and before we start drinking, which often has the effect of dimming cognitive sense among all parties involved. Rebecca, 23, of Chicago, who is a virgin, tells her partners up front something to the effect of: "We can do everything else, but we can't have intercourse. So, if you still want to be with me, that's up to you." She asserts: "It's fun to do other things without the pressure of trying to figure out whether or not you're going to have sex. It also forces the guy to figure out other ways of making me feel good." This is also a brilliant tactic for exploring your sexuality with a new partner, since intercourse is not always the most efficient way to get us girls going. But more on that in the next chapter.

If sex is within your boundaries, experimenting with new positions, various partners, multiple partners, and other erotic or downright kinky curiosities that you harbor will also help you form a sense of what you like and don't like when it comes to sex, helping to define that sexual identity you're in the process of molding. The only rules about experimenting are that you (1) must feel comfortable with what you're doing and (2) must trust your partner to delve into the unknown at the same pace as you *and* be willing to call it off, if you so desire, mid-experiment.

Confront the Enemies

As with any revolution, we must battle a few enemies in the campaign to get in touch with our sexual identity. Our enemies in the sexual revolution are our inhibitions, which typically derive from three sources: a fundamental upbringing that purports that certain (or all) sexual practices and desires are bad; negative body image; and past sexual abuse, assault, or trauma. Most of us have to conquer at least one of these inhibitions; the more deeply they weaken your artillery, the more necessary it is to seek professional counsel. "A therapist can help women understand how the past has influenced her present feelings about sex. Once she makes a connection, it's easier to see that she has a choice on how to deal with these feelings," says sex educator Sari Locker.

Getting over those frightful notions—"Sex is something bad girls do" or "Sex is meant only for procreation."—placed in our impressionable minds by our concerned but perhaps opinionated parents or the community in which we grew up generally comes about after we separate from our childhood caregivers and their ideas. (Chapter 11, "Family Knots," is devoted to this topic.) Of course, if your identity is rooted in these views toward women's sexuality, by all means, stick to them. The last thing I want to do is add another conflict to your adult identity-in-progress.

Being an American-born-in-the-'70s kind of girl, however, I take the stand that you should challenge your beliefs throughout life. Since your position on sex will be forced to come to a head during your 20s, I'm just suggesting that you take a deep and meditative look at why you believe what you do. If your upbringing is creating conflict in your blossoming sexual self, just know it's OK to question that.

Getting over bad body image is another huge challenge for us 20-something girls, and the curse infiltrates our lives in more ways than sex. (I've devoted a chapter to this topic, too, so skip ahead to Chapter 9, "The Body-Image Demons," if you're dying for details now.) Conquering the slings and arrows of body hatred is a gruesome, exhausting battle for us girls. Sex therapist Dr. Dennis Sugrue, clinical associate professor of psychiatry at the University of Michigan Medical School and president of the American Association of Sexuality Educators, Counselors and Therapists (AASECT), explains why: "For many women to feel sexual desire, they must first feel desirable. Those who struggle with body image—they look in the mirror and don't like what they see—feel less desirable, and therefore, feel less sexual desire. So, body image has a direct impact on women's sexuality."

A bad sexual experience in the past can also hinder our sexual development. Overcoming the trauma—whether it is incest, rape, an unwanted pregnancy, or a sexually transmitted disease that makes you feel undesirable—really warrants professional counsel and a whole lot of self-loving that I can't even begin to provide in this book. All I can do is encourage you to seek the help you deserve.

Remember, facing the enemy isn't easy. But, believe me, with conscientious soul-searching, these battles will be won, and your sexual identity will emerge victoriously. And victory is sweeter than chocolate!

CHOOSING OUR COMRADES IN BED

For many of us, getting in touch with our sexuality requires learning how to share our eroticism with someone else. Everyone has different criteria for determining who to sleep with, and these standards can often be traced to our personal views on what sex means to us. For instance, if you believe sex should be shared only with your lifelong mate, you will obviously have different standards from girls who believe that sex is a natural human expression to be explored at every stage of life with whomever strums their web. Therefore, I'm not going to even attempt to give advice about who you should or shouldn't sleep with.

However, those of us who have been around this block strongly suggest you mull over the following questions before you hop into the sack with whomever the pheromones are pointing you to:

Will This Person Be a Good Partner for Me?

When ticking off the pros and cons of your potential bedmate, start with the basics: trust and respect. Both of these qualities need to be present, visible, and proven in your partner-to-be before you ever let him near your private chambers. Trust and respect should be evident in the way your partner makes plans with you—he asks what you want to do and then always follows through—as well as the way he has treated you in the exploratory phases of your sexual encounters. For instance, does he linger in all the right places? You can also assess these character traits by looking at how well he respects your boundaries, another vital ingredient when it comes to sex. So, make trust and respect two prerequisites in your decision to sleep with someone.

While you're at it, think about how well you communicate with each other. After all, telling each other what you like and want more of, as well as registering your partner's desires and requests, is one key to a satisfying sexual experience. A good way to assess communication compatibility is to engage in a few discussions about sex before you pass the point of no return. One such talk should include the pros and cons of various birth control methods. It's wise to find out long before you get too far into the act where your partner stands on the condom issue, keeping in mind that some men could compose an entire aria of verbal grunts about wearing them. Another discussion is the whole sexual-history talk, in which each of you discloses whether or not you've been tested or treated for sexually transmitted diseases. Some women also like to know numbers of previous partners, but, personally, that's way more information than I need to know. If you have trouble broaching the subject of past experiences, you're probably not ready to sleep with whomever you have in mind.

To be better able to tell your partner what turns you on, it's a good idea to engage in various types of foreplay long before you progress to the more advanced stages of lovemaking. If, in your ventures with foreplay, you are able to coach your partner and have an orgasm with him, that's another good sign that this person is a good bedmate for you. If you can't, you probably won't have an orgasm *with* sex, and you may end up disappointed. Besides, if your partner learns how to make you come, it's obvious that he wants you to enjoy sex as much as he does—a very good sign.

It's equally important to never allow a body Nazi anywhere near your sacred sexuality. You know these guys—they are the ones who make a sport out of objectifying women's bodies, or who find warped pleasure in making offhand but traumatizing remarks about women's weight, size, or shape. Even if these types are complimentary about your own physique, their remarks about other women's looks will no doubt leave you feeling that they may one day discover your tiny patch of cellulite or PMS-induced bloat and start making the same horrible cracks about you. I once dated such a bastard, and believe me, that mistake did more damage to my self-esteem than three years of middle school. (In a world free of legal retribution, I would gladly include his name and E-mail address for all women reading this book to collectively harass, but in this world, I will refrain.) Avoid these guys like the plague they are to our society. There are so many other amazing men out there; channel your sexual energy to seeking them out!

Why Do I Want to Have Sex?

Your answer to the "Why?" question may be pure, unadulterated lust, a simple salute to the ole female hormones. And in many instances, such reasons are perfectly acceptable (we'll talk details momentarily). But even during hormonal moments, it's always a good idea to pause (ideally before you and your potential sex machine have started drinking, when all reason becomes a swirl of vodka and freshly crushed mint) to consider what you want out of the affair. If the answer is no-strings-attached sexual relief with someone you're dying to get to know in that kind of way, then by all means, get to work. Just take appropriate safety precautions.

But if the answer is to progress a little further in the intimacy department of your relationship, then you must—I repeat, *must*—find out if your partner is on the same page. If not—for instance, if he wants a casual fling, while you want a steady boyfriend—sex is not a wise move. The only way even the most titillating of your bedroom party tricks is going to have an effect on the progression of your relationship is if both of you are in forward mode. If you do have sex under such unbalanced desires, you will likely be fraught with insecurities, something of which we all have enough already without dragging our sexuality into the mix.

As you're weighing such heady thoughts, conduct a quick self-esteem check to make sure you're not wanting to sleep with the mate in question in order to gain his approval or love. We women are far too high at risk of using sex, sometimes not even consciously, to bolster our esteem. More often than not, such tactics leave us feeling worse about ourselves. Believe those of us who are personally familiar with this dysfunctional song and dance: a more fulfilling source of esteem is having the guy we're crazy about laugh at our jokes, cook us dinner, or engage us in a stimulating debate on the possibility of life in outer space.

THE ONE- (OR TWO-) NIGHT STAND

I know plenty of women will disagree with me on this treatise, as well as on the preceding ones, but I believe there is a place for casual sex during the early stages of our great debut into adulthood. There's something thrilling and triumphant about revealing the most carnal side of ourselves to someone we've been lusting after, even if we don't find much of a connection with the person otherwise. But this is true only for those among us who don't have moral dilemmas relating to the matter of sex for sex's sake. Those who do will find themselves with a bad case of identity crisis if they throw their values to the wind on this delicate occasion.

There comes a point, though—usually during the mid 20s—when one-night thrills turn into a bore, even among the very same girls who pounced on them during their early 20s. The change of heart goes something like this: I want more from sex than a fleeting ego boost; I want meaning and intimacy; I want to make love with someone who knows my body inside and out. Until this mental shift sedates the phenomenal explosion putting your young libido into overdrive, I say enjoy an occasional night or two of gorilla sex, taking the obvious precautions: never with a complete stranger or anyone you don't trust, and always with 10 condoms on at once for protection.

Exploring your sexuality with someone you trust but may not love, since love's arrow might not hit you for some time, is a great way to indulge a part of yourself that needs a little attention and feedback from others now and then. Still, several considerations are worth ruminating over if a crazy night of meaningless sex tops one of those millions of to-do lists we girls love to make:

The Sex Probably Won't Be That Good

Trust Elsie, 23, of Los Angeles: "I was once teaching a class abroad, and one of my students was a 25-year-old guy who was a total hotty. He had an amazing body, but his personality didn't appeal to me at all. I just wanted to sleep with him. That went on for two months. Finally I planned this whole conspiracy to hook up with him. I invited the entire class to a party at my friend's, who was going to help me work it so that the other students didn't see us get together. That was the most stupid thing I've ever done. The party turned into this huge event—everyone brought friends—and the guy I was after started coming on to every single woman in the room. Eventually, the party got out of control, the cops broke it up, and everyone left except for him. Then, we *finally* got together. But the sex was awful. He made this horrible face, and the whole thing was over in 90 seconds."

Lesson learned: Virtual strangers, who don't know the first thing about the way your body works and what turns you on (and probably don't care too much about finding out), are not the greatest lovers. Intimates who know every nuance of your body are. Just something to think about.

Veterans of Meaningless Sex Are Often Just Avoiding Intimacy

Since sex can be such a personal expression of affection and love, the idea of sex as an act of intimacy *avoidance* may be a strange concept to grasp. Nevertheless, some women are more comfortable baring their bodies in the company of partners they'll never rendezvous with again. They have trouble relating to people through the more traditional means of courtship: dinner, long walks, endless conversations, getting to know the guy's friends and family, and then gradually moving on to passionate, clothes-flinging, howling-at-the-moon sex. This isn't always the case when it comes to one-night stands, of course, but think about it if you start having more meaningless sex than you really want but aren't sure why and, more important, don't know how to put your voracious appetite on hold until you get to know your partner a little better.

Never Consider a One-Night Stand with Guy Friends or Ex-boyfriends

Why, you ask, when these should be the perfect partners because we know and trust them so well? It all boils down to the obvious: there's a *reason* you are "just friends" or *ex*-lovers.

When you sleep with an ex, you will wake up the next morning feeling awkward and sluttish and stay unforgivingly annoyed at yourself throughout the day until your friends—who *will* let it be known that they told you so—take you out for conciliatory drinks and become drunk enough themselves to admit that they, too, have slept with their exes. Then you will feel purged, and you will probably consider the whole affair a good lesson learned. But it's better to avoid this day or so of mental anguish. Leave sex with your ex in the past where it belongs.

When you bed down with one of your guy friends (unless you live in Scandinavia, where such behavior is considered as fraternal as sharing a swig of moonshine on a Saturday-night pre-pre-pre-party), you will just feel regret. Natalie, 26, of San Francisco, who slept with a friend in college, admits that their camaraderie fizzled soon after. "One night I was at a party with this friend of mine, and we got really drunk," she recounts. "He took me home, and we slept together that night. Afterward, we did the token dinner date, but there was nothing between us emotionally. We clicked in a great friendship way and had really good chemistry, but it was obvious there was nothing more. I didn't want a relationship with him, and we were too new as friends to just laugh about it, so being around him became totally uncomfortable, and we stopped hanging out." Again, just another flashing light to alert you as you explore all the opportunities awaiting your sexual soul.

THE SEX HISTORY TALK

In this day and age, the sex history talk is a pretty standard prelude to new sexual encounters, but that doesn't make the subject any easier to broach, particularly if you have a history of a sexually transmitted disease (STD) that needs telling. In my experience, along with that of many of the women with whom I spoke on the subject, it's usually up to us to broach the dreaded conversation and ask, "Have you ever been tested for AIDS or any other sexually transmitted diseases?" Guys generally don't bring it up—in some circumstances, even if they have a history that needs to be told. I'm being grossly general here, but anecdotally, that seems to be the case.

Likewise, women who have acquired one of those dastardly incurable diseases—such as herpes, human papillomavirus—which causes genital warts or cervical cell abnormalities—or the potentially fatal HIV can also find the subject too daunting and laced with fears of rejection to bring it up. However, we all know the ethical thing to do: talk *before* any exploratory ventures below the belt—even if you take necessary precautions to avoid spreading the disease. "If you don't," warns one 26-year-old who has grappled with this problem throughout her 20s, "the next question will be, 'Why'd you wait so long to tell me?'"

The reaction could also be distrust and anger. One 28-year-old I interviewed, for instance, waited three years to tell her husband that she had acquired herpes when she was a teenager. She explained: "I never got outbreaks, so it was easy for me not to mention it. But what it boils down to was that I was terrified my husband would leave me because of it. When I finally told him, he was furious I'd waited so long."

When you share the information with your partner, the straightforward approach is best, says sex educator Sari Locker. "Say it in a positive way: 'I'm really looking forward to having sex with you, but I need to tell you something. It's not a big deal, but I have this.'" Then be prepared to share everything you know about the disease, especially if it could be transferred to your partner, and tell him how you and he can still have a normal sex life with proper protection. If you've already had sex, this talk will obviously be harder for the above-mentioned reasons, so come prepared with a sincere apology, since you know you owe one.

After the talk, one of two things can happen, explains my 26-year-old source: "Men will either run away or stay. Those who stay will ask a lot of questions. One thing you have to accept is that the decision is up to your partner, and there's nothing you can do to prevent him from rejecting you for whatever it is you have. Once you've been rejected, you learn how to deal with it." And, of course, it's important to keep in mind that there are men out there who won't reject you for whatever it is you have. But your mate may need a few days to take in the news. "When I told my current boyfriend about herpes, he didn't call me for the next two nights, and he didn't want to have sex for a few days," says my 28-year-old source. "Later, he apologized, and we worked through it. But during that time, I decided that if he'd leave me for that, I didn't want to be with him, anyway."

If you're faced with the opposite quandary—your mate tells you he has something—the talk and resulting decisions can be equally difficult. Knowing all the facts of how various diseases can be transmitted, and then taking proper safety measures, will help you and your mate figure out how to live with whatever he has.

So, without further ado, let's go over the basics of keeping our sexual health in top form and protected from those nagging reminders that our bodies are vulnerable and mortal—even (perhaps I should say, *especially*) in our youthful prime.

OUR SEXUAL HEALTH

As with the rest of our bodily functions, taking care of our sexual health involves three efforts on our part: proper nutrition, to keep our ovaries and related machinery functioning; a few reliable disease-prevention strategies; and regular checkups, whether we're sexually active or not. Unfortunately, we 20-something females are at high risk of messing up on all three counts. Most of us don't know proper nutrition from a Power Bar; nearly two-thirds of all cases of sexually transmitted disease frequent the under-25 crowd; and, personally, I don't know too many of us who eagerly anticipate the annual, in which we're forced to lie atop a cold table, spread-eagle, and make small talk with a nurse practitioner whose head is bobbing up and down between our thighs. So, a lot of us put that task off.

Aside from reviewing the basics of proper nutrition, which we'll do in Chapter 10, "That Whacked-Out Body Feeling," most of us can concentrate our sexual-health endeavors on two strategies during these highly reproductive years: condoms and STD awareness. Let's talk condoms first.

These latex shields offer much-needed protection not only from pregnancy but also from major diseases when used each and every time you have intercourse. To be truly effective, condoms must be on the penis before, during, and after intercourse, with no penile dabbling in the forbidden zones without latex firmly in place. That includes using condoms during fellatio, because the bacteria and viruses associated with chlamydia, herpes, and HIV can be transmitted through oral sex. Likewise, dental dams—which are square sheets of latex designed to drape over the vulva during various sexual encounters—must become temporary fixtures when we're on the receiving end of oral sex. (Unfortunately, some people are allergic to latex. If this is the case for you or your partner, consult your health care provider for other options.)

To avoid such inconveniences, you and your partner can, of course, get tested for all STDs before engaging in any reckless sex. Even if your partner believes he or she has never been exposed to an STD, testing is imperative because some people unknowingly carry such common diseases as chlamydia and human papillomavirus but never get symptoms that might alert them to the fact that they were exposed somewhere down the line. (See Chapter 10 also for a list of screening tests.)

As for STD awareness, know your risks, and see your doctor if you think you've been exposed to something. Knowing symptoms of various STDs may help: the four basic alarm signals are bumps, burning sensations, abnormal secretions, and unaccountable pain during sex. If you experience any of these symptoms, give your gynecologist a buzz. Your vaginal distress may be only a yeast infection, swollen lymph nodes, or some other harmless irritation. But why risk your lifelong health?

If you do contract a virus or bacterial infection, the good news is that most STDs are treatable with antibiotics or other drugs. Others are manageable with medication and education about living with them. But if left untreated, some diseases can cause all sorts of serious problems and reproductive disasters, including pelvic inflammatory disease, which can lead to infertility. And while I'm in mother mode, here's one more piece of advice: If you're sexually active with a variety of partners, it's even more mandatory to take these safety measures seriously and get screened each time you're at the gynecologist, since you could acquire a disease and never even know it. Yes, do this even if your roommates have nicknamed you Latex Queen, because the only 100 percent fail-proof protection against STD is celibacy. And if you've read all the way to this point, I'm assuming that's not an option.

A WORD OR TWO ON BIRTH CONTROL

The fact that we are at our fertile peak in our 20s slightly complicates the field of sexual exploration, since so many of us these days want to hold off on having babies until we've whipped our careers into some sort of recognizable shape (not to mention find a proper child-rearing mate!). Luckily, our generation has a variety of birth control options from which to choose. There are pros and cons to just about all the contraceptive methods out there, so if you're in the market for one, plan to have a serious discussion with your doctor about the best one for you and your sexual lifestyle. The two main considerations are how effectively the method protects against pregnancy and disease and how likely you are to use it correctly. Let's talk shop.

In my book, condoms (male or female) are the only acceptable birth control methods for casual sex, since they offer protection against both pregnancy and sexually transmitted diseases. The female condom is neat in theory—you have ultimate contraceptive discretion and sufficient disease protection, which is especially nice for women whose partners complain of male condom discomfort—but there are several drawbacks. For one, female condoms (which look like a combination of a jellyfish and a headless ghost) are difficult to insert. One end consists of a closed ring that resembles a diaphragm and must be fitted over the cervix. This takes a little practice. Two, the open-ended ring descends from your vagina in a ridiculous, not to mention irritating, sort of way. Three, the condom must be removed immediately after ejaculation to avoid leakage problems. Last but not least, while you can actually turn the male condom-donning into a sexy moment during lovemaking, there is absolutely no equivalently seductive manner in which to insert a female condom.

Male condoms are quicker and simpler devices. However, they, too, have their issues. For instance, it seems that in the most passionate moments of love making, these latex sheaths inevitably either slip off and disappear into the void of the vagina, break, or leak, which makes them completely counterproductive and annoying. Proper prevention against such disasters—and condom mishaps are psychologically disastrous—is important. When your partner puts one on, make sure he allows room in the tip to avoid breaking. During sex, periodically check the condom to make sure it hasn't started to slip off. Also, your partner should hold the condom in place when he pulls out (which should be right after he comes). Then relax and enjoy yourself, because condoms, when used correctly, especially in combination with spermicide foam, gel, or cream, can be effective up to 98 percent of the time.

Two other barrier methods are the diaphragm and cervical cap, which are rubber domes fitted over the cervix to prevent egg-seeking sperm from entering the uterus. Both devices act as reservoirs for spermicide, which is squirted into the dome before the diaphragm or cap is inserted. That way, any wily sperm that manages to sneak past the barrier and get anywhere near your sacred cervix will be destroyed upon contact. Both of these methods allow sex to be a little more spontaneous, because you can put in a diaphragm several hours before sex and a cervical cap up to 48 hours prior to intercourse, and you can have repeated sexual encounters before removing them, simply by adding more contraceptive gel into the vagina using a tamponlike dispenser.

One drawback to these forms of birth control, which are effective 82 to 94 percent of the time, is that they don't offer adequate guard against some sexually transmitted diseases. For that reason, you should use them only after you and your partner have fully disclosed your histories and are aware of the risks that such contraceptives pose. Also, these little rubber demons are often difficult to put in and take out, and if they're not inserted correctly, they can do disconcerting acrobatic feats inside your vagina. Sometimes I wonder if, centuries from now, our descendants will view these contraceptive methods as a crude and cruel as chastity belts in medieval times. Only history can tell.

One of the most popular forms of birth control is the pill, largely because of its uncanny ability to prevent pregnancy and its relative simplicity. When taken correctly, the pill is about 99 percent effective. However, like the diaphragm and cervical cap, the pill won't offer protection against sexually transmitted diseases, so it should be used as the sole source of protection only if you are in a monogamous relationship and you and your partner have exchanged sexual health statuses.

There are two general types of pills on the market: combination oral contraceptives, which are made of synthetic estrogen and progesterone (or progestin), and progestin-only pills, which, as the name implies, contain only progestin, and very low levels of it, at that. Combination pills work by preventing ovulation, thickening cervical mucus to inhibit sperm from traveling into the uterus, and inducing changes in the endometrial lining to prohibit implantation if, by remote chance, an egg is fertilized. Progestin-only pills, also called minipills, work primarily by inducing changes in the cervical mucus, making it virtually impossible for viable sperm to swim to the egg.

Within these two categories of pills are a variety of hormonal combinations from which to choose. Detailed discussion with your doctor about your cycle and the potential side effects of the various combinations is necessary when it comes to deciding the right pill for you. There's quite a bit of trial and error involved, so if you opt for the pill as your source of birth control, prepare for a few months of experimentation—all of which should involve other birth control methods until the right combination is determined and your body responds to the hormonal influences according to plan.

In addition to the pill, two equally effective hormonally based methods of birth control are worth mentioning: hormone injections and implants. The injection method prevents ovulation with a simple shot of progestin (Depo-Provera) in the arm or butt every three months. The dosages are low, but they must be administered four times a year, which calls for a lot of office visits. Implants are match-size silicone tubes containing progestin that are surgically inserted just under the skin in the arm. Small amounts of hormone are released each day, preventing ovulation and making cervical mucus incorrigible to sperm.

Implants are effective for five years unless removed. The convenience of not having to take a pill every day or mess with barrier tactics makes these two methods attractive, but both have minor side effects, so get the details from your doctor. If you are in a monogamous relationship and know you don't want kids tomorrow, one of these may be the exact method you've been looking for.

Two more popular types of birth control exist but aren't broadly recommended for us fertile-but-not-ready-to-be-mothers-yet girls. The intrauterine device (IUD) is a small plastic device that is inserted into the uterus by your doctor. Through a slow release of copper or progestin, an IUD can prevent pregnancy for up to 10 years or until it's removed. Though IUDs are an effective form of birth control, doctors aren't in complete agreement as to how exactly the devices prevent pregnancy, which seems frightfully suspicious to me. Therefore, they're one form of birth control we should avoid. Besides, IUDs have been associated with an increased risk of pelvic inflammatory disease in women who haven't given birth yet, so if you're in that category, your doctor probably won't recommend it to you anyway. If he or she does, scratch that one off your list, and then find a better doctor.

The last form of birth control we have to cover is the old Russian roulette, a.k.a. rhythm method, in which you avoid sex during times in which you believe you're fertile. Most women who use this method figure out their fertile days through a combination of activities: (1) They check the calendar (most women ovulate 14 days before their next period, but the length of our cycles changes all the time, often due to stress, so basing the length of your cycle on last month's length is risky); (2) They measure a subtle changes in body temperature, which drops, then rises steadily right before we ovulate; and (3) They observe changes in their cervical mucus or vaginal discharge. When the mucus is runny and stretchy, like egg white, we are at our most fertile. This stretchy substance is what helps the sperm swim up into the cervix. When the mucus is sticky and clumpy, like cottage cheese, that's a sign that ovulation is over and done with, making sex a little less risky.

When combined with spermicide and your mate's flawless withdrawal before ejaculation, this method has better success. But to be considered a reliable form of birth control, the rhythm method takes lots of practice and a lot of abstinence (or use of barrier birth control) during those 10 or so days of stretchy mucus discharge. So, unless you like the adrenaline rush that accompanies that underlying fear that you might be pregnant, I wouldn't recommend it.

One more thing: In the big birth control headache, there are often mistakes—forgotten pills, condom ruptures, diaphragm failure, drunken stupidity. Most of us will trip at least once or twice in our debut to adulthood. Such is part of growing up. Hopefully, the consequences won't be tragic, but if they do result in a sexually transmitted disease or an unwanted pregnancy, the important thing is not to ignore it or beat yourself up about it (mistakes happen), but see a doctor immediately. Early drug intervention is the protocol for treating many STDs, since your fertility may be at stake. In the case of a possible pregnancy, you may be able to prevent conception or implantation after such accidents by taking high dosages of certain oral contraceptives or the proverbial morning-after pill. Since several factors are involved in the effectiveness of these after-the-fact birth control tactics, and more important, since I'm not a doctor, you must get professional consultation on this one. Just keep in mind that there are such options out there if you act quickly.

Then, promise yourself you'll be more careful next time, and always, always, always carry a condom. That way, you help ensure that exploring your sexuality won't sentence you to a lifestyle you wouldn't choose to live.

7

The Unpredictable Female Orgasm

t's hard enough to feel good about our sexuality with images of Sharon Stone and the likes cluttering our impressions of what's considered sexy in our society. Well, Hollywood's depiction of female orgasms are even more discouraging when it comes to our sexuality, since most of us would *never* be able to reach ecstasy the way female actresses appear to in choreographed sex scenes. Based on what I know about female orgasms and how most of us achieve them, which is rarely through intercourse alone, I'd bet good money that these actresses couldn't climax in real life the way they do on the big screen, either. Unless you're looking for pointers on how to fake an orgasm, which is not advisable for reasons we'll discuss, consider Hollywood's techniques for bringing on female orgasms as true to life as Pamela Anderson Lee's breasts.

To be fair to the movie industry, since I'm as much a sucker for erotic sex scenes as the next girl, the movies aren't solely to blame for some of the misconceptions that both men and women have about triggering female orgasms. (And there are quite a few misunderstandings percolating among the sexually active crowd, many of which I, myself, shared before researching this chapter and comparing notes with other girls on this matter.) Our culture, in general, doesn't talk truthfully or openly enough about sex, especially in terms of what *really* appeals to the female half of the population. It's high time we did some talking. In hopes of shedding a little light on the dark corners, I will try to be as frank as possible about the seven truths of female orgasms, which I've determined through all my research with sex experts and interviews with other 20-something women (the real experts). By the way, I highly recommend sharing these truths with your lover, who may also have a few wayward notions about the way in which our fire is best lit.

TRUTH #1: ALL WOMEN CLIMAX DIFFERENTLY

Some of us have ticklish feet. Others get body chills from having our necks lightly stroked. That's because the nerve endings in our bodies are all sensitive in different ways, and the manner in which we respond to touch is dependent upon our unique physiques. Nothing could be more true when it comes to the way in which we are sexually aroused. Some of us have orgasms from clitoral stimulation only, others by stimulating the G spot, or Grafenberg spot, which is a sensitive, nerve-intensive area about two inches back inside the front wall of the vagina. And some women experience orgasm through both the clitoris and G spot, though rarely at the same time unless they are lucky enough to have been born with bionic genitalia.

Because our bodies are all unique, there's no fail-proof recipe for bringing on a female orgasm. We must discover what works for us through trial and error. I was 21 when I figured out what all the talk was about; to be perfectly frank, it was through my own private investigation (prompted by a certain innate feeling that there *must* be more to sex than I was experiencing). It took me two hours to determine exactly what rang my bell, but it was well worth the time and frustration—and it *was* frustrating not knowing if what I was doing was ever going to trigger that sexual release so heralded among the more sexually advanced women I knew.

Sloane, 21, of Syracuse, New York, in an attempt to enlighten herself and friends to all our female orgasmic capacity, also took the matter into her own hands, so to speak. She reveals: "I ended up buying a Betty Dodson video from Good Vibrations about achieving orgasmic ecstasy, and I had a screening in my dorm video room. We served mango and angel food cake, and everyone was completely sober. The video talked about moving your hips, deep breathing, using your PC muscles, touching your clitoris, and rocking your pelvis." The moral here is that female orgasms are not something we girls experience miraculously and spontaneously. They are physiological responses that we must learn how to trigger through specific types of stimulation and movements. The submoral is that everyone should rent or buy a Betty Dodson video. Betty Dodson, Ph.D., is a sex educator and author of *Sex for One: The Joy of Selfloving*. She is the goddess of female sexuality, and if you're at all uncertain about how your body works, she'll help you figure it out for sure.

Since there is some expert debate on the subject of female orgasms, I'll review the general arguments here in case you haven't yet determined what types of stimulation turn you on. Some experts claim that the only way women reach orgasm is through constant external stimulation of the highly sensitive clitoris or surrounding area. The stimulation can be applied with your own hand, with your partner's hands or whatever other creative body part he might think to use, or with an electric vibrator, which most women who've used one agree is pretty much a guaranteed thing. Other women reach climax by continuously stimulating the G spot by way of the methods just mentioned.

The controversy surrounds the sensitive matter of whether or not the G spot is a viable source of female orgasms. Some experts say that the nerve endings around the G spot are connected to the web of nerves that feed into the clitoris, and that it's the clitoral stimulation that actually triggers the orgasm. I'm not here to choose sides, but I have spoken to several women who are brought to orgasm through repetitive stimulation on this spot, so I'm convinced it's as good a source of orgasm as any, though I can't boast of having had the pleasure myself.

What works for some women doesn't work for others. Figure out how *your* body works (if you don't, who will?), communicate those tips to your partner, and once you get good at that technique, stay open to trying new variations. With practice, you may discover many rather fabulous things about your body that you didn't know were possible.

You can also review a wealth of books and how-to videos about our female erogenous zones as well as techniques for learning how to tap into their powers (see the "Go-Girl Resources" section for a few good ones). One thing for sure about the great G-spot-versus-clitoral debate: G spot orgasms aren't more "sophisticated" than those triggered by the clitoris. Nor is one necessarily better than the other. According to Sari Locker, research shows that the nerve impulses resulting from various orgasms all look the same regardless of how they were precipitated. The result is generally three to five vaginal contractions followed by full-body release of muscle tension that leaves you more serene than an hourlong massage. Of course, whether women all experience the same feelings with orgasm is not something any girl or expert could know for sure, just as we don't know if Granny Green apples taste alike from one person to the next, or if everyone sees the same shade of blue when looking up at the sky.

TRUTH #2: ORGASMS DON'T (PARDON THE PUN) COME EASILY

Life would be so divine if orgasms were as predictable as our credit card bills. Dream on. Unlike the case with men, who can't seem to relate to us on this one, female orgasms with a partner require harmonizing four components: mechanical know-how, savvy communication skills, a certain comfort level with the partner, and complete mind and body receptivity. Like getting to Carnegie Hall, it takes practice, because even if we know every nuance of our clitoris or G spot, there's no guarantee we'll get the orgasm goddess dancing.

One of the reasons orgasms can be difficult to achieve is that we tend to need different types of stimulation at different times when we're making love, explains New York City sex therapist Carolynn Hillman, author of *Love Your Looks: How to Stop Criticizing and Start Appre-*

ciating Your Looks. "Small differences of touch make big differences with women," she says. Sometimes we need harder pressure, other times more delicate strokes. The clitoris has as many nerve endings as the penis, but they are concentrated in such a small surface area that sometimes even the slightest touch can be too much, explains Hillman. What's more, the approach that worked magic yesterday may have little effect on us today. While it would be dreamy to have a lover who, in an osmosis kind of way, knows exactly where to touch us and with what degree of vigor, here in the real world there's no way our mate can know if what he's doing is right on or all wrong . . . unless we tell him, which conveniently leads me to my next point.

TRUTH #3: OUR PARTNERS NEED POINTERS ON WHAT TURNS US ON

What may have sent our mate's previous partner flying across the room from pleasure (although such images of our lover's past sexual encounters do horrific things to the esteem and therefore, in general, should not be conjured) may do nothing for us. Such is the nature of the unpredictable female erogenous zone. Our job is threefold: first, we must realize that such differences are perfectly normal; second, we must educate our mates about the variances in female anatomy and orgasmic propensity if they don't already know; and third, we must explain and even (*eek!*) demonstrate what turns us on.

If you are bold, the direct approach, during or prior to the act of making love, is the most effective, rather than bringing it up on the subway the next morning as you're both on your way to work. Tell your partner outright, "I want to show you how I come," suggests Sari Locker. Then try to cast aside all modesty and get on with the show. Guys not only love the demonstration but also greatly appreciate the up-close and personal lesson, since they are often at a loss for what to do if none of their previous tricks have worked. Such frankness will also relieve the anxiety that you both may be feeling about bringing you to climax, namely because such show-and-tell sessions will give you a real chance to get some sexual release. Of course, if you don't know what makes you come, you will need to do some experimentation.

After your private showing, the transition from self-stimulation to partner participation can be somewhat tricky. Sex therapist Carolynn Hillman suggests this prescription, which she calls a bridging technique: "First hold your partner's hand and guide his finger until you have an orgasm. Next time, guide his finger until you're close to orgasm, then let go and have him bring you to climax alone. Finally, let him go the whole way without your assistance." As you're showing your partner the ropes, keep the lines of communication open, advises Bethany, 26, of San Francisco: "Guys have no way of knowing if what they're doing is right, so it's up to us to let them know." With that in mind, keep talking while you're making love, telling your partner gently, so as not to seem demanding or critical, "That's not good now; do more of what you were doing before," or whatever it is that triggers your orgasm.

If you're so shy about expressing your sexual desires that the idea of putting on such a brazen demonstration is enough to make you want to run to a nunnery, try warming up to the conversation slowly, suggests Elena, 23, of San Francisco. "One way to approach the subject is to ask your partner what he likes, and then tell him what turns you on. It can be awkward to say what you like—you don't want to sound too experienced—but if you can't talk about it with your partner, the sex might not ever improve," she says. One caution regarding wading into the water versus jumping right in through hands-on coaching: Be very clear when describing what you need. If you're too subtle, your partner won't get it.

TRUTH #4: INTERCOURSE, ALONE, DOESN'T CUT IT (AT LEAST, FOR MOST OF US)

For many of us, foreplay is the real play when it comes to making love. Intercourse on its own is often more of a pleasant afterthought or an erotic prelude to what really gets us going, which, more often than not, is manual stimulation or oral sex. In fact, according to some estimates, close to half of all sexually active women *don't* have orgasms regularly through intercourse. While oral sex and deft finger maneuvers are not how the entertainment industry generally presents us girls as primarily reaching orgasm (probably because closeups would be rated triple X!), such techniques are the favored vehicles for climaxing in the real world.

"Men and women's sexual experiences are very different from one another," explains sex therapist Dr. Dennis Sugrue, clinical associate professor of psychiatry at the University of Michigan Medical School and president of the American Association of Sexuality Educators, Counselors and Therapists. "There's a tendency in our culture for women to conform to the male sexual experience, which is intercourse. But intercourse is not an effective way for women to reach orgasm. The two major erogenous areas in women are the clitoris and the G spot, and intercourse isn't efficient at stimulating either."

Because of the female orgasm's rare appearance during penetration, it's pretty seldom that we're able to climax in unison with our mates, a feat that many men believe is the gold standard in sex. It shouldn't be, though, because such demands put a lot of pressure on both partners. Sure, it may be nice to strive for, and when it comes, we can howl at the moon in erotic harmony, but such events shouldn't be forced. This will require fighting the ideas that the media put into our heads about what real lovemaking looks like. In reality, the simultaneous climax takes knowing each other's bodies inside and out, a perfect (and learned) sense of timing, and lots and lots of practice. Not that any of us are complaining.

Of course, certain sexual positions—girl on top, giving us all the control, and doggy style, to name a couple—are better than others at hitting the right spots during penetration. And, of course, practice with an eager-to-please partner will help spur those wild horses to gallop across our pelvic floor. Having a partner whose anatomy complements yours (meaning that your pelvic bones bump and grind in just the right spot, stimulating your clitoris in the process) will also improve your chances of reaching orgasm through intercourse. So will the simple act of manually stimulating your clitoris during penetration. Also, experiment with holding off on intercourse until your mate has been able to bring you to orgasm through means other than his penis, as much as you may love his appendage of masculinity. Rebecca, 23, of Chicago, who has never had intercourse, tells her partners they can mess around but not have sex, which forces the guy to focus on what makes *her* feel good.

If intercourse is painful, you're due for a visit to your favorite female physician. According to some surveys, about 20 percent of women in their 20s experience pain regularly during sex, and another 26 percent do not find sex pleasurable at all. While pain during sex could indicate some internal problems, your discomfort may just be lack of lubrication, especially if you're having intercourse before you get properly warmed up. Vaginal dryness can definitely plague us 20-somethings, but it doesn't mean you're becoming frigid. It could, however, be the side effect of certain medications you're taking, including some birth control pills. In such cases I would recommend Astroglide, the lubricant of choice among several of the girls I interviewed.

TRUTH #5: NOT ALL ORGASMS HAVE THE SAME OOMPH

Orgasms can be as varied as good wines. Some spark a quick flutter that doesn't stray far from the source, like a crisp sauvignon blanc on the tip of the tongue. Others ignite a full-body experience with a long, luscious finish, similar to an aged cabernet swirled around your mouth; when swallowed, they're felt through every vein in your body, starting with the tips of your toes. These are the ones that tend to trigger those powerful vaginal contractions (at least three to five good ones) and muscle spasms in the thighs that leave our lower halves trembling.

However, one type of orgasm should never be considered more desirable than the other, especially because we just don't have a choice on which one will come. "Orgasms can vary tremendously from one sexual encounter to the next. One may be a tidal wave over the body, and another may be gentle water lapping the shoreline. But both of these orgasms should be valued," says Sugrue. If stronger orgasms are valued more than the flightier ones, performance anxiety and frustration to achieve them will surely contaminate our enjoyment of whatever does end up coming. So, when you find yourself making a note of your orgasm's Richter scale rating, stop, let that thought flutter out the window, and be happy that your body was relaxed enough to give you what it did.

That said, some authorities on the subject contend that there are a variety of ways to enhance our orgasms. So, they're worth a try if you're curious. Kegel exercises, which involve repeatedly squeezing the pelvic floor (PC) muscles, much as you do when you really have to pee on your way home from an extended happy hour, are one technique to build those muscles that surround the vagina, rectum, and urethra. This presumably puts the gas back in your or*gas*ms. (I've never had the patience to stick with these for more than five seconds, so I can't attest to the actual value of doing them, but hey, give it a shot and let me know if it works.)

Certain other techniques, such as almost bringing yourself to climax but then switching your source of stimulation from, say, your clitoris to your G spot, may also enhance your orgasms when you allow yourself to finally come. Breathing deeply into the abdomen (not something most of us stomach-sucking girls are used to doing, especially when naked and within such close proximity of our lover) relaxes the erogenous area and increases the pleasure, as does rocking the pelvis. And, of course, many women are able to have multiple orgasms to double or quadruple their pleasure.

On the topic of multiple orgasms, allow me to offer a little clarification about this amazing, but often misunderstood, phenomenon. According to sex educator Sari Locker, the actual definition of a multiple orgasm depends on who's describing: "For some women, having a multiple orgasm means they have one orgasm and five minutes later have another one if they continue to stimulate themselves. Or they may have one orgasm that continues longer than usual or feels as if it's rolling over into another one." Most women are capable of having more than one orgasm within the same lovemaking session, but, like learning to have one, some practice and knowing a few trade secrets can help. For one, the clitoris is usually way too sensitive after our first orgasm to get direct stimulation again and doesn't want to be touched, so if you want to go for doubles, wait at least a minute before picking up where you left off. Then, when you're not so hyperaroused, continue on doing what you did when the first one arrived.

TRUTH #6: THE MIND HAS MORE VERVE THAN A VIBRATOR

You're probably well aware of the mind's uncanny role as gatekeeper to sexual release. A big part of our mental capacity to encourage or withhold those desirable pelvic rumblings revolves around trust. To get into the orgasmic state of mind, we must, for instance, trust that our midnight cowboy (a) won't point and giggle at our unleashed display of sexual ecstasy in the nude; (b) will remain as concerned about the status of the condom as we are throughout sex (one woman I know, in the midst of making love one time, opened her eyes and to her horror saw the condom she had so carefully placed upon her partner's penis stuck to the wall by the bed; how it got there—the guy claimed he was as baffled as she—was the big question); and (c) will consider the boundaries that we set prior to the act as holy as Monday-night football. So important is trust in the mind's ability to give the go-ahead to our orgasms that it's a warm winter in Antarctica when we girls can reach climax during a one-night stand, since it's impossible (not to mention insane) to trust a stranger.

Orgasm is also more likely if our emotional connection with our partner is fully functioning. Foreplay, once again, is what sparks our emotional kindling. Eye contact, talking, and loosening up the old erotic joints, so to speak, through gentle and suggestive massage, will help shift the mind into lovemaking gear. Without an emotional and mental connection to our partner, it's pretty near impossible to warm up the nether regions properly and give our orgasms even a fighting chance.

Why the mind connection is so necessary for us girls in particular remains one of the mysteries of human sexuality. Perhaps there's some evolutionary rationale: maybe before the invention of birth control, girls needed that extra peace of mind that our mate would be trustworthy and emotionally connected enough not to leave us high and dry if our ventures below the belt happened to result in offspring. Regardless, the mind-body connection can produce some amazing rhythms when both components are working in unison. Unfortunately, that's not always the case.

More often than many of us would care to admit, the mind starts wandering when our body and partner are otherwise willing. We start thinking about bills, errands we have to run, that nightmare project due tomorrow at noon. When such mental disasters strike, we can either kiss that orgasm goodbye or lasso those distractions and, once they're contained, refocus on the erotic here and now.

Easier said than done, but a few tricks are worth a shot. Nina, 26, of Miami, concentrates on her boyfriend's sounds and his breathing if her mind dares to wander. Vanessa, 23, of San Francisco, focuses on all the different sensations she's feeling, blocking her mind of everything else, as though she were taking a test on her own sensuality. Elena engages her partner in conversation, sometimes just talking about what they're doing, when her thoughts start to drift. Just don't stray the conversation too far away from what's happening, she warns after once bringing up the subject of what they might have for dinner the following night: "It kills the mood." Thinking about erotic images and scenarios or, better yet, sharing them with your partner will also get your mind in proper orgasm mode when it starts fixating on such unsexy thoughts as the recycling bin you forgot to put out on the curb for morning pickup.

Since stress is often one of the culprits behind mind wandering, I'd like to mention one sex-related anxiety that can and should be ignored, in hopes of lightening your anxiety load and allowing at least a sneeze of an orgasm to sneak in. Due to our intrepid anatomy and all the other reasons previously discussed, many of us become stressed about taking so long to have an orgasm. Because so many of us have been socially engineered to please others (especially men) and think of ourselves and our own pleasure last, letting go and allowing our orgasms to come on their own accord can be psychologically challenging. This can cause all sorts of anxiety, all the more if we're simultaneously worrying that our mate is getting bored, discouraged, or antsy for his turn.

Here is a little secret: Most guys (unless they are sexually selfish, in which case I suggest you immediately go back to Chapter 5 and read

"When It's Time to Dump a Guy") get exorbitant amounts of pleasure from watching and helping their mates become sexually activated. Most of them are not looking at the clock, either. In fact, many men feel an equal amount of pleasure watching their partners come as when they have their own 30 seconds or so in the orgasmic limelight. As Melanie, 28, of Austin, puts it: "You don't have to worry about guys. You will turn them on regardless of what you do. Focus on your own pleasure. It's so erotic to be with someone who's sexually aroused." So, don't feel guilty about all the attention being lavished upon you, and just ignore any notion that sex is only about pleasing your partner. Making love is all about giving *and* receiving.

TRUTH #7: ORGASMS AREN'T PROOF OF GOOD SEX

Some women might wildly disagree with me on this one, but the rest of us often find the tender caresses, the naked bonding, and the undivided attention that precedes or follows a hearty romp just as pleasurable as those spine-tapping pelvic throbs. I know that some men, too, might not be able to comprehend this female concept of passionate lovemaking, but that's their problem. Dennis Sugrue explains a common dynamic: "The male ego often gets bruised if their partners don't have an orgasm. The issue gets even more complicated if a woman feels as though something is wrong with her if she doesn't climax. "As a sex therapist, I try to help dispel these myths and explain to men and women that it's not that common for women to have orgasms during intercourse. Lovemaking needs to be broadened to a fuller experience, not just limited to penetration. Intercourse is just *part* of lovemaking."

Orgasms, however, are important to achieve with your partner on a somewhat frequent basis. After all, your mate is the only one who gets to see this completely sexual and vulnerable surrender, and sharing your orgasms with the person you love *is* a spiritual thing. Don't shortchange yourself if you're not getting them. It can be easy to convince yourself that orgasms don't matter in the big scheme of your relationship because it takes you so long to come and you can just masturbate alone later, but when you do that, you're denying yourself a truly unique and soulful

Three Words on Faking

DON'T DO IT! When you fake an orgasm, you are taking two steps backward. Not only are you giving up your chance of getting any sexual relief with your partner that night (or morning, or midday), but you're also giving the impression that whatever your partner was doing worked, when, in fact, it didn't even come close. Next time you're both in the mood, your partner will likely put into play whatever he thought worked last time, and, before you know it, you're faking again. The more you fake, the harder it will be to broach the difficult conversation wherein you concede that you're, actually, not having orgasms. Also, to throw in a little "All women unite!" feminism, consider this: When we fake our orgasms, men get the general impression that female orgasms are easy to bring on, when we all can attest that they are not.

I know, I know. Most of us have done it now and then because faking is easier than telling your valiant partner that his tireless efforts aren't working or that you'd rather (ouch!) go to bed. But this harks back to my earlier point about redefining what sex means: making love shouldn't be judged on how loudly we scream or squirm. The true measure is how connected we become to our partner during the act. If orgasms are deemed the entire goal of our sexual liaisons, we'll be putting an awful lot of pressure on ourselves to perform each and every time, which will probably stress us out, and there is no room for stress in the bed. So, if you're getting tired and you know for sure that an orgasm is not going to happen, just slow down and move on to kissing and cuddling instead. That's OK. When it comes to our fickle orgasms, honesty is always the best policy.

connection with your partner. It would be a sin to ignore this amazing pleasure that your body can give you and your partner. Don't be a sinner.

The long and the short of orgasms: They get easier with practice, especially when you're training with the same partner. You see, monogamy has its merits on many fronts. And rumor has it that orgasms become even more powerful and predictable in our 30s. Hallelujah!

THE LIBIDO CRASH AND REVIVAL

While many of us have libidos as revved up and fine-tuned as a jazzy little red Ferrari, some of us take a detour during our 20s into the low-libido zone, in which our sexual desire becomes stalled. Sometimes a libido crash is just a temporary response to the flurry of hormones making their monthly rounds, such as when our lack of passion coincides with our period. Other times, a low sex drive can be traced to the ubiquitous psychological stress, such as depression, anxiety, anger at your partner, exhaustion, sexual insecurity, or negative feelings about sex due to a bad experience in the past, such as sexual assault, rape, or abuse. There may even be external influences that are stripping the *rouse* from your arousal. Certain medications, including antidepressants and some birth control pills (if that doesn't win the irony award of the century); a bad body image; and gynecological problems that cause pain during sex could nip any girl's desire in the bud. Or the lower-than-usual drive could just be due to the simple fact that sex has become a tad predictable.

To jump-start a crashed libido, you must first narrow down possible causes in order to seek appropriate counsel from a gynecologist, a psychologist, or even a sex therapist. Sexual trauma in the past must be dealt with professionally, since so many layers of pain are involved. Be wise, and seek help now so that you can begin to enjoy this vital birthright of sexual pleasure.

If psychological or physiological trauma isn't the issue, perhaps all you need is a little passion revival with your lovemaking mate, especially if you're in a long-term relationship. Ninety-nine percent of all couples go through periods—from weeks to months or longer—of boredom in the bedroom. Sex, similar to our career ambition, ebbs and flows. Being creatures of habit, many of us get lazy about trying new things that might revive our satisfying but unspontaneous sex lives. This condition is more likely the longer you date and the more time you spend with your mate. And if you and your partner move in together, don't be surprised if the frequency of your exploratory excursions beneath the sheets dwindles dramatically. It just does. I have a theory as to why, which I'll attempt to explain through this analogy:

You know how in the mornings we can douse ourselves with perfume, only to become completely unable to sense the fragrance after an hour or two? Other people, however, can smell us 10 cubicles away. That's because our noses, having detected the scent and determined its harmlessness, stop registering it after a while in order to reserve our sensory power for other smells that might indicate danger, such as a fire blazing by the copy machine, or our boss, who smells like stale coffee and cigarettes, sneaking up behind us to see what we're working on.

Though I haven't confirmed my theory with anyone medically knowledgeable, I suspect that our sexual responsiveness might just behave in similar ways: That is, once we've gotten into a routine, our sensory sex nerves don't have to work quite so hard to register the stimulation. Thus, what may have felt divine with our partners upon first encounter is old hat after six months. According to my theory, reviving those sexual sensations calls for a few wily diversions: namely, confusing our senses just enough to keep them alert and responsive.

This can be effected through a simple change of scenery. Having a little rumple with your mate in unfamiliar surroundings (aside from the exhibitionist/thrill factor of roommates or even strangers, depending upon how public you go, suddenly catching you in action) will alert your body to stimulation that it might otherwise choose not to register based on the familiarity factor. If you have roommates (and aren't interested in the dubious thrill of getting caught), the privacy of the bathroom is always an option (unless you live in a Manhattan apartment, in which case, it's unlikely the two of you will be able to squeeze into the minuscule space and still appear erotic to each other while getting it on). In spacially challenging circumstances, you might try this little tactic that Melanie and her partner occasionally employ: "We sometimes make love with shared fantasies in our minds. I'll start in a low-key way by saying something like, 'We're in a car,' and then we both imagine we're there. You can be doing the same positions you always do, but with this fantasy in your head, the sex feels very different."

Another technique to try when the sex becomes a tad too pre-dictable is to give your senses a jolt. One of the best sensory jump-starts I know is good ole Mother Nature. There's nothing like a little romp in the woods or along a deserted shoreline to reactivate the lovemaking senses. With no distractions of full-length mirrors to reflect your mor-tality (not to mention your body), no tangled sheets to restrict move-ment, no clocks to remind you that it's way past your bedtime, and no headlights in the window to startle you back into the reality of urban animus, pure, organic sex can be a true fix for sensual deprivation, which can flummox an otherwise perfectly satisfying love life.

Of course, revival tactics don't need to be so exotic. The essence is simply to engage in different and creative exploits. Marie, 27, of New York City, who has been living with her boyfriend for several years, sug-gests such commonplace diversions as wearing a satiny nightgown to bed instead of boxers, or wearing your hair differently. If stress is getting the best of your love life, try going to bed at 9 P.M. or setting the alarm early in the morning, to give yourself plenty of time to get into the mood and make love before you fall asleep or start the day, Marie suggests.

Whatever you do, don't get into the frame of mind that your sex life doesn't matter. "You've got to recognize that sex is an important part of your relationship—it's something that you can't share with anyone else," says Valerie, 29, of Boston, who has been with her (now) husband for more than 10 years. "If you let your sex life go, it may affect your relationship in other areas. That can happen without your even realiz-ing it, the way habits are formed. If it does, making love becomes this huge event and turns into anxiety, causing you to shy away from phys-ical intimacy to avoid those feelings." So, make your sex life a project, even if the concept seems wrong and frightening in a self-helpish kind of way. You've got to start somewhere.

The upside is that, like romance, most sexual lulls come and go. After a cold spell, the old fiery flames come flying back into your nether regions. Take advantage of the roaring times, and keep the lines of communication open during the more stagnant periods so that one of you doesn't become resentful or interpret the lack of sex as overall dis-interest. A good talk with your mate is sometimes all your sex life needs.

PART 3

Our Body and Soul

8

Emotional Theatrics

ental meltdowns are an unwelcome side effect of excavating a career and tracking down potential mates (or at least a good lover here and there to get us through those dry spells). Most of us go through about 2,001 emotional spasms a day during our early 20s, which are challenging to our mental health. The condition is progressive.

I know. I had little sobbing breakdowns all through college, triggered by lack of sleep, snarly spats with girlfriends, uncontrollable annoyance at my parents for reasons I can no longer remember, and heinous fights with the occasional boyfriend who dared visit me at my all-female campus. But those emotional theatrics were only dress rehearsals for the melodrama that strained my serenity in the following years.

My first great emotional meltdown occurred not long after I had graduated, about the time I received my 10th rejection for a newspaper reporter position. I was supporting myself with occasional freelance writing assignments and a part-time job, where I spent entire days opening other people's mail, a demoralizing entrée into the working world, considering I had thousands upon thousands of dollars of college debt to repay. Days off, I'd wander from café to café, perusing the want ads discreetly (so as not to appear a *complete* loser) between sips of nutmeg-besprinkled cappuccino (my only reprieve from the job-search debacle).

I was bored. I was angry! This wasn't what my 20s were supposed to be! Where was that glamorous and important job I was supposed to have been actively recruited for while I was still at college? Where were all the sophisticated dates? What was *up* with my stomach lately? And why did my depressed roommate have to spend every single day, dawn to dusk, sprawled across our living-room couch wearing nothing but scraggly underwear?

Now that I'm safely on the other side of the early-20s nightmare, I can chuckle about those former torments. The 20s are like that old adage about spring: We enter the decade like roaring, aggressive lions and exit like fluffy lambs with comparatively predictable lives, unless, of course, we start going schizoid about turning 30, which is another book. The 10 years in between this evolutionary transformation are tender times, considering how many life-altering decisions we have to make and all the transitions we face. That's why it's more important than ever to pamper our emotional selves. To every other 20-something out there, I offer this reassuring bit of reality: despite the lack of evidence from the media, which like to portray us as carefree priestesses of youth, most of us are just as lost, stressed, lonely, angry, envious, confused, and neurotic as you.

Luckily, we also possess a handful of tools for getting through the various manifestations of 20-something anguish, as detailed in this chapter. Let's talk about how to use them to our best advantage.

THE IDENTITY CRISIS

As much as we may wish that all the random pieces of adulthood would magically fall into place the day we turn 21—an entirely overrated birthday, by the way, since most of us have been drinking since high school and are still, technically, adolescents—it takes about eight years to get the hang of being a woman. Earning our adulthood stripes (wrinkles across the forehead, parentheses around the mouth, and hairline crow's-feet radiating from the corners of our eyes when we smile) is a gradual process that starts in our late teens when we begin to crave autonomy from our parents—remember all those nasty fights about what we were wearing and who we were hanging out with?—and then continues on through the decade, until two things happen: (1) We become financially and emotionally independent from Mom and Dad, usually sometime in our mid-20s; and (2) We develop a sense of who we really are, which typically doesn't happen until we're about ready to sneak into our 30s, or even later.

Growing into a woman is a taxing endeavor, because we are, in essence, reinventing ourselves. First of all, there's our professional identity, which we begin to mold when we accept our first jobs, commit to graduate school, or quit a nightmare employment blunder and pursue an entirely different vocation. Then there's our social identities, which we cultivate by meeting new people and experimenting with different ways of interacting with friends, coworkers, family members, and lovers. Next, there's our sexual identity, which we form by getting in touch with our erotic orientation, boundaries, and expression. Finally, there's our physical identity, which goes through a metamorphosis of its own, which we'll discuss a couple of chapters down the line.

Many of us also take on the scary task of folding motherhood into the web of identities that make up our womanly selves. This is one of the hardest identities to master, because becoming a mother competes directly with the other identities we've been trying so hard to establish. (I know this from my years as an editor at a parenting magazine, *not* from personal experience, in case you're wondering.) Learning to juggle all these identities is what renders this decade so emotionally wearing and probably why I have a secret (though embarrassing to admit) fascination with the Spice Girls. (Remember them?) If only we could have a single image, a single prerogative in life, a single way of relating to the world, like the girls of spice, life in the 20s would be far more bearable. For one thing, it would simplify our wardrobes!

During this evolution of identity, most of us experience a crisis or two, which is not at all surprising when you think about all the competing identities we're dealing with. The first crisis typically hits during our early 20s when we're bewilderingly trying to establish a professional persona. We either don't know what we want to do with ourselves (start up a cyber-chic website? go to law school?) or can't seem to transform our idea of what we want to do into reality (how *does* one become a world-famous travel writer who journeys from one land of lush to another investigating such intriguing topics as orangutan rehabilitation in Bukit Lawang?). If we base our entire identity on vague or unobtainable plans due to lack of experience, we are ripe for crisis.

Those of us who don't have a backup plan for the chance disaster that our dreams don't unfold as imagined—as when I received my 50th and final rejection for a newspaper reporter position (those bastards!) and hadn't come up with an alternative job option if the inconceivable happened—are particularly vulnerable. On a brighter note, those of us who enter crisis mode will find that the trauma is temporarily subdued soon after we accept our first job, which in my case was an administrative assistant position at a magazine, a far cry from the roving reporter image I had visualized. That's because when we accept a job, we have at least some form of professional identity to cling to while we rework that "Pre-30s Plan." And for escapist pleasures, we can finally feel free to focus on our other identities, like that of "sexy girlfriend" or "cool and aloof single-something chick."

The second crisis usually hits during our mid to late 20s. After we've established a crude model of adulthood by which we've been living, we finally regain enough strength lost from our first crisis to acknowledge that the model we've created is not working. Various external influences typically propel the second identity crash: a friend gets a huge promotion, making us uncomfortably aware of the fact that we've had the same unglamorous job since graduation and still can't afford a vacation in Hawaii; or the guy we thought we one day might marry goes on a three-day "vision quest" in the Rockies, comes back, and breaks up with us, forcing us to reenter the singles lifestyle we had long since happily abandoned; or a friend gets pregnant, and due to pheromone influences beyond our control, we are overwrought by primal urges to get married and procreate, making us burst into tears at the mere thought of buying tiny baby socks. These moments stir up a storm of emotions we thought we'd left behind in those wretched two or three years after college, spawning a renaissance of reassessment, during which we examine the adult lives we've created and attempt to make appropriate changes.

My second identity crisis overcame me two years ago, when I finally accepted the fact that I hated being an editor. I wanted to be a writer, which was my original plan all along. Precisely at that time, I sensed a primitive longing to take another step forward with my boyfriend and move in together to see if we were domestically compatible. I also realized that my heart, as the song goes, was pining away back in San Francisco, not New York where I was living at the time. So, I headed back West, signed a lease for an apartment with my boyfriend, who was heading back West from a stint in New York, too, and became a freelance writer. That's where I am now, ensconced in Identity #2.

Most girls who've entered this stage agree that it feels way saner than Identity #1. The reason is that we've acquired a few tools for dealing with the emotional trauma and insecurities that presage that second crisis. While there are no crisp blueprints for hammering all these various personae into one happy, successful woman—but if there were, I promise I'd pass them on to you—I can relay the following six suggestions. They'll help you get in touch with your fledgling adult identity and all her various incarnations so that she won't harm your mental health too drastically.

#1: Hit the Road Solo

One of the absolute best ways to get in touch with our core beliefs, strength, values, and dreams is to travel by ourselves to (ideally non-English-speaking) parts of the globe that are totally unfamiliar to us and therefore challenging to our comfort zone. In fact, if you only do one thing in the way of trying to figure out who you are, let it be travel.

Even if the thought of traveling alone terrifies you, spending a chunk of time outside of anything familiar forces you to rely on your intuition and instincts, which most of us ignore in our cushy existence. Plus, traveling opens up a whole new world of thinking, which can only influence our adult development in positive ways. Lauren, 23, of Santa

Barbara, who recently spent four months teaching English in Venezuela, puts it philosophically: "Travel takes you out of your present place and allows you to look at life from a different perspective. You become more yourself when you're gone."

My own perception of life drastically changed during the nine months I spent while in college traveling through parts of Southeast Asia (partly through an exchange program and partly alone, just me and my backpack). My American-style rational way of thinking was forever altered, for instance, when I saw a group of men in trances run spears through their cheeks *without screaming or gushing with blood*! My sense of possibilities was forever expanded when I saw a family of five and their entire belongings pass me on a dirt road *on a single motorcycle*! When I came back to the States, everything around me seemed far too rational, disgustingly stiff, and oh so decadent! I was appalled when I was visiting back home and saw a dozen or so cans of Diet Coke lining our refrigerator door.

"At home, you take many things for granted, but in a foreign environment, you don't have support from your family and friends, so you have to make your way on your own," says Miranda, 24, of Nashville, who spent three and a half months working at a clinic in Haiti and two months working at a Nigerian clinic through programs associated with her studies in medicine. "Seeing how other cultures interact with strangers and learning about their views of America and the rest of the world makes you reevaluate everything you know. One thing I realized from those experiences is how rushed we are in the United States. When I was living abroad, I'd meet people and end up talking to them for two or three hours. That's so uncommon here. We don't even have time to sit down." And that's exactly what travel gives us: time to sit down and think, which is something most of us never do, with all the distractions and convenience of home entertainment brought to us by modern living. But now I'm starting to mourn a past that only my great-grandparents knew, so let's move along.

Just one more point of order: Don't use the excuse of having no money. I don't doubt that it's true, but in the case of travel, it's just not valid. So vital are the benefits of exploring the world, now in this transitory and relatively responsibility-free decade of our lives, that credit card use is OK (as long as you don't go overboard and you stay at the cheapest hostels along the way).

#2: *Know Who You Are Not*

Sometimes, you'll find, the best way to figure out who you are (a hard-nose sales rep? a fabulous cook? a passionate lover? an adventurer? a member of the Green Party?) is to figure out who you are *not.* For instance, you know you are not your mother, who is terrified of highways and of pumping her own gas. Nor are you your brother, who supports Pat Buchanan and goes on holiday to Las Vegas. And you're definitely not your best friend from high school, who dropped out of college and delivers pizza for a living. This process of elimination is handy for narrowing down the choice of identities we might wish to try out in the next three or four years.

#3: *Find an Idolette to Guide You Through the Mental Muck*

In the same way we need advice from professional mentors to bush-whack through the jungle of our fledgling careers, we are at an advantage if we can find a few good role models for helping us through the stickier moments that threaten our newly established adult lifestyles and identities. Developing relationships with women in their 30s whose lives we'd like to duplicate gives us a real-world perspective of what we might create for ourselves in one short decade, such as having a stimulating group of friends, a job that lets us travel four times a year to parts of the globe where bananas grow in the wild, an adorable family, and a house near hiking-accessible parks.

Moreover, these relationships can provide us much-needed direction on how to work through some of the setbacks we're bound to encounter. "If you meet someone who is successful and has a life you'd like to have yourself, ask her how she got where she is," recommends Leslie, 26, of Seattle. She has several role models whom she consults regularly for advice on various life questions, be it work, money, or friendships. According to her: "You can always tailor their advice to what you want to do. There's nothing wrong with doing something your own way, but it helps if you can get ideas for what you're trying to do from others who have been there."

Our generation is coming of age in a country stalled at a cultural crossroads. Gender roles are more androgynous than ever before in recent history—both sexes are earning money for the family and sharing child-care responsibilities, for instance—and predetermined roles to which our female identities can automatically cling are no longer in vogue. A good role model, a woman who's had some success with the juggling act of working and mothering *and* living an active lifestyle, is invaluable if and when it becomes time to merge vocational and familial identities into one happy professionalmama. Even if you're far removed from motherhood, getting pointers during your first career moves will help you out with the big-picture planning.

#4: Find Your Voice

One of the tragic by-products of female adolescence is a dulling of our instincts. Parents, because they love us and want to protect us from all the dangers of the world (or perhaps are terrified that if something happens to us, they'll be left to face the world alone), often go overboard in the protection mode during these formative years. They laden us with rules and regulations that prohibit us from exploring the world in our own natural way. Why they wouldn't focus their efforts, instead, on teaching us assertiveness and self-defense skills is beyond me. That's yet another book for another time. If you're in your 20s, it's far to late for advice on your upbringing, but file this memo away for the future when you're raising girls of your own.

My point is that sometimes, during the course of our overly protected girlhoods, we stop trusting our instincts, or worse, we're never given a chance to experiment with our intuitiveness in interacting with the world at large. If you were raised by domineering parents, you also may not have been allowed to express your feelings or beliefs during those formidable years. "When I was growing up, my opinion never mattered," recalls Anna, 27, of Seattle. "If I ever questioned my parents, I was 'a rotten kid.' They never explained why I was in trouble, so I never learned to trust whether my anger was founded or not. Now I'm always doubting myself because my 'mad' was always wrong."

Part of this buried-voice epidemic has to do with the way girls are socialized in general. "Women are cultivated to adapt. When we're constantly adapting, we don't know who we are, and, consequently, we never learn what we want," says clinical psychologist Dale Lillak, M.F.C.C., of San Jose. Part of the identity-establishing process is forming opinions of our own, vocalizing them, and standing behind what we believe. If you were never given the opportunity to assert your opinion or experiment with success and failure while growing up, trusting your decisions and asserting your will is going to be a tough lesson to learn.

Go-Girl Guidance *Live alone for at least one year during your 20s, even if all you can afford is a teeny studio where the bathtub sits next to the refrigerator. If you think creatively (or have friends who know something about interior design), you can transform any questionable apartment into a stunning living space. "Having your own apartment gives you so much time to reflect upon yourself," says Tory, 26, of Hoboken. Even better, you will finally be able to hang your pictures, entertain guests, and explore your culinary whims without skeptical looks from roommates.*

#5: Stake Your Boundaries

Being able to maintain a sense of who we are and what we believe in, in the face of the often persuasive powers of family members, friends, and boyfriends, is another giant step to establishing a solid adult identity. But establishing and maintaining the boundaries needed to protect our voice and decisions is also one of the hardest lessons. Recognizing when your boundaries are being crossed is a prerequisite to learning to assert yourself around others.

"Listen to your body," counsels Allison Benton-Jones, L.C.S.W., of Tampa. "When you become nervous or tense, dig deep and ask yourself, 'What about the situation is making me feel this way? What does it remind me of?'" For instance, does your stomach cramp up when your parents start asking too many probing questions? Does your heart race and body temperature rocket if your boss yells at you? Does your forehead become tight if your boyfriend, in a fit of malfunctioning distrust, does something vile like read your journal? If so, your boundaries are clearly being overstepped. Lillak emphasizes, "Once you become aware of what makes you uncomfortable, you must learn to express your discomfort." For instance, tell your parents to stop with the interrogation, inform your boss that you will not accept his outrageously unprofessional behavior, and tell that suspicious boyfriend of yours to respect your privacy or move on.

#6: Run Within Yourself

I ran my first marathon just a few months ago, and one of my running partners—who was undertaking her 15th marathon!—gave me a tip that I have since been applying to just about everything else in my life. "Run within yourself," she told me, meaning don't get caught up in others passing you by. Stick to a pace that works for you. The same brilliant mantra should be muttered repeatedly during our 20s, when we're ferociously trying to get to the finish line of adulthood. If we don't focus on ourselves, we'll spend our entire 20s running someone else's race. The winning formula is to slow down, and let your identity evolve at its own speed. "Give yourself a chance for your life to fall into place," advises Zonya Johnson, Ph.D., a clinical psychologist in Oakland, California. "It takes time to figure out where your passions lie and what's important to you. Trust that the time will eventually come." When it does—and it will—you'll feel like a marathon queen.

THAT SELF-LOATHING FEELING

You know how thigh-high stockings with garter-free elastic lace tops do horrendous things to our legs? At certain angles in certain mirrors, these stockings make our legs actually look like the model's on the package. But just when we're starting to feel sexy, we turn, and the elastic part squeezes our flesh into bulging-over-the-top sausages. Self-esteem plays the same confusing trick during our 20s, offering a submelodrama to the emotional theatrics in which we're caught up.

One day, we're completely high on ourselves because we get an offer for the job we so desperately wanted, two guys ask for our phone number (OK, one had a scary looking nipple pierce, but oh well), and that girl with hip hair we met at our mailbox invites us to a party that promises to be swimming with titillating conversation and stunning men. The next day, though, we're wretched losers: the sort-of boyfriend who told us the night before that he had never been so in love dumps us due to commitment issues, the job for which we so enthusiastically competed turns out to be 90 percent low-level support (and on top of it, our boss is a patronizing egomaniac), and our nemesis at work gets a raise, while we don't. These fluctuations in esteem make us feel even more out of control than when the neighborhood pervert stole our underwear right out of the spin cycle at the local Laundromat.

Since plummeting confidence is as much a part of the 20-something existence as starting our first real jobs, learning healthy esteem-boosting comebacks is fundamental to our mental well-being. When your confidence is shot—you're at your first review and instead of the promotion you assumed was in the bag, your supervisor gives you a low rating on "attention to detail" or something else administratively lame—do a quick mental rundown of all of your recent accomplishments, suggests Melissa, 28, of Houston, who takes such opportunities to remind herself of the projects she's done well and the ideas she's come up with that have been successful. Another standby confidence-booster is to rally our own personal cheerleading squad. Call the supportive people in your life for a genuine pep talk, advises Astrid, 26, of Vermillion, South Dakota. She relates: "When my husband and I split up, I reminisced about good times with family and friends. Remembering who I was before things got so bad in my life, and thinking about all my past success, helped me rebuild esteem."

Getting to the root of your low confidence will help you determine how to improve your status. "I process things through writing in my journal, self-reflection, and talking with friends," says Caroline, 21, of New Salem, Massachusetts. "Usually I can pinpoint what's causing my lack of confidence through that." Since low esteem often has its genesis in girlhood, you may have to think back a few years. If you had controlling, overly protective, or absent parents, for instance, your confidence figures to be a notch lower than that of most other 20-something girls. That's because you probably didn't get adequate amounts of positive support or opportunities to make your own decisions, let alone learn how to be assertive or feel comfortable in positions of power. According to psychologist Zonya Johnson, those are two necessary ingredients to developing confidence. Working on your assertiveness skills and volunteering for projects that give you a chance to exert some power are means to boosting esteem.

Getting in touch with your creativity and spirituality can also restore a bad sense of self-worth when you need a fix due to an unfulfilling job and/or boyfriend and/or life in general. Our creative and spiritual sides need just as much pampering as our intellectual and emotional sides, but we 20-somethings are particularly neglectful of them due to more immediate tasks: finding a job with benefits, getting an apartment, scoring a date for Friday night. When I was most miserable at my first job, I remember doing crafty things, like making a wreath of cranberries around Christmastime in an effort to pretend I was Martha Stewart, and writing letters to my friends in Europe while sitting in a café in an effort to pretend I was a mysterious intellect/writer. The goal was to get my mind off the gloomy reality that my job and love life completely sucked. These little creative outlets made me feel that I was at least doing *something* worthwhile.

Working on the spirituality void may also do esteem wonders. If your soul is rooted in nature, spend time with the Earth. Hike with a group of nature lovers, do trail maintenance at local nature reserves, or even take up gardening. If your spirituality lies in the church, synagogue, temple, or mosque, start attending evening worship services. If helping others strengthens your sense of purpose, volunteer at a convalescent home, a children's center, or the SPCA, where you can try to cheer up forlorn-looking cats and dogs with a good belly rub. Paying attention to that do-gooder inside will make you feel good about yourself, which is exactly what you need when self-esteem has sunk lower than mercury on a February morning in Anchorage.

Believe it or not, the ups and downs miraculously level out, usually at a much higher level of satisfaction than we've ever experienced before, except perhaps during prepubescent girlhood when we were confident empresses. Satisfaction grows because the 20s, with so many occasions to succeed, offer us a gold mine of opportunity to prosper. And developing a strong sense of worth comes from building one success upon another.

"I'M SO STRESSED OUT"

Stress, like low self-esteem, can creep under our skin while we're trying to sculpt our adult lifestyles. Here's how it works: First, our bodies have to experience a physical change (we have three martinis in the course of one hour; we're suddenly hit with an allergy attack; we start PMSing) or a drastic shift in the emotional state (we're flooded with betrayal when our supervisor passes off our ideas as his own; we plunge into despair when our credit card statement arrives; we boil with wrath when our roommate leaves a nasty note complaining about the noise we made at 2 A.M., when she makes noise *all the time*). Next, our brain sends signals telling our bodies to release certain hormones that provoke the proverbial "fight-or-flight" syndrome. This then causes our blood pressure and heart rate to rise, muscles to tense, and breathing to accelerate. In evolutionary terms, this physiological reaction to stress would presumably give us the strength and courage to fight off a hungry tiger about to attack. Today we just tense up and get irritated at our boyfriends.

Of course, not everyone responds to life's upsets in the same fashion. Many people thrive off of the adrenaline that stress pumps through our arteries. Others (myself included) experience more despondent responses: our mental reserves break down, and we become fatigued, depressed, or weepy. Our perceptions sometimes get wildly twisted, verging on paranoia, and we lash out at cab drivers who we suspect are taking us the long way home. Other times, our immune systems collapse, and we get sick and develop all sorts of physical ailments, including aches and pains, digestion problems, insomnia, cramps, rashes, acne, chest pains, headaches, shortness of breath, sexual dysfunction, and even more serious disorders along the lines of high blood pressure, abnormal heartbeats, and sometimes heart attacks (though rare for girls our age).

Since the 20s are, in essence, one long decade of stress, we must learn a few tactics for reducing the tension and anxiety that go with the territory. The first approach is to try to identify the main sources (usually work, a despondent lover, overbearing parents, or money) and tackle them directly. For instance, when work began to dominate her life, Rosie, 26, of Los Angeles, switched positions within her company to a less stressful job so she could spend more time doing what she loved: rock climbing, hiking, and volleyball. And when Tory, 26, of Hoboken, New Jersey, began suffering insomnia and stomachaches from working in a hostile office environment with a sexist boss, she began looking for a new job. "Sending just one résumé was so liberating," she says. "Doing something to change my situation made me feel instantly better."

If you're the type of girl to take on more than you can chew (and who among us isn't?), you are suffering from commitment overload. Practice setting realistic limits for yourself. "I have to consciously think about how much work I can take on and how much I really can do socially in one night—not try to go to five different friends' houses, for instance," says Hannah, 24, of Los Angeles. "Learning how to say no is key to reducing stress, because not being able to finish all my work or canceling plans when I realize I can't do everything I thought I could can be even more stressful."

Training the mind to chill out and not obsess over the things that are causing us anxiety is something many of us have to learn, because our gender is wired to ruminate over the littlest things. To help free your mind of worry and anxiety, carve out some time every day to deal with the particular aggravations that are causing you to tense up or to fantasize about throwing a stack of papers in your boss's face, screaming, "Fax *this*!" Knowing that you will have a time in the day to mentally massage these cricks and hopefully find some repose will prevent anxiety from haunting your brain for 24 hours on end.

It worked for me, anyway. There I was, 26 and suddenly faced with one of the more stressful decisions I've ever had to make: relocate to Manhattan with my job (and attempt to live in expensive NYC on a paltry salary, knowing practically no one) or accept unemployment and pursue a new job in San Francisco. This was all within the same couple of weeks, might I mention, that a former boyfriend had the untimely nerve to tell me he wanted to date other women! I spent half an hour every morning writing in my journal about all my worries. With my mind purged of those darting anxieties, I was able to get through the day with clarity and purpose.

One more idea for nailing down the source of your stress: ask your pack of girlfriends for their input. "Talking to my friends when I'm under stress helps me organize my thoughts, even if I'm not really asking for advice," says Judy, 24, of New York. Besides, group venting does wonders for the soul.

Until we can eliminate, or at least tame, the source of our stress so that it doesn't make us break out into hives or toss and turn all night, we must calm our bodies and minds. Being well-experienced with stress, I have a seven-step program for that,

Step 1: Think Regularity

Making your day-to-day schedule as predictable as possible will help relieve tension and anxiety. Start by establishing a regular bed and wake-up time that allows you at least seven hours of shut-eye a night. Stick to this schedule as best as you can, at least during the week if you blow it on the weekends, which you probably will.

Step 2: Avoid Making Dietary Blunders

I've listed some general nutritional guidelines in Chapter 10, "That Whacked-Out Body Feeling," but here are the basics: Strive for five different veggies and fruits a day, along with a good mix of whole-grain breads and cereal, and reduce your consumption of refined sugar, caffeine, nicotine, and excessive alcohol, all of which cause disruptive physiological changes in the body that can lead to stress. Also, tank up on those eight glasses of water a day. Make it more exotic, if you like, by chilling filtered water in the fridge or adding a slice of fresh lemon so that you can pretend you're on vacation or at a fancy restaurant.

Step 3: Work It Out at the Gym

For reducing stress, aim for at least 30 minutes of aerobic exercise *every* day instead of the recommended three times a week, with a yoga class at least once a week. Yoga not only teaches you how to relax your muscles through deep breathing but also helps you temporarily relieve your brain of those racing thoughts and worries that are causing much of your anxiety.

Step 4: Just Chill Out

Take frequent 10-minute breaks: a walk around the block, a few shoulder or neck stretches, even a minute or two of deep breathing to relieve muscle tension and to trigger a physiological relaxation response in the body. Put off big changes until the main sources of your stress have been alleviated. That means no big moves, no fad diets (a useless endeavor anyway), and no major projects that will add more stress to your life. Save those for later days when you've got some of the stressload under control.

Step 5: Stare at the Sun (But Not Directly)

Expose yourself to morning light. Take a long walk every morning before you shower, or read the paper by a window with plenty of eastern exposure. Lack of natural light may lead to chemical malfunctions in the brain which can trigger stress.

Step 6: Experiment with New Ways to Unwind

The power of a bubble bath to soothe the nerves is nothing new to us, but try taking one first thing in the morning during those times when you're about to lose it. "The only way I can relieve stress is to get up at 6 A.M. every morning and take a bubble bath," says Astrid. "During this time, I make a point not to think about work or my one-year-old daughter; I just think about myself." Caroline says that part of her stress is not having time to de-stress, so she tries to make time to unwind by going into her room, shutting the door, turning on some music, watching TV, or taking a nap. Sloane, 21, of Syracuse, New York, gets haircuts when she's overwhelmed by stress: "Nothing makes me feel better than a new haircut. I feel renewed," she says. "But I also do ridiculous things to relax, like draw a tattoo with a pen on my arm or redecorate my room."

Those Sleepless Nights

Can't sleep in your perpetually stressed-out state? Well, join the club. Insomnia is one of the first signs that we are, indeed, stressed out. Consequently, most of us frazzled 20-something women are as familiar with sleeplessness as we are those teeny cracks on our bedroom ceiling. It doesn't matter which variation(s) of insomnia you experience—the "I can't fall asleep until 4 A.M." insomnia, the "my eyes pop open for good at 2 A.M. every morning" insomnia, or the "I slept the whole night but still feel as if I spent seven hours tumbling down a jagged cliff" insomnia—all versions add to our general fatigue, grouchiness, and neurosis, which heightens the stress in our already stressed-out existence.

To battle insomnia successfully, we must first attempt to reduce whatever stress is infiltrating our lives, so be sure to read the stress-reducing suggestions in this chapter. Then try a few of the following strategies for getting those doctor-recommended seven to nine hours of nightly slumber:

- Exercise regularly, but not right before you hit the sheets. An exception is sex, since orgasms are nature's most perfect relaxation tactic. For all other forms of physical exertion, allow at least three hours before attempting sleep. Likewise, cut out caffeine, nicotine, and heavy drinking before bed—or ideally altogether when you're *really* stressed out. Stimulants shake the brain and body all night long.
- Design a bedtime routine filled with mindless activities, such as listening to that tape of desert sounds that your transcendentalist coworker gave you for your birthday, reading technical essays on Sherman's march across the South, watching *Dick Van Dyke* reruns, taking a steamy bath doused with marjoram oil (which knocks you out), or whatever else makes you sleepy. Try to go to bed and wake up around the same time every day; otherwise, your body clock gets wound up at all the wrong hours. If notions of work, money, or freakish ex-lovers dare seep into your predoze ritual, light a candle and mutter an incantation to exorcise those thoughts, which have no

business sneaking into bed with you. Note: When you're really under stress, you must observe these rituals on the weekends, too—your body is telling you that you need a break!

- Buy a relaxation tape (they work if you take them seriously), and do the suggested breathing exercises—but explain to roommates ahead of time, lest they wonder what those gaspy sounds emanating from behind your door are all about. One of my faithful breathing stand-bys is this: Lie on your back, and place one hand on your stomach and the other on your chest. As you inhale, concentrate on making the hand on your abdomen rise higher than the one on your chest, as though you are blowing up a giant balloon in your large intestines with each inhalation. (The mental image is enough to distract you from all those random and alarming thoughts that threaten to keep you up all night.) Extend your exhale twice as long as your inhale, using your diaphragm to squeeze excess air out of your lungs. Mind-body gurus claim such deep breathing practices force your body into a physiologically relaxed state.

- If you haven't fallen asleep after half an hour of fluffing your com-forter out of boredom, get up and occupy yourself with your favorite bedtime activity until you feel sleepy again. Or take the VCR apart in an attempt to figure out why it makes weird clicking noises in the middle of the night as though it is possessed. Then, try to nod off once again, but if another 30 minutes pass by without a wink, get up and repeat the cycle until you drift off for good, which is hope-fully before your alarm clock goes off.

- When all the foregoing tactics fail in the wee hours, thrash violently beneath the sheets, as though having a fitful nightmare, to wake your sleeping-beauty boyfriend (who never has trouble sleeping despite the fact that he drinks espresso after dinner). This will likely earn you a two-minute empathetic neck rub until your lover drifts back into deep slumber. At least you'll feel loved, if not sleepy.

- If the entire night has gone by without sleep, take a very cold shower, eat a protein-rich breakfast (you'll need the extra energy), and don't dwell on your ferocious, lost night. Work hard, work out after work, be mellow, and take another stab at sleep in about 14 hours, when you'll be so exhausted that you can't help but pass out the minute you hit the bed.

- No matter how tempted you may be, never resort to sleeping pills or supplements, which can do more damage than good to our sleeping habits. Instead, see a doctor when insomnia threatens to get the best of you. Underlying medical conditions or drugs that you are taking (even the legal ones) may be causing all those sleepless nights.

Step 7: Imagine Life Without Stress

Last but not least, make a habit of visualizing yourself in your most relaxed state, such as on a pristine beach in Bora Bora.

"IS THERE ANYBODY OUT THERE?"

Loneliness is another mental-health threat most of us have to contend with as we go through the emotional theatrics that accompany our debut into adulthood. Friends abandon us—literally when they move away to claim professional turf, and figuratively when they become pre-occupied with their own identity-establishing rituals and love lives. Likewise, many of us abandon the roots of our support systems in an attempt to sow our professional and romance-seeking oats, not to mention figure out who we are, which is a taxing and exhausting quest of its own. The end result, more often than not, is an empty weekend spent imagining that everyone else in the world is at an outrageous party in which we did not even make the B-list of guests.

Though culturally humiliating to admit, since we don't want others to infer that we're socially inept or friendless, loneliness is something we have to learn how to conquer. Three reasons: One, loneliness never disappears on its own; social interaction is the only way out. Two, if we don't deal with loneliness, we're ripe for depression. Once we're depressed, our natural tendency may be to withdraw from others, so social engagement often becomes even *more* difficult. Three, social support is not only good for our souls but also good for our bodies. Studies show that those of us with strong social ties live longer, get sick less often, suffer from less stress and anxiety, and have higher self-esteem. So, in a sense, getting connected could be the one treatment we need to appease all the mental drama that marks our 20s.

Getting connected, however, takes effort, and you'll find a few suggestions for making new friends in Chapter 12, "Our Surrogate Family." For now, let's concentrate on getting out of the cave of solitude when you feel as if you're stuck behind a big, fat, immovable, desolate boulder. Here are 10 ways:

1. **Have a garage sale.** This is a particularly good way to meet your neighbors, who, believe me, will *love* to pick through your personal belongings while sharing neighborhood lore and gossip. You may even discover that the cute guy next door was also a fan of the obscure bands you loved in high school, whose CDs you're now trying to peddle at two for a dollar. Note: If you are moving to a new area, consider having a garage sale in your new hood *after* you've moved. Even though it might be nice to get rid of your junk before you haul it all the way across town, saving it for your new neighbors to rummage through is a good way to scope out who on your block might be worth inviting to the housewarming.

2. **Join a sports team that meets weekly.** A master's swim group, a running club, or the office soccer team could expand your circle. Or train with an organized group for a local marathon, triathlon, walkathon, or bike tour. You will meet people who have similar interests, and you will become part of a Greater Cause, in which bonding is inevitable. Signing up for organized sports or athletic events will give you at least one weekly social outlet on which you can steadily rely if all your plans lately seem to be falling through at the last minute.

3. **Take a city college class.** A course that lasts several months will give you the time you need to establish acquaintances. Make sure

that the class intrigues you enough that you won't get bored and drop out. The best classes for meeting people are those that offer plenty of interplay among students: wine tasting, improvisational theater games or acting, cooking, Zen and the art of stripping (just kidding!), and foreign-language workshops.

4. **Chitchat with local merchants, neighbors, coworkers, and other people you see throughout the day.** When Judy first moved to Manhattan and knew no one, she set a goal to talk to one new person every day and to go to one cultural event every week, which helped her feel less lonely. Kelly, 28, of Brooklyn, suggests introducing yourself to the neighbors. "When I first moved to New York, I ran into one of my neighbors and introduced myself," she says. "We started talking and hanging out. Now he's one of my best friends. There's also an old retired guy who sits around my neighborhood. I always stop on the street and talk to him. He keeps me informed about what's going on around the block." If you're not a chitchatty kind of gal, take small steps by saying hello to the locals and striking up conversation when it feels natural—casual chatter with neighborly folks will give you a sense of belonging.

5. **Volunteer for a neighborhood-improvement weekend project.** Painting a community center or planting flowers along a local street divide can be another great way to tick off the number of foreign faces around the block and make you feel like a vital thread within the neighborhood fabric. If the fabric of your hood is more like scrap material with random loose fibers, it may be time to move to a friendlier part of town where other 20-somethings congregate. You'll hate boxing up your stuff again, but you'll thank me for it later.

6. **Join a spiritual group.** A religious congregation will also do, if you're affiliated with a particular denomination. One of the premises behind these gatherings is to establish a sense of community among those with shared faiths. Just one request: Please don't go out and join a local cult out of desolation. Make sure that whatever group you choose to associate with doesn't want you to move into

an isolated community, fork over all your money, wear black Nikes, or terminate all ties with family and friends.

7. **Ask someone you'd like to get to know for a favor.** The favor in question could be taking over a project when you're away from the office, patting your cat while you're on a weekend camping trip in the Ozarks, or lending you an extra chair when you have one too many guests for dinner. I got to know one of my neighbors this way when she knocked on my door one evening to ask if she could borrow two chairs. She had just moved into the apartment across the hall and was trying to impress some guy she had met by making him dinner, but she didn't have any chairs to go with her new dining-room table. I immediately liked her because she wanted to include me (or at least my chairs) in her seduction scheme. Living an entirely self-sufficient, self-reliant life breeds all sorts of loneliness, so retrain yourself to think of requesting favors as offerings of friendship, rather than impositions. Establishing connections with others requires learning how to receive as well as give.

8. **Enhance your idle hours.** Since we all go through bouts of loneliness, learn how to enjoy the time you spend by yourself so that when you find yourself alone, these solitary moments won't seem so damn dreadful. Sloane, for instance, went to dinners, movies, and even the ballet alone when she was studying abroad in Scotland. "Doing things by yourself reaffirms that you can enjoy life without being entirely dependent on others for your entertainment," she says. The next time you find yourself alone, make yourself a gourmet dinner, go see that foreign film you can't persuade anyone else to watch, take a long walk in a beautiful part of town, or plant some potted flowers for your kitchen windowsill.

9. **Pick up the phone.** Dish with old friends, who are likely going through similar feelings of isolation in the cities where they now reside. If no one is around, call your parents, who are, undoubtedly, always eager to talk to you.

10. **Make plans immediately.** The best way to nip the bud of loneliness is to surround yourself with supportive people. Book your Fri-

day night early on in the week—with someone who you *know* will not cancel. Or plan a trip back home as soon as you can get the 21-day-advance discount tickets. You know that your parents will be ecstatic, and who else but those with whom you made your very first connections in the world can make you feel less solitary in this great big universe?

MOVING 101

If there's one thing we 20-somethings are experts in, it's moving. Moving to a new place—especially if we know no one there—ranks as one of the loneliest and most stressful things to do. But personally, I think moving is also an excellent way to figure out what type of lifestyle we'd like to live, because so much of who we are is influenced by our surroundings. If we never question our environment and try new things, we may be living the wrong life!

When I was living in New York, for instance, my emotions and intellect were on stimulation overdrive. I loved it, but one year was plenty. My senses had retreated into some sort of protective hibernation from the city noise, smell, and grime—the attributes that make New York as raw and intense as a city can possibly be. I craved open space, nature, a view of the sky larger than the square footage of my midtown apartment kitchen, which I shared with four other intense Manhattan transplants. Back to San Francisco I came.

Moving around can sure impede our efforts to get our lives in order, though. Not only is it expensive to pack up and float around from one city to another, but also, the more we move, the less likely we'll form lasting bonds with the people we meet along the way. So, if we're always moving around, we probably won't have the same strong friendships that we so desperately need to cultivate during our 20s as we would were we to stay in one place. (Of course, if we stay and our friends leave, we may have the same problem.) To top it off, it can take a long time to make a new city feel warm and familiar enough to call our home.

That's why I've provided several clever ways of speeding up the process:

- **Be choosy.** Move to a neighborhood that is safe, fits your personality, is close to areas where you think you might like to spend a lot of time, doesn't cause commuting hell, and has nearby commercial areas so that grocery shopping, coffeehousing, and all-purpose bumming around is immediate and enticing enough to get out of your apartment and interact with your new surroundings. When you move to a new area, don't hole up in your house by yourself. With nothing external to influence you otherwise, you'll hate your new city within three weeks.

- **Live with roommates.** Living alone teaches you all sorts of things about yourself, but the best time to experience this intense form of self-awareness is not when you're new to a city. Roommates are great for meeting other people, going out with, getting invited to parties, and getting the inside scoop on neighborhood bars and restaurants. If you're moving in with strangers, be sure to ask prospects three probing questions before signing the lease: (1) how they've resolved roommate problems in the past (if they say they've never had problems, they're lying—look for the telltale signs of fidgeting and subject changing—but if they say they have adult discussions and talk until they find a satisfactory compromise for all parties involved, ask if you can sign the lease today); (2) how often they are home, especially if you know you'd like to have the place to yourself now and then; and (3) how many nights their significant others typically crash there, so you don't end up sharing the kitchen and bathroom with more roommates than you bargained for.

- **Call everyone you know.** Be aggressive about asking people to hang out with you—even if initiating plans feels weird, advises Stephanie, 26, of San Francisco. She lays it on the line: "When I moved to San Francisco, I met some cool people at work and said, 'Hey, I just moved to the city and live nearby. Do you want to hang out?'" The very fact that you're new helps you deal with the reality that you have no friends in the area, and it's a great icebreaker: those who have been in your shoes will take the cue and invite you to join in their activities.

- **Call everyone your friends know.** In your attempt to establish a brand-new social life, definitely follow up with all those friends of friends, whose names you started getting by the dozen as soon as you told people about your moving plans. Being shy, I know how excruciatingly painful it is to ring up virtual strangers and ask them to meet you, but if you don't follow up on those referrals, your friends will keep asking you if you've contacted their friend yet, and you will be forced to admit that you haven't and will probably miss out on meeting some cool people. After all, if your friends like them, why wouldn't you? Most friends of friends are happy to meet for a drink and tell you all the quirky places they frequent in the city they know much better than you. And if you click, you've found a new playmate.

- **Mark your turf.** Decorate your new apartment with a few things that have always been with you, suggests Marie, 27, of New York City, who has moved about eight times in the past five years. Her version: "I have some candles and crystal vases I bring wherever I move."

- **Establish a routine right away.** Lori, 23, of San Luis Obispo, California, advises newcomers to go to the same store, same laundry, same gym, same dry cleaner, same deli. "You have to have a routine to get a sense of your environment," she says. Routines also help lower stress, one thing we could do without when we're trying to establish new bearings. As much as I loathe to admit it, being a supporter of independent mom-and-pop shops, I found Starbucks a haven of comfort when I first moved to Manhattan. Not only was it the only place where I could find a decent cup of coffee (on the West Coast, we like it *strong*!), but it was also somewhat comforting with its familiar, though generic, surroundings.

- **Get involved in your company's social life and outside organizations.** Choose activities that offer lots of interaction. Diane, 27, of Chicago, joined a couple of Jewish organizations, a movie screening and discussion group, and a book club when she moved to the windy city after college graduation. You won't have to stick with these outlets if you find out that a connection doesn't exist, but at least the activities will keep you out there meeting people until you start cultivating a group of friends with whom you bond. These doings will also get you through those early bouts of loneliness that always accompany a move.

- **Get lost in your new city.** Says Mary, 25, a med student in Washington, D.C.: "Spend a day walking around an area that you don't know. I once came upon a used bookstore run by a little old Greek woman and found some amazing classics and an original version of *Gray's Anatomy*. Every time I explore an area, I find something new—an ice cream shop, a music store. You can discover so many little gems just by wandering."

- **Give a part of yourself to the area.** Participate in a local fundraising drive; volunteer at a community center; plant flowers in your yard, or set up a window box; register to vote before the first municipal elections. When you commit a part of yourself to a new environment, you'll inevitably feel more connected to it. When Marie's job took her to Puerto Rico, for instance, she signed up for Spanish lessons and went to restaurants frequented by the locals.

- **Go to places far away from your neighborhood to get some of the stuff you need.** "No place is too far. This will help you get to know the city well," says Elsie, 23, of Los Angeles.

- **While you're at it, do the "sights."** Adds Elsie: "Every city has them. When I first got to L.A., I wanted to see the Hollywood sign, so I drove there and spent some time cruising around the Hollywood hills. If you're curious about anything, do it while you're new to the area." Doing the sights has another extraordinary effect: they're probably familiar to you from exposure through the media, so when you visit you'll feel as if you're a part of a supreme club of people who've been there too, which can make you feel like a local. One of my favorite New York experiences occurred within a few weeks after I'd arrived in the city. I was walking home after having drinks with one of those many friends of friends whom I had contacted and found myself at the bottom of the Empire State Building. There was a full moon that night, so I took the elevators up and spent about an hour walking around and around the top gazing upon my new town. It made me feel intimately attuned to the city in a way I hadn't felt an hour before.

- **Maintain relationships with your old friends.** This tip comes from Stephanie. Until you make new friends, she points out, you'll need their support and companionship—even if it's only over the phone. Proven friendships remind you that you're not a friendless loser, despite the fact that you feel like one, and that you *are* able to bond closely with others. For the same reason, put up pictures of your old friends immediately upon moving into your new place.

- **Give yourself time to feel settled.** It may take a year to feel vaguely comfortable in a new city, and even longer before you can start calling it home. Don't automatically assume that you've made the wrong decision if you don't love your new community right away. You may just not feel like an integral part of it yet.

WHEN YOU HAVE THE BLUES

If we dwell too long in a state of loneliness, stress, or self-worthlessness (hemlock to our mental serenity), we're ripe for depression. Doctors believe depression is caused by inadequate amounts of certain neurotransmitters in the brain, brought about by a variety of factors over which many of us have no control. These include genetic predisposition; reactions to certain medications, drugs, or alcohol; and even physical illness. As life would have it, women are twice as likely as men to get the blues. Moreover, the usual onset for clinical depression, in which symptoms are severe and begin to interfere with normal eating, sleeping, and daily functioning, is in our late 20s. Dysthymia, a milder form of depression that comes and goes throughout life, also common among 20-something women, usually begins during childhood or adolescence.

As with stress, getting daily exposure to natural sunlight is one good way to help draw us out of melancholy. Some researchers believe it may help raise our levels of serotonin, the mood-regulating neurotransmitter in the brain. That's why those early-morning walks and runs are so good for us. Getting together with friends will also help brighten our mood, even if our instincts are telling us to withdraw from the world and stay under our covers all day.

If sad, hopeless, hostile, apathetic, guilty, or even self-destructive feelings last longer than a few days or weeks, professional counseling might be the next logical step. Depression is best treated with cognitive and behavioral psychotherapy. In these sessions, a qualified counselor teaches positive patterns of thinking (for instance: "My boss doesn't think I'm incompetent; she's just too busy/arrogant/controlling to delegate more interesting work to me") as well as ways of dealing with life's setbacks and stress (such as: "I'm going to approach other supervisors in the office and ask for more interesting projects" or, "I'm going to update my résumé").

Antidepressants, such as Prozac, Zoloft, and Paxil, which raise serotonin levels, alleviate depression in many women when combined with therapy. But without help from professional counselors, depression is very hard to overcome. The sooner we reach out, the quicker we'll be back on track with our lives. Now, let's move on to cheerier matters, shall we?

RAGE

OK, OK. Rage is not cheery, I know. But at least rage, another headbanger of an emotion that afflicts our 20-something minds, is visceral and passionate, unlike depression. What *is* depressing is unexpressed anger, which is usually directed toward our parents for their child-rearing inadequacies, from which most of us suffer, no matter how saintly the folks were during our youth. Those of us who harbor such anger must begin to get in touch with these emotions and their source, rather than ignore them. Otherwise, we will project our rage onto undeserving people, such as our boyfriends, siblings, bosses, and very close girl-friends, which does no one any good at all.

Rage, like low self-esteem, is just one of those mental dramas most of us have to work through as we evolve from girls to women. After all, there are so many things to tick us off and hinder our evolution: dis-couraging bosses, spiteful roommates, and controlling boyfriends, to name a few. There's also still a fair degree of role confusion and gender inequality, not to mention sexual harassment at work and on the street in the form of lewd catcalls, which can turn an innocent evening walk into a mental-health nightmare. And, of course, financial disparity in the workplace breeds waves of anger as it hinders our female dreams, even at the dawn of the new and seemingly progressive millennium. All of this is enough to drive a girl to wrath and back. That's why it's a good time to learn how to manage our rage.

The best way is through (you guessed it) therapy and anger-man-agement workshops, since trying to change some of the bigger social structures that cause so much of our anger is best achieved through the polls and women's-rights advocacy groups. Therapy teaches all sorts of strategies for getting in touch with our anger and its causes, as well as for calming ourselves down before rage takes over our entire con-sciousness. This knowledge could then be applied to help us avoid such instances as, to pick a *totally* arbitrary example, when we are gathering our coat at the end of a dinner party and in front of a stunned hostess and her embarrassed-looking group of guests, we lash out at our horri-fied boyfriend and crazily accuse him of not paying enough attention to us during dinner.

Therapy can help deduce what's really going on in such circum-stances. Let's move on (*please!*).

ENVY

I have yet to meet a girl who hasn't been at least somewhat tormented by the green-eyed monster at some point during her 20s, which makes envy yet another terrifying catalyst for mental meltdown. Me, I've been downright deranged. *She* makes more money. *He* has a better social life. *She* loves her job. *He* got accepted to grad school. *She* just lost 5 pounds. *She* has orgasms every time she has sex (she's lying). *She* gets asked out left and right *and* has a devoted boyfriend who sends her flowers at work on Valentine's Day. *He's so damn happy all the time and I'm not!*

As human emotions go, envy isn't an easy one to shrug, especially when most of us are feeling so vulnerable and insecure to start with. If life were fair, we'd all be making the same amount of money, we'd all have adoring parents who take us on exotic vacations to Spain, and we'd all have a date on Saturday night. But life's not fair, and the injustice that many of us feel, knowing that our peers or even close friends whom we love and adore possess something we long for, can bring out the most primal and urgent form of malcontent.

Unless you're pathologically questionable (and in case you're wondering, my friends assured me that I wasn't, though I had doubts around age 24), one way to handle envy's wrath is to heed the wisdom of Sadie, 23, of Queens: "I remind myself that everyone has just as hard a time as I do and just as many problems. Then I tell myself, 'I'm me. I'm here. This is what I've got. There will be better times.'" Another route is to think about what you have that other people might envy, such as a supportive family or boyfriend. "I have a friend who lives in an awesome loft downtown," says Maureen, 28, of San Diego. "When she moved in, it drove me crazy for two weeks, but then I realized that by living in a cheap apartment, I can afford to do so many other things that she can't."

Once you've calmed your envious feelings down, make an effort to build self-esteem. A shot of confidence may or may not reduce envy, but one thing's for sure: our sense of worth often plummets when we compare ourselves with others and realize we're holding the shorter stick. Go back and reread those tips for boosting self-esteem, because you'll need them. Here's another possibility: If you can get beyond the bitterness, use envy to motivate yourself to make changes in your life. For instance, if you're envious that your best friend just got promoted to the fast track while you're still raking the coals in entry-level hell, update that résumé you've been procrastinating over, call those contacts you keep meaning to farm, and schedule those interviews that will lead you to the job you've been dreaming of. What else can you do (that won't terrorize your conscience)? Exactly.

A MENTAL-HEALTH CHECKUP

I'm a huge proponent of therapy for those of us having a hard time with family stuff, work trauma, or relationship ins and outs, especially if our health plans cover it. A good therapist will help you work through baggage that might be preventing you from excelling at work or engaging in meaningful relationships. "The younger you are, the easier it is to work through past conflicts and change your relational style and behaviors," says Josie Levine, Ph.D., a clinical psychologist in San Francisco. "If you don't deal with some of the problems that keep recurring in your life now, they'll pop up later on at a time when you may be less flexible and less fluid to deal with them."

True, it is emotionally draining, exhausting, and a trifle scary to squeeze those hourlong weekly sessions into our already crammed lunch hours. And sometimes those painful discussions will put us into an incredible funk with which we must live, or attempt to disguise, for the remainder of the day. Still, if you think you need professional counsel, get names of therapists from friends, family, or your health-care plan. Or call your local mental health hot line, listed under government or community services in your yellow pages. Interview a few potential counselors, social workers, psychologists, or psychiatrists to find out what they charge, what type of approaches they use, and whether you're likely to click with the practitioner's personality. Therapy does not mean you've a freak or failure. Seeking help through this highly emotional time of life just means you're a hip chick who's got an incredible amount of respect for herself and passion for life. Give your mental health the care it needs. You deserve that, girlfriend.

9

The Body-Image Demons

*A*nother "issue" that imperils our female souls (not to mention our health) during the great debut into adulthood is the ghastly body-image obsession. I can vouch for this because I've spent a chunk of my 20s making sacrifices to the body-image demons. Even now in my pre-30s, supposedly wiser state, I get flashback obsessions. These usually occur right before my period or whenever I spot evidence that I'm no longer 22. (I'll spare me the details.) Well, in case you haven't heard, let me be the first to tell you what I have learned during this highly body-conscious decade: It is not normal to obsessively count calories; exercise compulsively for two hours every day; deny yourself food; or fixate on body size, shape, or weight 24 hours a day.

Yet, according to some estimates, 80 percent of us don't like the way we look, and as a result, many of us engage in body-hating rituals. We're taunting our reflections, haunting the scale three or more times a day, scrutinizing the contents of everything we eat in search of hidden fat or calories, or forcing ourselves to tread the mill an extra half hour because we devoured two (OK, ten) Hershey's Kisses during a post-three-o'clock-meeting-with-ornery-boss panic attack at work.

The tragedy of it all lies herein: Deploring our bodies and basing our entire sense of worth—and our identity, in some cases—on how little we weigh or how hot we look in a red tankini devastates our budding creativity, our capacity to feel, our energy levels, and our maturing sexuality. It also contributes to other manifestations of emotional torment, including stress, depression, and low self-esteem, with which we all are more than familiar without goading from the body-image demons. In severe cases, the preoccupation can also become destructive to our health. Clinging to a distorted perception of ourselves increases our risk of developing an eating disorder, for which we 20-something girls, along with our adolescent sisters, are also statistically among the highest at risk in our country.

What really gets me wound up (as if that's not enough!) is that many of us who suffer from a bad body image have healthy, strong, and beautifully unique women's bodies; we just can't see or accept that reality. The obvious question is "Why?" The other obvious question is "How do we make the negative thoughts and obsessions stop?" They aren't easily answered, but let's discuss some of the diabolical contributors to our body obsessions and how to assuage them.

THE VALUE OF BEING CUTE

You are doubtless familiar with the feminist observation that women in our society are often valued for our looks more than our intellect or talents. The horrible truth is that looks *do* matter in our society, especially when it comes to attracting a mate. That's partially why so many of us are obsessive about our appearance during these prime mate-seeking years. "We live in a visual culture that, despite all the advances made during the women's movement, still values women for their looks more than their minds," says Sharlene Hesse-Biber, Ph.D., associate professor of sociology at Boston College and author of *Am I Thin Enough Yet?: The Cult of Thinness and the Commercialization of Identity*.

When looks are what is most valued in our gender, it's difficult *not* to use physical appearance as a basis of our sense of value, esteem, and worth. It's also difficult not to berate ourselves when our looks don't subscribe to the cultural standard of beauty, because that means, in essence, that we're not valuable. Perhaps after we've witnessed a few more generations of women in the working world, a few more progressive politicians who are dedicated to legislation that benefits women's rights, and a lot more awareness circulating throughout our culture, things will change. Until then, our task is to learn how to derive more esteem from what we produce, create, say, or believe in, and less from our looks.

REAL WOMEN AND THE AIRBRUSHED

The symmetrically proportioned, outrageously skinny women idolized in magazines, on TV, and in the movies are genetically rare creatures. And, let's not forget, they spend big bucks to enhance their genetic endowments, if not through plastic surgery, than through expensive trainers and nutritionists. Most of us knocking on womanhood's door can't help but compare our never-been-airbrushed looks with the likes of these women who are hoarding the cultural spotlight. In a primitive kind of way, we are bound to feel bitter and inadequate that our sub-supermodel looks aren't being idolized, too. That's why, to preserve a healthy body image (and our esteem, which gets so dangerously mixed up in the self-image crisis), we must avoid comparing our bodies with the genetically rare, half-starved females that our culture unjustly worships like fertility goddesses.

How can we *not* compare ourselves, when such images dominate every ad we come across, not to mention the entire entertainment industry? Well, start with the magazines. If you love women's magazines, but looking at glamorous models drives you nutty (or straight to the freezer for a calmness-inducing spoonful of ice cream, which then makes you feel three times as bad), do what some of those men who read *Playboy* say they do: skip the pictures and just read the stimulating articles, for which a few women's magazines are still worth buying.

As for movies and videos, make sure you balance your intake of Hollywood flicks with foreign films, in which women actresses, in general, tend to look healthier and more realistic. If you are renting a movie because your boyfriend broke up with you and everyone else has plans, or because you are in PMS hibernation mode, the last thing you need is to spend two hours wishing you had someone else's anorexic look or glamorous life. Head to the classics section instead of toward the latest Gwyneth Paltrow release. Remember, movies are for entertainment, not for evoking the body-image demons.

Then, for inspiration, seek out women in the real world who are healthy and who eat well, rather than comparing yourself with a twig, advises one 26-year-old woman. As an athlete in college, she became obsessed with having a perfect body and has had a few battles with bulimia, anorexia, and diet pills—despite the fact that she has always been fit and thin. Real-world role models should ideally have a similar body type and ethnicity to yours, and be approximately the same age as you or slightly older. In other words, if you're a 28-year-old, big-boned woman, don't look at a 21-year-old waif for examples of what a healthy and fit body should look like or you will feel like a worn-out tire.

Finally, take a good, honest look around the next time you're at a shopping mall or walking down a busy street, and note the variety of women out there. Doing so will give you perspective (and probably an ego boost), which is exactly what we all need to dilute the idealized Hollywood female body images. Taking this type of reality-check survey had a lasting effect on Liza, 26, of Brookline, Massachusetts: "When I was 21, I worked at a summer camp, which provided me an opportunity to see a bunch of female bodies at once. I also saw how greatly the body changes at different stages in life. In the communal showers, there were girls from ages 6 to 24, and all of us had such different types of bodies. To see how different one woman's form can be from another was a very affirming experience for me."

ADS THAT PROMISE THE UNIVERSE

If you haven't realized this yet, I'll let you in on the secret: many advertisements are designed to make us feel inadequate. That's how advertisers convince us we need to buy a triple-boosting bra (or else we'll never snag a lover in this bursting new world of silicone breasts) or to join the local gym (or else we're destined to plumpness, and no one will ask us out for a cocktail). Many body-image experts and scholars, in fact, implicate the fashion, cosmetic, plastic surgery, and weight-loss industries as having a heavy hand in the cultivation of body-image problems. This indictment applies more among young women who are in active pursuit of attracting a mate and, consequently, more concerned about their looks (and possible inadequacies that might complicate the mission) than, say, women who are out of the competitive mate-seeking race.

"Many corporations use advertising to create an insecurity that women might not have, had advertisers not called whatever the product is targeting 'a problem' in the first place, like vaginal freshness," explains clinical social worker Allison Benton-Jones. "At the same time, these corporations make themselves and their products look like the rescuer. This becomes even more problematic when women use a product and it doesn't work. Many turn on themselves and assume there's something wrong with *them*, rather than whatever it was they purchased."

That doesn't mean we should stop spending money on things that make us feel happy and beautiful, if they really do make us feel happy and beautiful—there's nothing wrong with that! Just keep the following in mind: When your bikini line isn't as flawless as the model's on the package of the hair-removal strips, that doesn't mean you're a hairy beast. All it means is that the strips are complete crap.

THE ROOTS OF BODY-IMAGE BLUES

The body-image saga often takes root early on. I can trace some of my demons back to kindergarten, when a skinny second-grader with freckles teased me for having curly hair and chubby thighs. Being ever impressionable, I convinced my mom to straighten my hair and began a decades-long crusade to attain the coveted status of *thinness*, which my mind equated with acceptance. My crusade was assisted by the fact that dieting around my home was as routine as watching the "After-School Special," and by the fact that my pediatrician (of all people!) seemed to conclude every yearly checkup by telling my mom: "She's a few pounds overweight. If she doesn't gain any weight this next year, she'll be right on target."

Then there was puberty, which made me feel uncontrollably grotesque and fat in general. And of course, it didn't help growing up in Texas, where, as in many parts of the South, a girl's looks are often considered her strongest asset. But what was my point? Oh yeah.

If we can identify some of the reasons why we formed the negative perceptions that we have of our bodies or why we put so much value on our looks, it's easier to develop a more accurate image, one that's free from the demons of the past. So think back: Was anyone in your family constantly insinuating that you were overweight? Did you pick up messages that a woman's greatest asset is her looks? During puberty, were you made to feel ashamed of your developing body or of your interest in dating? (If your parents were uncomfortable with your budding sexuality, you probably internalized some of that and may feel uncomfortable with your sexuality as a result.) Were you ever sexually abused? Have you had a physical disability, an illness, or a sexually transmitted disease that made you hate your body? Did your parents fixate on how much weight you put on in college? If so, you could probably benefit from individual or group therapy to rid yourself of all the dross.

THE SCAPEGOAT FACTOR

For many of us, the fact that our lives feel so out of control plays a diabolical role in some of our body-image negativity. Most of us are undergoing the complex transition of starting a career, establishing adult relationships, and getting our financial lives out of the chaos into which they slipped during our credit card experimentation in college. Preoccupying the mind with food and weight therefore often serves as a comparatively easy way to feel in control over *something* in our lives. The body preoccupation also conveniently distracts us from dealing with pressures that are making us feel so painfully vulnerable, such as having a job we hate or being in a relationship we know is not right for us.

In tackling body-image demons, take a measure of what's going on in your life that's making you feel so much abhorrence toward your poor, undeserving body. I, for instance, can almost always trace bad body image to PMS, boredom with work, or feeling disconnected from others. When I address these conditions directly instead of plucking my brows until they are specters of their former selves, chewing my nails, or scowling at my reflection every time I pass a mirror, I almost always start feeling better about my body again.

If you're not sure what problems are triggering the body hatred, keep a journal (what would we girls do without them?). Write down your body-hating thoughts as they arise, as well as what is going on around you—for instance, if you and your boyfriend just got into a fight, if a coworker just berated you, or if your mom just called and complained for half an hour about your being a selfish daughter. This will help separate the real problems from the scapegoat that our bodies often become.

Just one more word on scapegoating, and then we'll shuffle on: being skinny does not guarantee happiness. "There is no proof that thin women have better lives," says psychoanalyst Carolynn Hillman, author of *Recovering Your Self-Esteem* and *Love Your Looks*. "There's a myth in our culture that being thin will solve all of our problems—you'll find a man and find a career—but weight is just an excuse for your problems or unhappiness." Don't fall for the myth.

THE BODY MORPH

You'll read all about the subtle changes that our bodies undergo in the next chapter. For now, keep in mind that most of us are destined to become curvier during this decade due to physiological developments over which we have little control. Many of us, as a result of hormonal influences, are also becoming more bloated during certain times of the month, and there's little we can do about that, either. As we enter our late 20s, for the first time in our lives, we get to experience the shock of growing older. Not only will we begin to *look* older (and witness younger 20-somethings taking over our former youth-goddess status), but we may also begin to feel older, with more aches and pains that we had strictly believed affected only adults our parents' age.

These unsettling developments may revive old body-image nemeses that quieted down from the early-20s rioting. Isabelle, 27, of Oakland, California, describes this phenomenon perfectly: "It's hard to make the transition to womanhood because aging is not considered sexy. When you suddenly realize that you look older than other girls at the beach or at work, it definitely affects your self-confidence. Suddenly, you're not as sexy as you used to be."

If we become pregnant, our bodies may also change in irreversible ways: "I went from perky Cs to a size A with big nipples after I had my daughter last year," says one 26-year-old woman. "Now I have cellulite and stretch marks on my thighs and butt." Before you vow never to give birth, remind yourself that many 20-somethings (depending on their genetic engineering) bounce back to their prepregnancy shapes with little evidence of their motherhood status. In fact, some women who have been stymied by bad body image their whole lives finally come to terms with their size and shape once they've witnessed their bodies produce a living, breathing baby, which has got to be one of the most amazing and body-affirming experiences we women could ever hope to have.

ONE WEEK WITHOUT OBSESSIONS

Consider this a science experiment: Live one week without the obsessive thoughts about your body. That means no calorie or fat-content counting, no working out three times a day, no scrutinizing your face or butt in every mirror or window you pass (always horribly distorted anyway!), no weighing yourself twice a day, and no whatever else you do that drains your energy. The goal is to spend the week not criticizing your body. Self-criticism isn't going to make you skinny, and being skinny isn't going to make you happy. Hopefully, this experiment will help you realize that life without the obsessions won't make you spontaneously gain 500 pounds, as feared.

"It's important to become aware of how much the obsessive thoughts are infringing upon your life and happiness," advises Allison Benton-Jones. "When you start obsessing about calories, stop and ask yourself how the behavior is helpful to you. A lot of women accept this obsession as a normal part of existence, but it's not. It's a problem. Ask yourself what food and weight represent to you emotionally and how you use them to deal with certain feelings."

Once you've tasted life without the body-hating rituals that dull your experience, try a few bolder moves to get over any unnecessary emphasis you place on your looks. Judy, 24, of New York City, distinctly remembers the day she took a leap: "I was in college, it was during finals. I hadn't showered in three days and was walking down the street, hanging my head low. I suddenly realized that no one was staring at me. People have bigger fish to fry—they don't care how you look."

So, be creative with those risks. Wear a form-fitting dress that shows off your fertility-goddess cleavage or womanly hips. Accept a compliment, for once, by smiling and saying thank you instead of smirking. Or go to a nudist beach, which is one surefire way to shock yourself out of body-consciousness obsessions. Besides having an exhilarating experience, you may even feel proud of your body and revel in the sensation of sun on skin. Do be sure to bring sunscreen.

A WARDROBE YOU LOVE

The clothing crisis is nothing new to most of us, but it has developed a new wrinkle. Our bodies are changing during our 20s, and if we don't update our wardrobes accordingly, we will hate the way we look in most of what we own. This has a not-so-surprising negative effect on the way we view our looks. Liza knows: "I love my body when I'm naked, but when I put on clothes, I hate it. Clothes are not made for people with curves." That goes double for trendy clothes. In fact, clothing may be a big contributor to women's negative body image, according to Allison Benton-Jones. "In my reading on the subject," she says, "some body-image experts point out that prior to the industrial revolution, clothes were hand-tailored to fit a woman's body. Mass production of clothing changed that. On the one hand, it gave women the freedom to leave the house instead of making clothes all the time, but it also has made it so that women must fit into predetermined sizes."

We all know how impossible it is to feel good about our looks if every pair of pants we try on either doesn't fit or makes us look pregnant. That's why it's important to create a wardrobe that makes us feel sexy and positive about our bodies—not a wardrobe that constantly reminds us that our bodies don't conform to the fashion industry's arbitrary mold or sizing scale. From your nightgown to your workout clothes, make sure that every piece makes your specific body type feel good. Otherwise, you'll set yourself up for putting yourself down.

Alterations have sort of dropped out of our ready-to-wear consciousness, but getting your clothes tailored to your body can relieve a lot of unnecessary body-image anxiety. It may make your wardrobe a bit more expensive, but it's worth the premium when you consider the reward of actually liking every item you own and even feeling sexy in everything you wear. If you plan to alter, buy items that fit the necessary places—hips, shoulders, waist—and then have the baggy butt, droopy crotch, roomy bodice, or whatever else needs a tuck, taken in. The corollary is: Never purchase an item that you'll "get" to wear if you lose five pounds. Why torture yourself? You'll likely hate what you've bought long before you ever "get" to wear it.

Go-Girl Guidance *When it comes to clothes, take the bloat factor into consideration. The 20s is 10 years of unexplainable bloat taking over our bodies at the most unappreciated moments. Be prepared by being sure you own at least a couple of items in which you feel undeniably gorgeous when you're bloated. Specifically, we can all avoid the horrendous nothing-to-wear debacle if we own an any-occasion pair of loosely fitting (but seductive) black pants to wear with a favorite top and an unrestrictive (but still suggestive) dress. For best fit, shop for these pieces the next time you're feeling pregnant.*

BATHROOM SCALE TORCH

The scale is a tool of the body-image demons through which they attempt to communicate to us. It is therefore evil and something we should avoid at all costs. "I've learned not to weigh myself," says Dara, 24, of New York City. She's the kind of girl who would look thin no matter how much she weighed, but after she gained 20 pounds during her freshman year, she spent her entire sophomore year obsessing about her weight, to the point that she sought help from a psychologist. Now, she says, "When I think about getting on the scale, I tell myself, 'What's the point?' I know I'm going to feel bad about myself if I do."

I, too, have stopped worshipping the scale, tempting as it is to see if I've miraculously dropped a few pounds since I last checked. Scales only make us more out of touch with our body than we already are.

Improving our body image starts with accepting our real shape and size—not by trying to attain or maintain an arbitrary number.

MIRROR, HATEFUL MIRROR!

Like scales, mirrors can unsettle those of us with shaky body image. Unlike scales, they are exceedingly hard to ignore. The last time I was at yoga, my instructor caught me suspiciously eyeing my backside in the wall-to-wall mirrors (so embarrassing!) and cooed, as yoga instructors do, "Look at your body *without* self-criticism." We could, of course, remove all the mirrors from our apartments or replace them with those skinny mirrors, but in real life, most of us are forced to confront our reflections daily in public bathrooms, store windows, and, of course, yoga class. That's why it's a good show to learn how to make friends with your reflection rather than begrudge it.

One way to do that is to actively compliment the aspects of yourself (physical and nonphysical) that you do like when you come face-to face with your reflection. Tell yourself how hot you look, how stunning your hair is, how smartly you answered that question your supervisor posed at the group meeting. (Note: This has never worked for me, personally, but I thought I'd include it, since so many body-image experts advise doing so.) Brainwash this may be, but so are we brainwashed into believing that we look bad in the first place, the thinking goes.

If you're not quite sure what you might say to yourself, Christine Hartline, membership director of 1-800-Therapist and editor of *The Eating Disorder Resource and Information Guide*, suggests making a list in advance so that you'll have a few compliments on hand the next time you catch your reflection. If that horrible, critical voice inside starts whispering in your ear that you're looking a little droopy lately, or are breaking out like a stressed-out teen, or have hair that looks as if you just fell off a truck, do whatever it takes to silence it. Critical thinking *will* get the best of your psyche if it can't be stifled.

Also keep two things straight about your reflection: (1) Some mirrors truly distort your appearance; and (2) Sometimes your eyes are the doing the distorting, like when you're PMSing. In search of perspective,

Isabelle often relies on photographs to get a better representation of how she looks: "When I get a new haircut, I sometimes have my husband immediately take a picture of me. It's the only way I can be objective."

EXERCISE AND PROPER FUEL

From all my interviewing, and from my own experience, I've found that the optimum way to master the body-image demons is to exercise regularly; eat healthy, natural foods; and tank up on water. Engaging in physical activity—the kind that makes you really, really sweat—helps refocus body-related thoughts from what your body *looks* like to what your body can actually *do*. Dara found that exercise helped her get back to feeling good about herself after her weight gain in college. "My goals changed from trying to lose weight to trying to build muscle and do things that are healthy for my body," she says. "I also began to see food as a fuel." That brings me to my next point.

When we eat crap all day long, we *will* feel gross about ourselves, if only because our bodies are reacting to the toxins and carbo overload in the form of intestinal cramps, nausea, or bloating. Hence, one way to avoid feeling bad about yourself is to eat healthy meals with lots of fresh vegetables and limit junking out to emergency occasions, such as when your boyfriend dumps you or your boss yells at you for something you didn't do, and when all other soothing tactics have failed. (Just remember, junking out is going to make you feel worse about your body; reserve this tactic as an absolute last resort.)

While you're at it, drink lots of water. Eight or more glasses a day will make your body feel clean and pure. And when your machinery is feeling good and purged of toxins, so will your head, where the body-image demons dwell.

BODY IMAGE AND THE BEDROOM

We all know there's not enough room in the bed for us, our lover, *and* the demons, because the demons prevent us from flaunting ourselves in front of our lover, which can be so sexually exciting. Unfortunately, the bedroom is often where the demons conduct most of their mischief, because sex is, well, so body intensive. "Bad body image has a direct impact on women's sexual enjoyment, because sexual desire and desirability are intertwined with women," says sex therapist Dennis Sugrue of the University of Michigan Medical School.

"When women become so focused on how their bodies look, that creates a lot of anxiety, and when women become uptight, they can't enjoy themselves," adds Carolynn Hillman. "Being self-conscious about your body limits your sense of adventure." For instance, if you think your stomach wrinkles when you sit up, or that your breasts are too small or droopy, you may not try being on top or any other position that you might truly enjoy if it weren't for the exposure. Or you may want the lights off when you make love, which limits your looking at your partner.

The first inroad toward exorcising the demons from the bedroom is to shift our thought process. "Think of your body as an instrument, not an object," advises Hillman. "Take the part of your body that you're self-conscious about—your stomach, for instance—and concentrate on the pleasure you feel when your stomach is stroked or when it's touching your lover's skin, instead of focusing on how it looks. Then, realize that your sexual partner isn't going to be surprised by what your body looks like without clothes, because clothing can't disguise that much. The insecurities woman have about their bodies are usually exaggerated in their minds, and they expect their partners to see what they see. But most sexual partners aren't concentrating on the size of your thighs." (But if he is one of the very tiny minority of men who do, you know where to aim your kick!)

This brings us to one of the thrusts of this chapter: Guys who are in love with us don't care about our weight, weight fluctuations, and all those parts of our bodies that we deem imperfect. They care about our happiness, our dreams, our souls, and our health. (You've got to trust me on this one even if you don't believe me; I've asked around and confirmed my theory with the women I interviewed who are in happy, healthy relationships.) Since this is the truth, we must also direct our energy to our happiness, dreams, souls, and health. One more tip: If you are self-conscious about your body, don't draw attention to the parts you are still insecure about while getting in the mood with your lover, advises Valerie, 29, of Boston. "That's the worst thing you can do, because it will totally impact your ability to feel sexual. It will also alter your partner's mood, because part of what's sexually exciting is being with someone who's excited about herself."

Many women told me that once they found a partner who loved their body (and was poignantly verbal about liking what he saw), they were better able to feel good about their bodies, too. That's all divine, but if you've found such a partner, don't get too reliant on that praise in order to feel sexual. "Getting affirmation from partners is a two-edged sword," says Sugrue. "On the one hand, having a partner tell you how beautiful you are is valuable and makes a big difference in women's feeling desirable. On the other hand, it externalizes your sense of worth. If you base your adequacy on your partner's assessment, you're giving him a lot of power. Affirming is an important part of a sexual relationship, but women also need to work on internalizing their sense of desirability, so they're not dependent on their partners for feeling sexually attractive."

THE MIND FACTOR

Most of us have wildly perverse images of ourselves that hardly come close to representing what we look like in reality. That's why we must attempt to chase the body-image demons from our minds, rather than attempt to change our bodies. Accept that what you think you see in yourself is horribly distorted, then concentrate all your efforts on being a healthy woman. You'll eventually eradicate these demons if you continuously work on it.

Mine, though still harrowing me now and then, have in general mellowed out as I've gotten older. (No fair counting this year, since I'm soon turning 30, the contemplation of which has stirred them temporarily, but let's not dwell on such matters.) In fact, refusing to dwell on those demons is the best way to send them back to hell, where they belong.

Eating Disorders

Up to 10% of American girls and women have eating disorders, including anorexia, bulimia, and compulsive overeating, according to estimates from Seattle-based Eating Disorders Awareness and Prevention (EDAP), a nonprofit clearinghouse of information and referral center for eating disorders. "The most significant time of onset is during puberty and the early college years," says program coordinator Holly Hoff. "Being away from home, many women for the first time are in control over what and when they eat, and eating disorders are often more about control and emotions than about food. Most of these women have low self-esteem," she says. "Many are also afraid of gaining the Freshman 15 and not living up to the 'ideal' image. What these women don't know is that they *should* be gaining weight during college. The body is becoming more womanly."

If you have an eating disorder, or suspect you're on the road toward one because you are obsessing over your weight, weighing yourself constantly, denying yourself food, bingeing, purging, or persistently agonizing over your body, get professional help immediately. "The consequence of not getting help could be long-term health problems or even death," says Christine Hartline of 1-800-THERAPIST. "Eating disorders are very difficult to overcome. If you can prevent a serious disorder from developing, you'll have a better chance of recovery."

Professional help usually involves a combination of psychotherapy and nutritional and medical counseling.

10

That Whacked-Out Body Feeling

*R*emember puberty? (Battling zits and feeling fat all the time.) Combine that adolescent *ick* feeling with increasingly bad PMS, an irritable stomach, a strand or two of gray hair, "smile lines," and a newly acquired roundness in the hips, tummy, and breasts, and you'll get a pretty good idea of what the 20-something body experience has in store for you. Luckily, the changes our bodies undergo as we enter the unknown terrain of womanhood happen so gradually that we barely notice them along the way. But then one morning, not long after our 25th birthdays, we wake up feeling a bit stiffer than the day before, look into the mirror, and *freak out* because a full-blown woman is gaping back at us, and we're not quite sure how she got there!

For many of us, welcoming this womanly creature into our hearts takes every ounce of self-respect within us, since our gut reaction is to want to hurl her out of the nearest window for making us feel so whacked-out lately. After all, the 20s are supposed to be the most vibrant and sexiest years of our lives. No one ever talks about the mood-disrupting, body-altering changes we must endure!

Ok, the changes aren't all that bad, but having experienced most of them, I can attest that they do add to the overall mental anguish and body-image distress we suffer during these years. To help you brave the metamorphosis, here's a head-to-toe sketch of some of the most common transformations our bodies go through, starting with our figures.

OUR SIZE AND SHAPE

This may come as a shock if your body hasn't changed much since high school, but many of us are still growing in our 20s. In fact, our last growth spurt, which usually begins during late adolescence, may continue right on up to age 25, when the bone plates typically close off for good, says Michele Olson, Ph.D., a professor of exercise physiology at Auburn University.

This final growing phase may prompt several unpredictable changes in our bodies, which most of us, quite frankly, assume stop growing around age 16. Many girls dipping into their 20s accumulate extra fat to accommodate the growth (remember, that happened during puberty, too). This natural plumping up partially accounts for the gnarly 10 to 15 pounds that most of us unwillingly gain as we enter college. So, you see that weight gain isn't solely due to the three helpings of lasagna followed by the lemon meringue pie *and* cookie we consume nightly at the campus cafeteria. Some girls actually grow a half inch or more during the spurt. As for the rest of us, the only skeletal development we witness is our hipbones cranking outward.

If you've always had boyish hips and are panicking right about now, keep in mind that the hourglass figure is due for a comeback. Until then, reevaluate what clothing styles look good on your new curves, suggests Veronica, 27, of New York City. She switched from wearing slim bottoms and baggy tops (her standard college outfit) to tight tops and looser bottoms once her womanly shape began to emerge.

After we've grown all we're going to in this lifetime, some of us shed the extra baby fat our bodies no longer need, giving us leaner physiques and, sometimes, more angular faces. The rest of us, more so during our late 20s, experience the opposite effect: our breasts begin to fill out (in which case, no need to complain!), and our abs, hips, butt, and thighs begin to take on a rounder, OK plumper to be perfectly honest, form. This is often due to the direct influence of cellulite, which we had, until now, falsely assured ourselves was not possible within our gene pool due to lack of supporting evidence. There are two physiological explanations for this plumping up, notably in our lower halves: First, our metabolisms begin to slow down 2 to 4 percent every decade after the age of 25. According to Olson, that roughly translates into an extra 75 calories a day that our bodies must work overtime to metabolize. Second, our bodies are circulating estrogen like there's no tomorrow (in case we decide to get pregnant), and in many women, estrogen directs extra fat to be stored below the waist.

As much as I'd love to tell you that all that extra poundage is due to these uncontrollable changes, the truth lies elsewhere. Physiologists and fitness experts have assured me that about 90 percent of this gradual plumping out has more to do with the fact that we're just not as active in our late 20s as we were when we were fresh out of school and starting our first jobs (and had comparatively less responsibility and more time and energy to hit the gym or go dancing until three every night). In fact, physical therapist Marty Mattox, of San Francisco, says we can generally offset our slowing metabolisms and get rid of excess fat by maintaining the daily exercise routines we established in our early 20s; or, if your idea of exercise back then consisted of projecting M&Ms into your mouth for neurological stimulation, by beginning a regular fitness program. This is covered in "Exercise Guidelines" later in the chapter.

I know how tough it is to stay active during our late 20s. Trying to get ahead at work, establishing close relationships with potential mates and new friends, and raising a family (if you're already in that space) can take its toll on our energy levels, leaving zero desire to change into workout clothes and pump iron for an hour in front of tell-all mirrors and body-obsessed people. But there are a few proven prescriptions for getting the blood circulating.

For starters, I'm convinced that walking an hour a day can prevent the extra pounds from creeping on, because as soon as I quit my job and started freelancing from home (and consequently stopped walking to and from work), I put on eight pounds in seven months, even though I was running, cycling, and hiking every week!

Another way to motivate is to pick exercises that you think are fun, such as dancing, in-line skating, tennis, volleyball, climbing, or kick boxing. Most of us are more likely to stick to workouts that we find inspiring.

Making workout dates with friends may also force you to stick to your fitness goals. It's harder to blow off yoga class when your girlfriend is expecting you, because then you'll look like a flake and a sloth!

A friend of mine uses this motivational trick, which I've tried and found works: She tells herself that she has to exercise for only 10 minutes and *doesn't* get down on herself if she stops after that, because at least she did something. More often than not, she ends up completing a half-hour workout, since by the time 10 minutes have passed, she's worked up a sweat and her initial resistance has miraculously disappeared.

Training with a group for a particular event—a marathon, triathlon, or century bike ride—is another way to keep your fitness motivation relatively consistent. The tangible goal of finishing a race often offers more incentive to hit the track than the intangible (and painfully slow) concept of losing weight or getting a better body.

If all that doesn't work, try using incentives. Amelia, 28, of Atlanta, got her navel pierced to boost her motivation. "When I'm too embarrassed to show it off, I'll *have* to exercise," she says.

OUR FACES

As mentioned, many of us shed baby fat after our final growth spurt in our early 20s and consequently lose the chubby-cheek look that always stopped us at the door of over-21 bars and clubs. What's much more disturbing for some of us is the fact that our noses are made of cartilage and, therefore, never stop growing. That means our noses may begin to stick out more than they did in high school. Keep in mind, these changes are *ever* so slight, and only you will notice them! Friends and family members will likely see (and hopefully keep to themselves) only the subtle changes in our skin. So, without further ado, let's look into it.

OUR SKIN

First of all, there are plenty of reasons to love our youthful skin, especially as we slip *into* the decade, as opposed to teetering dangerously on the opposite edge, denying the reality of where we're headed. During our early years, our skin is supple, firm, vibrant, and relatively wrinkle-free. Women in their 30s and beyond can't compete (*ha, ha!*) with our youthful glow, unless, of course, they spend all their money on the dermatologist, but let's not think about that right now. If you want the full scoop on skin changes that occur during our 20s, though, a few unlovable facts must be accepted.

Even if you never had acne as a teen, you may suddenly be accosted with some of the most inflammatory and tender pimples imaginable, usually along your jawline, chin, lower cheeks, and neck. Your skin type may also change: some of us turn into oil wells; others develop dry or combination skin for the first time. And no matter how diligently you avoided the sun all these years, tiny lines begin to immigrate across our foreheads, around our eyes, and on the sides of our mouths, like parentheses. Let's pore over these skin horrors, shall we?

Acne

Because the pimple look is neither professional nor ego boosting, it can be particularly troublesome for us career-climbing, mate-seeking women. Some of us are genetically engineered to develop acne as adults, so if Mom or Dad was pimply at your age, you have one more reason to loathe the parental unit. Others can blame fluctuating hormones, such as progesterone (which rises right before our periods and during pregnancy) and androgen (which increases with stress or hormonal abnormalities). Both hormones accelerate oil production in the skin, which can clog pores and cause pimples or those painful, slow-surfacing cysts that manage to resist all efforts to be covered. Oil-based hair or facial products and cosmetics, pollution, and certain drugs, including some birth control pills, may also give rise to these dastardly bumps. So, examine your beauty arsenal, lifestyle, and drug use if the acne deluge is confounding your morning getting-ready-for-work routine.

Even if you're one of the lucky few to get only one or two pimples now and then, resist the urge to scrub, pick, or squeeze. Our youthful skin is resilient but not scar resistant, and picking, as tempting as it may be, can aggravate our already inflamed pores and make the problem worse. Instead, the general rule for dealing with pimples is this: Wash your face two to three times a day, using mild cleanser; disguise your bumps with an oil-free concealer, foundation, or powder, and don't look in the mirror for the rest of the day except for a quick touch-up. These occasional bumps will eventually dry up or pop on their own. For more pervasive pimples, start with an over-the-counter topical lotion, gel, or cream containing benzoyl peroxide, which helps dry out the skin and kill bacteria that cause inflammation. Products containing salicylic or glycolic acid may also help unclog pores and exfoliate the skin.

If after a couple of weeks you don't see improvement, visit a dermatologist, who can pinpoint the cause of your acne and prescribe an aggressive oral or topical drug treatment. Whatever you do, don't sit around waiting for your face to clear up on its own. Advises Kelly, 28, of Brooklyn: "When I got acne for the first time last year, I spent four months feeling horrible about myself before I saw a dermatologist. Once you start treatment, it takes time for your skin to clear, so take care of it sooner than I did."

Dryness

As many of us enter our late 20s, oil production begins to slow, and our smooth, silky skin turns dull and flaky. The darker your skin tone, the later this drying-out phenomenon tends to occur. The only redeeming quality to dry skin is that it's less prone to breaking out. However, dry skin is not pimple-proof, and acne medications designed to control excess oil may agitate sensitive skin. Dry-skin treatment strategy involves a slightly different approach: Use a gentle cleanser once or twice a day, and apply topical medications only to individual zits instead of the whole face.

To keep dry skin as plump and elastic as possible, moisturize when you're still damp from a shower or after washing your face. An all-purpose lotion is fine for both the body and face, says New York City dermatologist Diane Berson, M.D. But if you tend to get acne, look for a "noncomedogenic" or "oil-free" lotion, which won't clog pores. For extra-dry hands and feet—which seem to get crackier the older we get—try a heavier cream or ointment containing lanolin, mineral oil, or silicone derivatives to seal in moisture. And to avoid dehydrating your skin inadvertently, forgo steamy-hot showers and baths (soaking in warm water with moisturizing bath oil is OK), use a vaporizer or humidifier in the winter if indoor heating makes you scaly, drink those eight glasses of water a day, limit yourself to one daily caffeinated beverage treat, avoid the sun, give up cigarettes if you smoke, and cover up head to toe on moisture-zapping windy or cold days.

If all of these techniques fail, hang up a picture of a turtle at work for you to stare at when your skin feels exceptionally reptilian during the winter. Your complexion will look and feel like a baby's bottom in comparison.

Wrinkles

Luckily, most of us have a good decade or two before furrows, sagging cheeks, patchy pigmentation, or sun spots begin to raid our complexions. But many of us start to spy suspicious creases around our eyes and mouths and across our foreheads as we gain momentum toward our 30s. Most of this prewrinkling is due to excessive sun exposure in our "never-grow-old" youthful denial and, if you smoke, to nicotine. Wrinkles tend to stake their claim even earlier if you have dry skin, live in a congested city (some pollutants can damage the skin's renewal process, experts say), gain and lose weight frequently, or constantly squint or crinkle up your face.

Because our lines are relatively invisible, our main objective is to immobilize them in their infancy, which starts by wearing sunblock every day. This also lowers our risk of developing skin cancer. For days spent predominantly outdoors, skin doctors advise spreading a thick layer of sunblock on exposed areas about 20 minutes before we leave the house, reapplying every two hours. On other days, a daily moisturizer with sunscreen is sufficient protection from cancer-causing sun exposure through windows or from taking short walks outside in an effort to liven up a boring day at work. Both daily moisturizer and sunblock should have a sun protection factor (SPF) of 15 or more, with ultraviolet

(UVA and UVB) protection. If you're prone to burning, avoid the sun altogether between 10 A.M. and 4 P.M., and reinvent your wardrobe so that all your outfits consist of a broad-rimmed hat, long sleeves and pants, and UV-protective sunglasses.

Recent research indicates that antioxidants, such as vitamins A, C, and E, and alpha-hydroxy acids, derived from fruit and dairy products, may reverse signs of aging. Many of these antiaging ingredients are being added to drugstore lotions that don't cost a fortune, and some dermatologist are all for them. According to Cleveland dermatologist Wilma Bergfeld, M.D., author of *A Woman Doctor's Guide to Skin Care: Essential Facts and Up-to-the-Minute Information on Keeping Skin Healthy at Any Age*: "Women—even in their 20s—should use a moisturizer with either an antioxidant or alpha-hydroxy acid. If you start using these agents early on, you can prevent the barnacles of aging."

Other Developments

Circles under our eyes, enlarged pores, varicose (spider) veins in our legs, and stretch marks on our thighs, abs, hips, or breasts are other common badges of womanhood that many of us earn for the first time during our 20s. Combined with our unpredictable complexions, these developments can be traumatizing. And they're not exactly the greatest conversation starters, either, observes Dara, 24, of New York City, who was once lying out on the beach in a bikini, when some guy asked her what "those lines" were on her legs.

Unfortunately, there's not an easy fix for these developments. Dark circles are primarily due to genetics, but getting plenty of sleep and finding a reliable concealer may help minimize the contrast. The only way to shrink our pores is to strip them of the oil and dirt that are keeping them perpetually open, so a reputable mask or peel formulated to do that is worth a try. As for varicose veins and stretch marks, well, these either are inherited from Mom or stake their claim after a rapid weight gain or loss. We can't control our genetic wiring, but we might be able to minimize their condition by maintaining a steady weight and keeping our skin moisturized to enhance elasticity. If you're really bothered by them, ask a dermatologist about reduction treatments, but you might want to hold off on getting these newly formed lines removed until you're long past child-bearing desires, since pregnancy exasperates them.

OUR HAIR

For many of us, the only hair complaint (besides an occasional bad hair day, which is universal to females of all ages) is a subtle change in color, sheen, or texture. The less fortunate of us, however, encounter more unnerving transformations: a strand of gray appears; we start shedding like cats in the summertime; the chin, neck, and nipples begin to randomly sprout dark, kinky hairs. Be brave, girlfriend, here's the lowdown:

Loss of Gloss

Twenty-plus years of sun exposure and abusive hair products often begin to strip our hair of life and luster, which is all the more burdensome if you have naturally coarse hair, like me. I have discovered one little trick for dry hair: pour a tiny drop of olive oil into your palm, rub your hands, then smooth out your hair. This not only gives some shine but also tames uncontrollable frizz for those of us whose hair is nonconformist. Just be careful not to use too much oil or you'll end up smelling like a Caesar salad.

Another peculiar hair change that many of us experience is altered texture: straight hair may develop a wave, and curls may loosen up. And many blondes must accept the fact that they can no longer call themselves naturally blonde, unless, of course, they've been highlighting for years, in which case this hair phenomenon is nothing new or horrifying. Why light hair tends to darken with age remains a physiological mystery, but it probably has something to do with the fact that our initiation to the office culture leaves increasingly less time for hanging out under the hair-bleaching sun.

Perhaps the most onerous hair-related event, however, is finding that first wiry strand of gray, a sign that the pigment cells in our locks have ceased to function and, to get a little dramatic, that our youth is slipping away. Most of us experience this jolt of mortality sometime during our 20s, though the exact timing of the Great Gray Debut depends on our biological makeup. Regardless, there's not much we can do except dye, pluck, or get over it. "I distinctly remember pulling out my first gray and showing it to my husband," notes Pamela, 28, of Chicago, who had her first sighting at age 27. "Now whenever I find one, I pluck it immediately." Kelly, who also plucks, offers this therapeutic advice: "I make a point to look around at other women. When I see how many of us have gray hairs and wrinkles around our eyes, I'm less fearful about getting old." Since my own scalp can't tolerate the brutality of plucking, I try to keep a flexible part: a quick flip of the hair is all it takes to camouflage stray grays that dare to surface from the depths of my thick mane.

To keep our tresses healthy and consequently more manageable in light of these changes, dermatologists recommend the obvious: washing with gentle shampoo several times a week, followed by a conditioner or rinse, which coats the hair shaft, giving it the illusion of being thick and shiny. The oilier your hair, the more often you can wash without causing dryness or damage. They also suggest that we reduce styling to an absolute minimum, since heat from rollers or dryers, overzealous brushing, and some gels or sprays encourage split ends or breakage. Another byword is to limit exposure to the elements—wind, sun, and chlorine. If you opt to lighten or dye your hair, keep in mind that the chemicals in these products can further the damage. Semipermanent dyes, which coat natural color instead of stripping it in the manner of permanent dyes, cause less trauma and often contain conditioners that enhance your hair's sheen and luster.

Thinning

Let's get one thing straight: there's a difference between thinning and balding, and very few women actually develop bald patches or a receding hairline. If you are among the unlucky few, you likely inherited the trait, but see a doctor anyway because balding could indicate a hormonal abnormality. More common among the 20-something crowd is gradual thinning, which is also hereditary and can start as early as puberty. Most of us already know the signs—our once-thick ponytails are now as thin as a pencil, and clumps of our hair clog up the bathtub drain, convincing us that we have been overexposed to radiation from too many dental x-rays and probably have cancer. Sometimes a change in grooming techniques is all we need to slow the avalanche of hairs falling from our head. Tight ponytails or braids, curling, drying, spiking, excessive brushing, or overusing certain hair products and treatments may increase the number of strands that end up sticking to your brush instead of your scalp.

If, however, you're shedding more than 100 hairs a day, see a dermatologist. (If you're not sure, collect a day's worth of strands from your tub, floor, and brush, and count them; I've done it, being a shedder myself, and it takes only about 10 minutes.) A doctor can help determine whether your hair loss is due to an underlying problem, such as a thyroid or hormonal abnormality, a nutritional deficiency, a medication you're taking, a recent illness or injury, or a change in birth control pills. Keep in mind that temporary thinning may also result from a recent weight loss, emotional stress, or hormonal fluctuations due to pregnancy or childbirth. Once the source of the problem is appropriately addressed, the hair usually returns.

Kinky Body Hair

You probably don't want to hear this, but divulging dirty details concerning womanhood is what this book is all about: Dark, coarse hairs may begin to appear (sometimes, it seems, overnight) on your neck and chin or around your nipples. I first learned of this phenomenon when I was 20 and found an inch-long wiry hair sprouting from my neck! The degree of hairiness can vary from one or two whiskers to a light patch. In most cases, these strays are just a product of normal hormonal fluctuations and are nothing more than an annoyance or embarrassment, as Kelly mortifyingly discovered when an overly enthusiastic shampoo attendant at her hair salon noticed a hair growing on her chin and proceeded to pluck it in front of curious onlookers!

If excessive body hair is accompanied by irregular periods, balding, acne, or a deepened voice, you may have an overabundance of that bothersome hormone androgen. Again, a dermatologist can look for underlying causes. Electrolysis procedures and new laser treatments may offer permanent hair removal for those who can afford them, but most of us delete these random strays by plucking or shaving. If you decide to take matters into your own hands, remember to remove the hair in the direction of growth to avoid irritating the skin. An infected hair follicle on your nipple is not attractive.

OUR DIGESTIVE SYSTEMS

To be perfectly blunt, the 20s are a gastrointestinal nightmare. For the first time in our lives, many of us are forced to contend with uncontrollable gas, perpetual bloat, and chronic constipation or diarrhea. Besides contributing to that whacked-out body feeling, these abdominal tantrums can present a huge social dilemma. For those of us who are dating squeezing a bloated belly into a tight minidress is hardly a turn-on, and frequent escapes to the ladies room to avoid an embarrassing situation won't enable prospective mates to get to know us better (at least, not in the way we'd like them to!).

More rotten news is that gastrointestinal specialists don't even know why so many women in their 20s develop abdominal distress or what exactly causes it. A hormonal connection may be at work, they say, since symptoms tend to get worse right before our periods. Another obvious contender is our diet which, let's face it, is often irregular, high in fat, and low in fiber—factors that may inhibit the food's fluid passage through the intestines.

For constipation or diarrhea, bulking up on fiber (see "Nutrition Guidelines" later in the chapter) often helps, but fiber is also a well-known gas offender; add it slowly so that your body can adjust. Eventually your intestines will get used to the increase in roughage and won't cause a stink (horrible, *horrible* pun, I know). Note: If diarrhea is keeping you up at night, see a doctor immediately; you may have an intestinal infection or another serious condition.

Some women develop sensitivities to certain foods during their 20s. Dairy products are among the most common perpetrators of gas, bloat, constipation, and diarrhea. High-fiber vegetables, multigrains, and beans may also cause bloating, abdominal pain, and gas. Identifying the source of our abdominal woes can be a taxing undertaking, increasingly so when *everything* we eat seems to make us feel sick and bloated. But once you know which foods to avoid and then readjust your diet accordingly, bowel angst usually turns into a mild form of intestinal contempt.

San Francisco gastroenterologist Martin Brottman, M.D., suggests conducting an elimination test to try to identify the foods that exasperate your system. First week, avoid all dairy products. If your problems cease, you're probably lactose intolerant, which means you have trouble digesting the milk sugar in dairy products and should avoid them (make sure you eat other calcium-rich foods and take a calcium supplement). If the problems persist, however, continue the test. The second week, cut out raw fruits and vegetables. If that does the trick, try adding back one vegetable or fruit at a time to see which ones are OK and which ones cause distress (and limit those from your diet). If most fruits and veggies give you problems, you're unfortunately going to have to learn how to live with them, since you need these valuable sources of nutrition. Some women find that the antigas dietary supplement Beano (as horrifying as it is to purchase) helps with beans and vegetables. But not everyone has such luck.

If the elimination diet yields no enlightenment, it might be time to see a gastrointestinal physician, who can help evaluate your diet and test for possible food allergies and other more serious conditions. About 15 percent of U.S. adults have what's called irritable bowel syndrome (IBS), a condition marked by exaggerated muscular contractions in the intestines, causing a hypersensitivity in the gut. And guess what? IBS is most often diagnosed in women under 30. Common symptoms—which vary in severity and often get worse after a meal or around our periods—include abdominal pain and cramps, constipation, diarrhea, bloating, excessive gas, and intestinal contractions. While there is no cure, IBS isn't serious, as painful and disrupting as it can be. A good gastroenterologist can help minimize the symptoms by analyzing your diet and lifestyle and possibly prescribing helpful drugs.

In any event, four activities will go a long way toward improving abdominal discomfort: eating balanced meals at regular times, drinking eight glasses of water a day (to help move food through the digestive tract), exercising frequently (I've found that doing 30 sit-ups a day helps minimizes that bloated feeling, when I motivate to do them), and learning stress-reduction techniques (many women swear that yoga helps with their digestion). And when all else fails, do what many of us do: ban all suspicious foods on days that promise hours of intimate interaction with others, and isolate yourself from human contact during those times when your symptoms are egregiously antisocial!

OUR REPRODUCTIVE SYSTEMS

The goal of our 20-something reproductive system hasn't changed since adolescence: ripen egg, project egg into fallopian tube for easy access to sperm, shed bloody lining in uterus if egg isn't fertilized, start process over. But what changes in our 20s is that we become fertility goddesses: almost every month, we produce a mature, sperm-seeking egg, and our risk of miscarriage or having a baby with a birth defect is lower than it ever will be. However, many of us experience nerve-racking changes in the way our bodies respond to our reproductive agendas, making us feel more whacked-out than ever! Let me tell you all about them.

Our Periods

Many of us entering our late 20s notice our periods becoming shorter, lighter, and more predictable (for instance, they start every 29 days, practically to the hour, and last precisely 4 and one-half days). This is especially true for those of us whose cycles are regulated by birth control pills. Doctors attribute part of this naturally increasing regularity to the fact that our hormones, which catalyze every phase of our cycles, have finally gotten enough practice over the years to monitor our systems like clockwork. Even so, it's completely normal for our cycles, which typically last anywhere from 21 to 35 days, to vary in length each month, or when we're stressed, sick, or traveling. If a normally punctual period suddenly becomes infrequent or stops altogether, see a doctor immediately. Uncharacteristically early or late periods may be linked to stress, illness, or excessive exercise, but missed cycles could indicate pregnancy (obviously!), a poor diet, or anorexia, which can have lifelong repercussions on our general and reproductive health.

Cramps

First, the good news: many women who suffered from cramps during adolescence finally get to kiss those daggerlike abdominal pains good-bye during their mid 20s. Doctors aren't exactly sure why some of us outgrow cramps, but in many cases, the bio-miracle can be traced to starting the pill or having a baby. Now the bad news: the less fortunate of us may develop cramps for the first time during our 20s or, worse, find that our periods are getting more intense, with headaches, back pain, and overwhelming fatigue accompanying our monthly misery. Zoe, 29, of Los Angeles, rationalizes her increasingly agonizing monthly pains in this way: "It's my body's way of getting mad that I haven't had a baby yet."

In most cases, cramps (officially known as dysmenorrhea) are caused by uterine contractions believed to be triggered by prostaglandin, a hormonelike substance produced when the monthly buildup of blood in the uterus breaks down at the start of our periods. Abdominal cramps may also result from a physical abnormality or infection in our reproductive organs, such as endometriosis, fibroids, or pelvic inflammatory disease. If cramps become really disruptive (you find yourself curled up on the floor in the fetal position once a month or are bedridden for a day or more), see an ob-gyn to determine possible contributors and design a treatment plan—*fast*! Common therapies include a dietary overhaul (some doctors believe cramps are aggravated by certain foods or deficiencies in various vitamins and minerals), taking over-the-counter or prescription painkillers, going on the pill, recommitting to your exercise endeavors, and learning stress-reduction tactics, since stress generally increases muscle tension.

I'm a true believer in the stress connection. Once, when I was flying back to college after a trip home, I got the worst cramps I've ever experienced. They were so bad that strangers passing down the aisle stopped to ask if I needed help. During the flight, I was totally stressing about whether or not my friend Angie was going to pick me up at the airport, since I had left only vague arrival information on her answering machine and, for reasons to which I can no longer relate, was horrified at the notion of taking a bus back to campus. (Too broke to take a cab.) By the time we landed, I was doubled over in pain. When I stepped off the plane and saw Angie waiting for me, my stress spontaneously dissipated, and within *seconds*, my cramps were gone! I was so stunned by this anatomical feat that I vowed to investigate every known stress-reduction tactic for future relief. Of course, that resolution lasted about as long as it took for me to claim my baggage, but I still contend that taming stress is the way to win the monthly battle with cramps.

If you've read through my advice for dealing with stress, you'll know some useful aids, but when it comes to period stress, a few more specific suggestions apply. Some doctors recommend cutting down on caffeine, refined sugar, alcohol, salt, dairy products, red meat, and eggs at least one week before your period (or in extreme cases, permanently), since these foods may aggravate cramps. Instead, they advocate loading up on fruits, veggies, fish, beans, whole grains, seeds, and nuts, as well as foods that are rich in calcium, magnesium, and potassium, such as many of the green leafy vegetables.

To help reduce overall moodiness, which can make anyone tense no matter what time of the month, increase your exposure to natural light. For instance, walk rather than drive to work, if you can, or eat lunch outside instead of at your desk. Also, when you've got your cycle's timing down to the wire, take two tablets of ibuprofen (doctor permitting) on the day you expect your cramps to start, before they do, as a preventive measure. I've found that if I can get my body in relaxation mode before the abdominal horror takes over, my muscles seem relatively oblivious to the start of my period. If you've missed the window of opportunity, and cramps have started doing their thing, try placing a heating pad on your lower abdomen to help relax the muscles, or soak in a warm bathtub for half an hour—that is, if you're at home.

Zoe, who experiences vice-gripping cramps each month, advises a regular commitment to gym therapy. "When I work out, my cramps aren't nearly as bad," she reports. And Katharine, 28, of Los Angeles, suggests doing a few sit-ups as soon as the cramps take their gut-wrenching hold. If anything, doing crunches, in which you have complete control, will distract you from the internal pain that currently has you at its mercy. When all else fails, try this distraction tactic one woman I know uses: take a piece of paper and write down potential names of your future children, boys and girls. This won't necessarily make your cramps go away, but it will remind you that they are all worth something some day.

PMS

Premenstrual syndrome, the physical and emotional changes that take over our lives one to two weeks (and in really bad cases, sometimes more) before our periods, ceasing only once the blood begins to flow, warrants a whole book—and there are many out there worth reading. But what's particularly relevant to us is this horrifying fact: even if we've never had PMS before, we may develop symptoms during our late 20s. Even more gruesome, veteran PMSers may notice their symptoms getting worse! Unfortunately, no one knows why these changes occur.

There's not an abundance of conclusive research on the causes or treatment of PMS. Most physicians agree that the symptoms may be triggered by a variety of unrelated causes: hormonal changes in the body, starting or stopping the pill, childbirth, decreased exposure to light (especially during the fall and winter), nutritional deficiencies, and of course, stress. According to the American College of Obstetricians and Gynecologists, common symptoms include breast tenderness, bloating, headaches, acne, appetite changes, fatigue, insomnia, irritability, crying spells, and depression. Personally, I would add a few more to the list: inability to concentrate, clumsiness, feeling like an ugly, obese loser, weight gain (which feels like the equivalent of 500 pounds suddenly dumped into our abdomen), low alcohol tolerance, nausea, nervousness, and an overwhelming need to hibernate from everyone.

As soon as the symptoms begin to interfere with your daily life, seek counsel from an ob-gyn with experience in treating PMS. I did at age 24 when my PMS symptoms began to stretch into three weeks of misery. For me, an intense dietary overhaul (which struck caffeine and refined sugar from my plate), along with a daily dose of progesterone supplements, evening primrose oil, and calcium/magnesium pills, dramatically improved my preperiod body and soul. Bonus: my cramps got better, too. That dietary formula worked for a good year. Then I got bored with it . . .

To help your doctor determine the best treatment plan, keep a PMS journal for three months. The easiest way to track your symptoms, I've found, is to set up a log marked Day 1, Day 2, Day 3, and so forth. On the first day of your period, Day 1, record the date and any physical or emotional discomfort you feel (I'm lethargic and ugly, no one likes me, nightmare stomach trauma, I can't concentrate), rating each symptom's severity on a scale of 1 to 3, with 1 indicating that the symptom is barely noticeable and 3 indicating that you're at the point where you want to quit your job and move to Siberia. Between each day's entry, be sure to leave space to record the following month's symptoms. (If you do this on the computer, you won't have to estimate how much space to skip, which helps because some days, the list could go on forever.) When your cycle starts over again, go back to Day 1, and underneath your first entry, write down the current date and relevant symptoms.

After keeping a log for three months, I was *amazed* at the monthly parallels in my day-to-day emotional swings. One thing I learned for sure was to isolate myself on Day 16. For some reason, my irritability level goes haywire. God help the poor soul who crosses my path on Day 16!

Once you've got an accurate record of your symptoms, including when they begin and end, a doctor may be able to match patterns with specific treatments. Common therapies somewhat overlap those for cramps and include eating a well-balanced diet (high in iron, calcium, magnesium, potassium, and vitamins B and E), exercising at least three times a week, drinking enough water to drown in, getting plenty of exposure to daylight, and practicing stress-reduction techniques. For bloating, doctors suggest cutting out salt, sodium, and caffeine about two weeks before your period, since these substances make you retain water; for serious cases, prescription diuretics may help. Many women also find that birth control pills help minimize the symptoms. Recent research suggests that calcium supplements may also reduce some of the physical and emotional upheaval, and antidepressants have been helpful for some women with severe emotional symptoms.

PMS relief comes down to trial and error. What does wonders for one woman may do nothing for another. Keep a journal, see a doctor, try a few therapies, and above all, don't give up the fight!

A few other dos and don'ts for getting through this disruptive time: "I've learned to avoid shopping," says Pamela. "When I'm PMSing, I buy random things that I would never wear, so I stay away from stores." Amelia hones in on reducing stress. "After work, I come home and just relax," she says. "I also avoid alcohol, which usually stimulates my symptoms and makes me want to fight with anyone who says anything that makes me mad." Kelly takes it easy: "Midcycle, I become tense, angry, and impatient. I try to cut myself some slack. And I *don't* get on the scale that week." While you're at it, try not to analyze your reflection too closely during this ultrasensitive time. Something strange happens to our vision when we're PMSing, making us look like Picasso women, which is actually quite fitting, since distorted and abstract is exactly how most of us feel.

OUR FEET

I feel incredibly hypocritical dedicating a section to our feet, when I've treated mine so brutishly by wearing three-inch platforms day and night for several years in a row during my early 20s. However, I feel obligated to warn those of you entering the workforce and the 20-something lifestyle of dancing until the wee hours that an ill-fitting shoe (one that forces you to bear most of your weight on your toes) can cause future problems, including arthritis in your toe joints and skeletal deformities in your feet, hips, or back. Of course, there are the more immediate disadvantages: bunions, calluses, corns, and that increasingly unrecognizable baby toe.

If you're like me, that won't stop you from buying a shoe that will instantly make you three inches taller. But at *least* find a pair of work shoes that are roomy enough in the tips to wiggle all of your toes and keep your heels from sliding in and out, advises orthopedic surgeon Dr.

Rosemarie Morwessel. To find the perfect fit, she suggests shopping in the afternoon, when your feet are usually swollen.

EXERCISE GUIDELINES

First, a few reminders on why exercise is so important in our 20s (just in case I haven't hammered them enough already in this book):

- Exercise reduces stress, something we're all too familiar with; boosts energy levels, which tend to plummet as we accrue more responsibility in our jobs and commitments in our personal lives; keeps acne and PMS under control; and may prevent heart and cardiovascular disease, diabetes, and colon cancer down the road.

- Weight-bearing exercise (any activity that puts weight on our bones, such as walking, jogging, aerobics, stair climbing, and, of course, weight training using at least 5- to 15-pounds weights) builds bone mass, which begins to plateau after our final growth spurt and even decline in our early 30s. The more bone density we can build now, the lower our risk of developing osteoporosis, which causes all sorts of skeletal problems later on.

- Building muscle mass in our 20s helps offset our slowing metabolisms and the natural loss in muscle size and strength that takes place soon after we turn 30.

- The fitter we are, the easier it is to get our bodies back after we have a baby.

- Working out makes many of us feel more in control over the changes in our bodies and appeases the body-image demons.

The official recommendation: the American College of Sports Medicine recommends exercising three to five times a week at moderate to high intensity for 20 to 60 minutes per session. Choose exercises that strengthen your heart *and* bones: fast walking, running, aerobics, stair climbing, dancing, circuit training, kick boxing. Swimming and cycling are excellent forms of cardiovascular workouts, but they won't build bone density, so if you can exercise only three times a week, go for the activities that pack the most punch.

Next, an insider tip: vary the exercises you choose. Running for 30 minutes three times a week may be more convenient than going to an aerobics class or finding a climbing wall, but the repetitive motion puts wear and tear on a select group of muscles and joints. This increases your risk of injury and also limits development of your upper body, which is just as vulnerable to muscle loss and osteoporosis as your lower half. To avoid these effects, dedicate at least one of your weekly fitness routines to the upper body: boxing, circuit training, or repetitions of push-ups, pull-ups, and crunches.

And finally, every 20-something should begin some form of flexibility training at least once a week. This could be a yoga class or extensive stretching before and after each workout. After our last growth spurt, our bodies slow down the production of the hormone prolactin, which helps keep us flexible, says physical therapist Marty Mattox. As our muscles lose flexibility, they become more prone to strain and tears.

Before starting any exercise program, consult your doctor or a fitness expert for personal guidance, since everyone's fitness level differs. More important, doing so much too soon can lead to muscle strain, which, those of us who are familiar with it know, is a great deterrent to turning over that new fitness leaf.

NUTRITION GUIDELINES

If you eat regular, balanced meals, you deserve a gold medal, because the 20-something lifestyle is simply not conducive to nutritious eating. Our unpredictable schedules—deciding on a whim to meet a friend for dinner or to hit the gym after work, picking up Chinese food on the way home because we're too exhausted to cook—guarantee that half of the fruits and veggies with which we dutifully stock our refrigerators will be rotten by the time we're ready to eat them. Thus, on nights when we find ourselves home alone, we down a bag of chips instead. And then, of course, there are other deterrents, such as not knowing how to cook or what exactly constitutes a healthy meal. Plus, many of us are so fixated on being skinny that we often compromise our basic nutritional needs.

Eating balanced meals with a variety of whole grains, vegetables, fruits, protein sources, and dairy products is essential for staying healthy; boosting our energy levels; controlling stress, acne, and some PMS symptoms; and preventing a whole slew of diseases from developing later on, including cardiovascular disease, cancer, and osteoporosis. Since our bodies are still growing, it's just as important to eat well in our 20s as it was when we were teenagers. And if we grew up eating Pop-Tarts and frozen pizza, we have all the more reason to reform our frightening nutritional habits. For all the time, effort, and money we spend grooming and primping the dead parts of our body (hair, nails, outer layer of facial skin), we can at least make a little effort on the parts of our body that are living, right?

I'm not suggesting that we eat pyramid-perfect meals every day (only freaks do), but here are some fairly simple things we *can* do to improve our diet:

- **Add variety.** When we eat the same foods every day, we limit our bodies to a small group of nutrients. Here's a sample menu to go by: For breakfast, eat a whole-grain cereal with nonfat milk or yogurt, topped with a different fruit every day—banana, frozen berries, raisins, peaches. When it's time to buy cereal, try a different high-fiber brand every time. For lunch, eat a different meal every day. If sandwiches are your typical fare, alternate turkey, chicken, hummus, vegetable, or tuna on *multi*grain bread. For snacks, eat a different fruit every day, and munch on nuts, popcorn, cottage cheese, or yogurt. And for dinner, vary your nightly sources of protein (tofu, fish, poultry, red meat, beans), vegetables (broccoli, zucchini, corn, eggplant, green beans, mixed greens, or spinach), and grains (pasta, wild rice, couscous, polenta).

- **Increase fiber.** Put the accent on veggies, fruits, beans, and a variety of whole grains. About 75 percent of what we eat should come from these food groups, and most of us don't meet the recommended daily 20 to 35 grams. Fiber not only helps decrease the risk of heart disease and possibly colon cancer but also moves food through our digestive tracts, which helps relieve diarrhea and constipation. Breakfast cereals are great fiber sources; for best nutritional value, go for brands that include both soluble and insoluble fiber. And remember, if fiber is relatively new to your diet, add it slowly so that your intestines won't revolt.

- **Drink milk.** Those of us between ages 20 and 25 need at least 1,200 milligrams of calcium each day, since our bones are still growing; those of us over 25 need about 1,000 milligrams. To get calcium to our bones, we must: (1) consume it through milk (one glass contains about 300 milligrams), yogurt, green leafy vegetables (especially broccoli), seafood (especially salmon), and nuts (if you think your diet is lacking, ask your doctor about taking a 500-milligram calcium supplement each day); (2) cut down on substances that prevent our bodies from absorbing calcium—namely, canned and frozen foods with preservatives, high-phosphorous soft drinks, caffeine (relax: one cup of coffee a day is probably OK), and cigarettes, since nicotine also prohibits calcium absorption; (3) aim for a body fat percentage between 18 percent and 22 percent, as we need a certain amount of fat to store estrogen, which helps us absorb calcium and prevent bone loss.

- **Pump iron.** We need about 15 milligrams of iron each day. Iron helps the body produce red blood cells, which carry oxygen to all parts of the body. Frequent dieting and our monthly blood loss (unless you are on the pill and barely bleed) put us at risk of anemia, or low iron levels in the blood, causing fatigue and weakness. Iron-rich foods include meat, poultry, clams, fortified cereals, oatmeal, legumes, and spinach; so load up.

- **Eat folate-rich foods.** Women of childbearing years need about 400 micrograms of folic acid a day—even before we conceive—to reduce the risk of birth defects. Folate-happy foods include citrus fruits, dark green leafy vegetables, whole grains, nuts, and legumes. So, if we're eating our fiber requirements, we're probably getting our daily folate dosage too.

- **Go easy on the junk.** Eschew fat (especially saturated fats), cholesterol, sweets, salt, sodium, and alcohol (limit yourself to one glass of wine a day).

- **Take a multivitamin.** For sure, if you know your diet is lacking. Look for a brand with antioxidants (vitamins A, C, and E) to help reduce your risk of cancer. Some evidence suggests that oral antioxidants may also lower our chance of developing cataracts and reduce visible signs of aging.

- **Quit smoking.** You know the reasons why.

Since most of us don't want to spend hours preparing food just to eat all by our lonesome, the nutrition gods have endowed us with these simple cooking techniques: sauté strips of meat and veggies in a saucepan using a teaspoon of olive oil; drip a little olive oil over raw meats and vegetables, wrap in foil, and bake at 350 degrees for 20 to 30 minutes; grill veggies in the broiler (dabbed with olive oil again) or steam them on top of the stove. In case you're wondering, olive oil is one of the healthy fats we can consume, so it pays to use it instead of butter when you're cooking. In moderate amounts, it will not make you gain weight. To avoid that common food-rotting problem, stock up on frozen vegetables and meats. It's not the ideal way to eat, but it's still healthier than having cereal for dinner and much better than skipping meals altogether!

Go-Girl Guidance Shop the walls. *"When you walk into a grocery store, shop around the walls, where they sell vegetables, fruits, milk, eggs, and meats,"* suggests Astrid, 26, of Vermillion, South Dakota. *"Only dip into the aisles for a few choice items, such as grains, cereal, bread, beans, and ice cream made from natural ingredients. When you shop this way, you will eat healthier and lose weight."*

The "I Just Want to Lose Five Pounds" Diet

Who among us hasn't attempted the "magic five pounds" diet at some point? The statistics make your stomach growl: At any given moment, 45 percent of American women are on diets. On a typical college campus, 91 percent of the female population has used dieting in an attempt to control weight. Here's the real clincher: 95 percent of all dieters regain the weight they lose in one to five years. Clearly, we are a diet-obsessed gender. What's the point if our efforts are ultimately useless?

This may sound obscene, but here goes: dieting is not an effective way to drop a few pounds. Why? When you begin to cut down on your caloric intake, your body metabolism slows down a notch. That makes it not only harder to lose weight but also, ironically, easier to put the pounds you lost back on. Besides, dieting makes us ornery. But if you really just want to lose five pounds, do two things: (1) Exercise 45 to 60 minutes every day instead of the minimum 20 minutes three times a week—building muscle will increase your metabolism, which will help you lose weight; and (2) Give up one or two high-caloric items that are regular parts of your diet, but not foods you'll really miss. This tip comes from New York City registered dietitian Riska Platt, M.S., R.D.

For instance, if you have a candy bar and soft drink every afternoon, give one of them up. If you have drinks after work every night of the week, order spritzers, and save the highly caloric alcohol beverages for weekends. While you're doing this, make sure you're not replacing the foods you've given up with other high-calorie items. For example, instead of having candy in the afternoon, you're inhaling half a bag of chips when you get home from work.

The beauty of this tactic is that you won't have to skip dessert all the time or live in a bleak world of nonfat. You'll just have to watch that candy bar craving come 3 P.M. and appease it with something a bit healthier, such as a few olives, a handful of nuts, or a few whole-grain crackers dabbed with peanut butter. The object is to reduce fattening foods in our diet in a way that won't make us feel deprived, resentful, or, ideally, even aware that our diet has changed. As soon as we become bitter about what we're eating (or not eating, as is more often the case), we set ourselves up for a massive binge, which will make us feel absolutely horrible.

If you want to lose more than five pounds, make sure you really could stand to lose the amount you desire (check with your doctor for your ideal weight, and don't consider guerrilla dieting unless you're about 20 percent over your healthy weight target); otherwise, you're just going to screw up your metabolism. Then, get proper nutritional and dieting counseling.

Whatever you do, don't take dieting drugs or diuretics, and don't jump on the fad-diet bandwagon. Fad diets and dietary props are not always safe, and they just don't work. Remember the stat: 95 percent of all dieters regain the pounds they lose through dieting within five years. The dieting industry is making huge bucks off of us 20-somethings who are obsessed with our weight. The most effective diet, meanwhile, is the one that allows us to savor food in moderate amounts while retraining our minds to treat food as fuel for our bodies rather than as the enemy.

SCREENING TESTS TO GET RIGHT AWAY

Among the items we don't want to have to squeeze into our sacred mornings, lunch breaks, postwork retreats to the gym, or, *God forbid*, weekends is a trip to the doctor—especially when we feel just fine. But annual checkups, self-exams, and a few screening tests have never been more important, since this newly acquired adult-ish lifestyle of ours (punctuated with stress, erratic sleeping habits, sexual exploration, nutritional ignorance, etc.) increases our vulnerability to a variety of diseases. Plus, many problems that develop later in life establish their roots in the 20s, and early diagnosis goes a long way toward prevention.

Following are eight tests every girl should get. Most screenings are covered by insurance (especially if you fall in the high-risk category), but many hospitals, local health departments, or community clinics offer lower rates for uninsured clients. If you blow off the tests, at *least* do the self-exams religiously, know warning signs of the diseases mentioned (and if you develop symptoms, put the exam on your credit card), and keep your eyes peeled for free screenings offered periodically by various health organizations.

This information is not meant to convince you that you're about to contract a fatal disease. We are, after all, at our physical primes. It's included to give you a sense of control over what's out there and encourage you to take a little precaution now.

Pap Smear

Once a year, every year! The more sexually active you are, the more important the test, which detects cervical cancer and precancerous cells on your cervix. Both of these conditions may develop due to undetected sexually transmitted diseases—human papillomavirus (HPV), in particular—but are treatable with early detection. This test, one of the standard procedures during an annual gynecological exam, takes only minutes, as annoying as it is. You spread your legs and stare at the ceiling while your doctor or nurse practitioner scrapes cells from your cervix with either a cotton swab, a scraper, or a brush. The cells are then placed on a slide for later analysis.

Sexually Transmitted Diseases (STD) Tests

If you are sexually active or have been in the past, ask your gynecologist to screen you for chlamydia, gonorrhea, syphilis, hepatitis, and HIV, the virus that causes AIDS. Most doctors don't perform these tests automatically, so be assertive and request the full gamut. Many of these diseases lack symptoms until the late stages, which makes early detection crucial, since drugs can get rid of chlamydia, gonorrhea, and syphilis, or, in the case of HIV, help prevent or delay the onset of AIDS. If you're monogamous (and your partner is too), you won't need these screenings again unless your sexual status changes.

Breast Exam

Only a tiny percentage of women develop breast cancer in their 20s, but it's never too early to practice a self-exam every month (it's best to do it on the last day of your period, when your breasts are less tender). Many women develop benign lumps in their breasts called fibroadenomas, which are made of connective tissue or clumps of cells. And quite a few of us have what doctors call "lumpy breasts" in general. Nevertheless, it's important to have a professional confirm that these knots aren't cancerous.

For a self-check, stand in front of a mirror, and look for changes in your breasts' size, shape, and symmetry, skin color, and nipples. Next, raise your right arm, and use your left hand to feel for hard, immovable bumps or thickened tissue with irregular edges on your right breast. Pressing firmly, circle each nipple, covering the whole breast's surface as far outward as your armpit. Then repeat with the other breast. Finally, pinch each nipple, looking for discharge. At your annual gynecological exam, ask your doctor or nurse for a clinical breast exam, which mimics the monthly checks you do yourself. The American Cancer Society recommends a clinical exam every three years for women under 40, but why not get checked every year for safety's sake? Your doctor will likely do it anyway, but if not, ask.

Skin Cancer Check

While the percentage of 20-somethings who develop skin cancer is low, it's important to take inventory of our freckles and moles once a month (do it right after your breast self-exam), because all three types of skin cancer—basal cell, squamous cell, and melanoma—can develop in our 20s and are curable if detected early on. Melanoma, which is the most common cancer in women ages 25 to 29, usually appears on the arms, backs of the legs, torso, and face. Look for new growths or the following changes in existing freckles, moles, or lesions: asymmetry (if you drew a line through the middle, the halves wouldn't match); irregular or ragged borders; inconsistent coloring; and a diameter larger than a pencil eraser. If you are at high risk (you have fair skin, a large number of moles or freckles, a relative who's had skin cancer, or a history of blistering sunburns), see a dermatologist once a year for a thorough body check.

Blood Cholesterol Screening

Get this simple blood test from your primary care physician, and repeat the screening every five years, to determine whether your body has a healthy amount of cholesterol, a fatlike substance circulating in your blood. A high cholesterol reading (more than 240 milligrams) may indicate that you are at high risk for heart disease. Additional tests and changes in your diet and exercise habits may be in order.

Gum Probing

In addition to twice-a-year cleanings and cavity checkups, ask your dentist to screen you for early signs of gum disease, the number one cause of tooth loss in adults. Using a special probing instrument, the dentist will check to see how your gums hold up to pressure. If the probe goes deep, you may have bacterial decay which, if left alone, can rot your gums as well as the bones that hold them in place. Regular brushing and flossing help prevent gum disease, but make sure you get this test to double-check your efforts.

Eye Exam

Many of us find ourselves staring into the eye chart at least once in our 20s because our computer screens have become an electronic blur or we're having trouble driving (especially at night). But even if your eyesight is 20/20, make an appointment to visit an ophthalmologist (a medical doctor who specializes in eye health as well as vision) for a comprehensive exam that will screen for diseases that may develop in early adulthood, such as glaucoma, which can cause blindness. If your eyes are healthy, you won't need another exam until you're 40, unless you are African American, have a family history of eye disease, or have had an eye injury in the past; in these cases, the risks for glaucoma are higher, so you should get tested every three to five years. Contact or glasses wearers should have prescriptions checked every two years (or sooner if your vision changes).

Diabetes

When most of us think of diabetes, we visualize insulin shots. But insulin-dependent diabetics represent only a small percentage of those with the disease. The more common Type II diabetes develops slowly, often without symptoms, and affects the way our body uses food, causing problems with the kidneys, legs and feet, eyes, heart, nerves, and circulation. The American Diabetes Association recommends the blood test after age 45, but recent research suggests that screening as early as 25 years—particularly for those in the high-risk category, including non-Caucasians, obese people, and people with a family history of the disease—may lead to early diagnosis and treatment.

PART 4

Our Support Group

11

Family Knots

*I*f you haven't grasped one of the recurring messages in this book, let me spell it out for you: Turning 20 does not miraculously propel us into full-fledged adulthood. The 20s are all about *transitioning* into scary womanhood, a process that can take years and that usually requires the following: (a) therapy, (b) way more mental energy than most of us are willing to expend, or (c) monthly splurges at expensive makeup counters as a form of mental distraction. Even psychologists these days generally agree that the formidable stage of adolescence stretches into our *mid* 20s, not up to age 21 as popular opinion contends. (For the record, I'm not at all implying that the drinking age should be increased to match our level of emotional maturation; I'm just saying we shouldn't all be so hard on ourselves about getting our lives together before our bones have stopped growing.)

One of our main tasks of the decade—at least for the All-American Lone Cowgirls among us who were raised to uphold individualistic and independent values—is to facilitate a shift from our support group of yore (our parents) to a new group of support, whose members include ourselves, friends, and, when our stars are properly aligned, a significant other. In order to finagle the shift, we must first separate financially and emotionally from Mom and Dad's influence. This, as you probably know, is not easy or natural, definitely not if you have parents who are reluctant to relinquish their roles as maternal/paternal advisers. Yes, separation requires that we make a few bold changes in these life-long relationships.

WHO ARE THESE PEOPLE (AND WHAT DID THEY DO WITH MY PARENTS)?

One of the first side effects of leaving home and becoming more worldly (which we do when we leave home) is a new awareness that our parents are not just parents, but *humans* with attributes and faults like the rest of us. During this shot of reality, most of us come to realize one of two things: (1) Our folks, as suspected during adolescence, are members of the wacko race; or (2) Our parents are actually less weird/embarrassing/psychotic than we previously believed, compared with our college friends' folks, who make our own mom and dad resemble the peaceful, loving Cosbys. If you're like Natalie, 26, of San Francisco, you may also come to the sage realization that your family is completely normal precisely *because* it is abnormal: "When I got older and talked to people I didn't grow up with, I realized that *everyone* has a dysfunctional family."

Right along with this sudden cognizance, many parents do a number on us and begin to morph into beings we barely recognize, which can be both inspiring and somewhat unsettling. "When I left home for college, so many things changed between my parents," recalls Sloane, 21, of Syracuse, New York. I'd come to visit, and my mom was suddenly eating roasted lentils and drinking soy milk. Or I'd come home for the weekend only to find out that my parents had taken off for the Catskills. It was hard seeing them not need me—I resented that at first."

Rest assured, this is normal parental behavior, according to Lynn White, Ph.D., professor of sociology at the University of Nebraska–Lincoln and an expert in families over the life course. "Many parents experience a brief euphoria, a honeymoon, when the kids leave home. They're often pleased to be relieved of their daily duties as a parent," she says. (And, by the way, it's OK to feel disturbed by it, too.) "In general, children don't like it when their parents change," White points out. "They feel uprooted. They may recognize intellectually that their parents are individuals and should live their own lives, but emotionally, they still feel wronged."

Though less common, some parents experience the opposite effect when they find themselves suddenly alone in the house with no one (namely, us) to distract them from their own relationship. With their roles as parents no longer influencing their every move, they may finally begin to examine the life they've carved for themselves and decide to make a few changes. If conflict was rife, such parents may separate or divorce, which can be just as psychologically traumatic to us not-quite-functioning-on-our-own 20-somethings as it would be had the separation happened 5 or 10 years before. My mom and stepdad, who raised me like a father since I was 4, separated and divorced when I was 22; though I can't say I was shocked by the divorce, it shook my world, all right.

If you, like me, are one of the relatively few women whose parents divorce during our 20s, try to distance yourself from the conflict as best you can, and don't get sucked into either parent's side, advises Teresa Cooney, Ph.D., associate professor of human development and family studies at the University of Missouri. Cooney, who has conducted studies on how recent parental divorce affects young adults, makes the case for independence: "In my research, the young adults who had left home were better able to shelter themselves from divorce-related conflict, such as being pulled in by one parent to act as the mediator or adviser. Those who went on with their lives and proceeded with their plans dealt with the divorce much better." But since parental divorce so late in our lives is rare, let's go on to one last major parental behavior change *all* of us can relate to.

Right around the time we leave home is often the same time our mothers enter that life-altering change, menopause. If they're not quite there yet, they're probably riding the subtler but still turbulent waves of perimenopause. Either way, the hormonal changes waging war in their bodies are likely going to have some effect on their behavior, which, in turn, will have some effect on our behavior when we're around them.

First of all, it's important to recognize what might be menopausal (as opposed to crazy): If, during a Sunday stroll, your mom midsentence, kicks off her shoes and bolts down the sidewalk to the end of the block, where she then pants until you skitter after her to catch up, that may be menopause playing a little joke on both of you. Or, if in the time it takes you to sneeze, grab a tissue, and say excuse me, your mom has scarfed down an entire bag of CheeTos, that, too, may be menopause (and how can we get annoyed at her when we do the same thing during PMS?).

While these behavioral quirks may seem disturbing and rude, try to remember the menopause factor. "Be cognizant of it and patient," advises Natalie, whose mother's menopause went on forever. "Understand what your mother is going through, and give her space." Claudia, 29, of San Francisco, handles her mom's menopausal grumpiness by letting her vent: "When she has mood swings, nothing will make her happy. She'll pick fights with me, but instead of reacting, I've learned to say, 'Well, we'll see what happens,' and leave it at that."

CUTTING THE CORD

As our parents morph into unrecognizable beings, we will initiate one of our biggest tasks of adulthood: separating ourselves from their influence, support, and expectations. Of course, our separation starts long before we turn 20, erupting most violently during puberty when our emerging sexuality makes it clear that we have made the irreversible leap from baby to babe. Our parents then go berserk and pull in the parental reins in a frantic attempt to control the inevitable. But most of us don't get the full satisfying effect of being on our own until we reach our mid to late 20s or even later, depending on several factors, including how fervently our parents resist the change in familial dynamics, how comfortable and capable we are relying on ourselves instead of them for *everything*, and how deeply our particular Ameri-ethno-cultural heritage cherishes strong family ties during adulthood.

Successful separation from our parents is contingent upon one ability: learning to derive esteem from within ourselves and our new support system of adult friends instead of from our parents. If we don't learn how to do that, we will get stuck in the stale state of childhood, trying to please our folks or get attention or approval from them for everything we do, be it choose our careers, our mates, or our lifestyle. And if we spend all of our time trying to gain their approval, we're at risk of ignoring our own dreams and beliefs. That would be a real tragedy, so let's not even go there.

Like every other change we instigate, weaning ourselves from a parentally based source of esteem can be difficult, especially if our parents resist our attempts, which isn't uncommon. "Some parents can accept the changes easily, but usually this is a combative time of fights and arguments in families," says clinical psychologist Josie Levine. "There is a lot of pain involved in trying to change a relationship that has gone on a certain way your whole life. It's really up to the child to take the initiative."

To help you initiate the separation, here are six tricks to cutting the cord once and for all.

#1: Listen to Parental Power-Advice with One Ear

Learning to trust our own decisions is one of the best ways to develop the esteem we need to fully separate from our parents. "It's important for women in their 20s to realize that they have their own wisdom and the right to make mistakes," says Arlene Foreman, Ph.D., a clinical psychologist in Philadelphia. Her advice on separation: "Begin to visualize yourself as an adult on the same par as your parents. Respect their opinions, but really explore if their advice is what you want to do."

If your parents have a hard time offering "take-it-or-leave-it" advice and, instead, prefer giving "do-as-we-say" advice or "you're-making-a-huge-mistake-if-you-don't-trust-our-opinion" advice, halt your consultation with them on the bigger decisions, advises Lori, 23, of San Luis Obispo. "When I decided to quit college after three years and accept the lead role in a Broadway musical I'd been offered, I didn't consult my parents at all, because I knew they'd try to persuade me not to quit school," she says. "That was a turning point in my life. I decided I had to take my happiness into my own hands. When I told my parents about my plans, my mom was especially upset. She thought I had made a terrible decision. She even went to the head of my school to see if I could be accepted back if I didn't do the show, which really upset me because it undermined my decision. I think she didn't quite understand what this show meant to me; plus, we had different points of view about when I should finish college." Eventually, their differences blew over. (Lori, by the way, did the show—she's so cool!—and is now planning to finish up school.)

#2: Discuss the New You

Knowing that our parents believe in us aids esteem building. To promote their acceptance, frank discussion about our new status as an adult may mitigate some of the uneasiness that many of our parents have about the big shift in roles and may even curb some of their paranoia about our independence. "It's hard for parents to recognize that we're able to take care of ourselves and make good decisions," says Kelly, 28, of Brooklyn. "When I told my mom I was going to travel through Europe alone, for instance, her immediate response was '*Ohhhh!*,' which means, 'I need to process this.' So, I decided to wait for her to bring it up again, which she didn't. Finally, I asked her if she understood how important this trip was to me. Turns out, she was really worried about me, so I reminded her that I'd been living on my own in New York since I was 25 and could take care of myself."

Though it may be tiring to constantly remind our parents of our new adult competence, communicating our wish for their confidence in our decisions (and then providing solid examples of what they could—and shouldn't—do to relay that confidence) may help our own fragile self-confidence. It needs all the external support it can get. Diane, 27, of Chicago, learned the possible scope of this lesson in an after-the-fact kind of way: "My mother became increasingly overprotective when I moved out of the house. Once, I was driving back to college after a trip home, got stuck in terrible traffic, and was delayed. When I finally got back to school, I didn't call home right away. Because my mom hadn't heard from me, she assumed I had been in a horrible accident and called the state police in most of the states I had been driving through. I was so angry that she had done that before even trying to call me. I told her that it would have been better if she had at least attempted to see if I had gotten home before calling the police."

#3: *Activate the Boundaries*

Back in Chapter 8, "Emotional Theatrics," we talked about boundaries and how they help us establish our identities. Never are they so vital to our adult identity as when we're trying to separate from our parents, some of whom by virtue of having brought us into the world feel personally entitled to our space and time. That's why setting up a few guidelines for how often the family should talk and get together— especially if you live near the folks—is practical. Most of the time, straightforward honesty about the boundaries we desire does the trick. When Diane moved back to her hometown after college, her mother got into the habit of stopping by her apartment to drop things off without notice. Diane told her point-blank: "This is my space, and I don't feel comfortable with your coming by to drop things off. Next time, I can come to the house and pick them up." Her mother understood and accepted her feelings.

If you've made a hearty attempt to set firm boundaries, but your parents make repeated efforts to challenge or ignore them, develop strategies for responding to these situations whenever they come up. Step back, don't overreact, and remind yourself that you're not being a horrible child for setting these boundaries in the first place. That insight is from Claire, 27, of New York City, who is learning the virtue of patience: "Once, I was about to go on vacation and stopped by my mother's house the day before to drop off some jazz tickets I'd gotten for her. She has a fear of being alone and always wants to spend more time with me than I have to give. That day, she blew up at me for just dropping the tickets off and not hanging out with her, too. I had to consciously tell myself that I wasn't doing anything wrong by just dropping off the tickets, and I told her that I didn't deserve her anger. After that incident and others like it where I stuck to my boundaries, she has slowly—*slowly*—begun to respect my boundaries."

Sometimes, unfortunately, the most effective way to maintain these boundaries is to separate physically from our parents and move out of the house or to another city. Doing so may not just help with the separation but also enhance your relationship. "Young women's relationships with their family of origin usually improve after they leave home," says sociologist and family expert Lynn White. "Parents tend to monitor girls and expect them to pitch in around the house more than boys. When women move out of the house, they're no longer constantly supervised, so there's less friction and tension with their parents." Moving away also gives us the independence we need to learn how to be confident with our own thoughts and decisions, as well as figure out what our ideal lifestyle may be without the influence of our parents.

#4: Establish Conversation Boundaries

Tilling new conversational terrain may yield a relationship that's more on par with the folks than ever before. Molly, 27, of Philadelphia, clearly remembers the day she forced her mom to see her as an adult: "We were at an Italian restaurant, and I told her I was going on the pill. That was my way of telling her I was having sex. She was stunned. In almost an instant, I could see our relationship transition from mother/daughter to friends." But what we decide to tell our parents about our adult life— be it the way we spend our money, our sexual liaisons, our career plans, or anything else—should be totally within *our* discretion, not theirs. Otherwise, we will likely feel that our privacy has been invaded, no matter how innocent the inquiry. Or, worse, the lifestyle we've been trying to carve out for ourselves could be disparaged before we're adequately confident about it ourselves.

Unless your parents are probing, manipulative nightmares (in which case, I'm so sorry!), they will simply be confused as to what they can and can't talk to you about. The solution is to take the lead and offer information you'd like to share, and respond vaguely when asked about something you'd rather not discuss. If they don't take the hint, or if they begin to pry, offer this comeback: "I love you, but I'd rather not talk about that." Many parents may be shocked and slightly wounded the first time you utter this powerful statement, but they'll probably accept your will with little resistance. If they try to argue or ignore your request altogether, keep repeating the sentence until they give up.

If they want to know why you don't want to talk about something, simply say, "Because (fill in the blank) makes me vomit when I think about it (just kidding, try 'upsets me')." Or, "I'm not sure, but I'll let you know as soon as I do." Then change the subject so you can process why their questions are bothering you and probably messing with that self-esteem you've been so carefully building. Your guiding principle here is that keeping parts of your life private is not a sign of dishonesty, lack of loyalty, or evil daughter's disease; it's a sign that you're a woman who knows her boundaries and trusts her decisions.

#5: Cut the Purse Strings if They're Messing with Your Dreams

If your parents are helping you out financially, you're very lucky. But if they're using money to manipulate you into doing something with your life that you're not keen on doing, such as go to law school when you'd rather open up a hip beauty salon/laundromat, then you are not so lucky after all. You need to detach those powerful strings immediately so you can begin living your own life.

Besides, financial independence is a powerful boost to our self-esteem. Take Sloane: "In college, I had an opportunity to do an internship in San Francisco over the summer. My mother forbade me from going, but I *had* to do it. So, without financial support from my parents, I took a train across the country—which was very symbolic of my making the decision on my own—and did the internship. That was the first time I realized how much control I had over my life. I felt joyful." Being our own financial supporters can also bring about some good changes in our relationships with the folks. "I felt guilty about accepting money from my parents, so I cut all our financial ties in my early 20s," says Jane, 25, of Chicago. "After that, I felt much freer talking to them about things I didn't feel comfortable bringing up before. My financial independence has made us more like friends."

#6: Recognize the Resistance if That's What You Face

Negotiating independence from our parents is all about control—our parents letting go of theirs, and our taking command of our futures. "It's helpful when young women have parents who support their leaving the family nest," says social worker Allison Benton-Jones. "Of course, it's normal for parents to be concerned about their adult children, and it's normal for a child to feel some degree of fear and guilt when she leaves, but it's significant for her to know that it's OK for her to venture out on her own. If she lacks that support from her parents, she should first recognize that she doesn't have it, then figure out how to give herself permission to leave."

UNRESOLVED "ISSUES"

Most of us have *some* problems in the form of baggage left over from our childhood that we must overcompensate for . . . I mean . . . *overcome* in our 20s. The baggage could originate from an overly intrusive mother, or it might appear due to an absent father. It could even come from something so horrendous and painful I don't even want to think about it right now. Whatever type of baggage we carry, there's one thing for sure: it gets very, very heavy during our 20s.

According to clinical psychologist Dee Marx-Kelly, revivals of unresolved issues that have been dormant for years are often triggered by major milestones, such as marriage or becoming pregnant, or by being in a situation that evokes feelings of similar situations that we've experienced in the past, such as being in an intimate relationship. And with our new jobs, new loves, new lifestyles, new everything dominating our 20s, those old ghosts from the past have many opportunities to reprise their haunt. As they do, many of us begin to feel an innate urge to right past wrongs.

Sometimes, in our quest to reckon with the past, we seek out those who will allow us an opportunity to fix what went wrong, psychologists say. "We often are attracted to people who have qualities that remind us of our parents," says family therapist Cynthia Belzer, M.F.C.C., of Monrovia, California. "It's the nature of human beings to try to resolve unresolved issues. It's like learning to ski: if you don't get it the first time, many people are compelled to try again and again until they master the skill." Perhaps this obsession also has something to do with wanting to feel in control now that we're in the position to actually influence the course of our lives.

Regardless, psychologists advise that we confront these issues as soon as they make their presence known. If we don't come to terms with old recurring pains and learn new ways of interacting with people who trigger relationship patterns that we're trying to escape, we'll continue the old behavioral habits and carry the emotional baggage we acquired as kids. In doing so, we stunt the development of our adult identity before it has a chance to grow. Whatever your issues may be (excessive neediness, fear of abandonment, control, uncontrollable anger), the process of overcoming childhood trauma requires some serious deliberation and a gutsy will to change.

If one particular stumbling block keeps impeding our relationships—for instance, every guy we date is a control freak (and so is our boss and landlord and best friend)—that's a clear indication that we have some baggage to contend with vis-à-vis a controlling parent. In like vein, if every interaction with our parents makes us crazy, we're probably ignoring a more troubling fundamental. To break the cycle and gain some clarity, examine these annoyances, how they make you feel, and how they make you react. Talk to your siblings, if you have any, to see if they respond in similar ways and what about your shared upbringing gives *them* the most grief. This will give you clues for understanding your own antics. Get some feedback from your friends. Talking through your baggage with others often provides the best perspective for what's going on.

Once we have an idea where our familial conflict stems from, it's important to talk to our parents about it, either in person or in a letter. Scary as that may be, this will help free us from the past. Claire recontacted her father during college after not having seen him since she was a child, when he and her mother divorced: "I wrote him an 18-page letter telling him everything I had felt since I had seen him last—how shocked I was that he could run away from his daughter and not try to keep contact, how I had worked so hard to compensate for his not being in my life. When we met in my early 20s after all that time, I tried hard to cultivate a relationship, but we had so little in common, and I realized he really doesn't want anything to do with me. This past year, I've put to death the dream of a father I couldn't have. Now I'm at peace and can let go of the quest. I know that no matter what I do, I can't change his ability to be a father to me."

Attempting to understand why Mom and Dad raised us the way they did that may help us through these emotionally tough times. "Women in their 20s need to demystify their parents and look at them as humans who've developed their own ways of dealing with the world," says Virginia Holmquist, M.F.C.C., as associate in family therapy with Belzer in Monrovia, California. "Once you've negotiated the differences between you and your parents, you can talk about what you're able to give and not give each other, and have that be OK." Ask your parents questions about their childhood: how they were raised, what their fears were, what their life was like when you were born.

"They're a product of their genes and their environment. They may not have grown up in the most opportune environment, either. If you blame your parents for your life, you can't move on," adds Belzer.

Looking at Mom and Dad in a more holistic manner will also likely give us some compassion, which will help us forgive them for some of the stuff they did that may have tarnished our childhood. This will aid our separation from them as well, because this holistic vision will help us see the differences between them and ourselves.

SIBLING RIVALRY NO MORE!

Your relationship with Mom and Dad probably isn't the only familial current experiencing a subtle undertow. Sibling relationships are going through their own metamorphoses during this decade of change. "In the early 20s, there's typically a period of readjustment among siblings, followed by a drop in contact as siblings move away from home—especially if they move across the country from each other," says sociologist Lynn White, who has conducted research on adult sibling relationships. "Contact then typically levels off at a relatively high level—getting in touch once a month or so—for the rest of their lives." In White's research, sisters are the most likely to keep in touch (but those of us with sisters already know that), and brothers are the least likely, with brother/sister siblings falling somewhere in between.

Many of us find that the older we get, the less antagonistic or competitive we become with our siblings. This is often due to the fact that we've finally separated from each other and have our own friends and lives and, consequently, are no longer being compared with (or overshadowed by) one another. That doesn't mean we won't still fight. In fact, fighting often coincides fervently with this readjustment, and the attacks are often just as passionate and cruel as ever (but now the most cutting sib-to-sib insult of all is: "You are just like Mom!").

When the fighting subsides and independence takes over, many of us are finally able to get over any genetic inequalities (like not being the one to get the gorgeous aqua-blue eyes, but instead, boring brown) and actually become friends. If that independence doesn't happen, a friendship will be harder to form. "One thing that gets in the way of adult sibling friendships is a concept that people develop in childhood that everything must be fair," says White. "For a mutual friendship to evolve, siblings must give up their expectation of equality. If one sibling has a more successful career, a better marriage, or nicer children, the other needs to stop thinking, 'That's not fair,' and instead just consider her sibling different from her, as she would relate to her friends."

Of course, there are also big sister/little sister roles that we must consciously shake. "I'm the bossy older sister, and my sister and I are just now starting relate to one another with mutual respect," admits Lori. "That's partly come about by my watching her grow up and feel that I can relax if she isn't doing something right. Now I can see that she thinks things out before reacting. As we get older, the age difference has also become less and less apparent. Now I ask *her* for advice and actually benefit from her opinions." Miranda, 24, of Nashville, and her brother, who is three years older, have also become friends: "Before my brother left for college, we were always fighting, but now we respect each other, and we're both really interested in each other's lives. When the family gets together around the holidays, we spend most of our time together doing fun things, such as snowboarding or skiing. There's a new bond between us."

Aside from the reliable-friendship factor, keeping tight with our sibs during the 20s has another priceless benefit. Having shared our upbringing and genetic pool, they are the only people in the world who can give us reality-check perspective on our childhood, which helps immensely as we begin to negotiate new relationships with our parents and deal with some of the familial baggage. "Growing up, my older brother and I hated each other," recalls Leslie, 26, of Seattle. "But around the time I turned 21, we started talking about things. I wrote him a couple of letters about how we'd been so distant and how I missed him. He sent me a letter back saying that he loved me. That's the first time I remember his telling me that. We both realized that we needed each other and that we understood each other in ways that no one else could. Only he can *really* understand our wacky family."

Make every effort you can to rework these very special bonds now so that they'll grow. After all, no one in the world will know us longer and probably better than our brothers and sisters! But while you're doing so, keep in mind that like all relationships, they may go through several readjustments. Hannah, 24, of Los Angeles, says of her relationship with her older sister of three years: "We became each other's best friend in college. We were both single, and we'd party all the time. Now that she's engaged, she's readopted the role of older sister, giving me advice about how to meet Mr. Right, which gets really annoying."

During these changes, talk about the kind of relationship you'd like with your sib in the future and what changes might need to take place before that can happen. For instance, if your older brother uses you to communicate for him to Mom and Dad, who, likewise, want you to translate for them, and you're sick of that responsibility, state your boundaries. Or if your younger sister and mother gang up on you every time the three of you get together, make it clear to both that behavior ain't gonna fly anymore. And, as we must do with our parents, establish how often you'd like to talk and see each other, and do your fair share of the maintenance (even if you are the younger sister and aren't used to taking the lead). Tell your siblings that you love them—they need to hear this as much as our parents do during this time—and plan fun things to do together that will allow the friendship to grow in bigger, better ways.

SHARING THE NEST

I haven't had the pleasure (or, as some girls would attest, the displeasure) of living at home as an adult. But since more and more of us are flocking back home after school to cushion the financially challenging times during our 20s, some sanity-preserving advice is in order. Here are five living-back-at-home rules compliments of those who have been there:

1. **Sit down and talk about finances.** Determine whether or not your parents expect you to contribute to rent, utilities, and food. "Even if your parents don't really need you to help out, suggest paying some share of the expenses yourself," advises Abbie, 25, of Palo Alto, California. "Have that be *your* idea; it will help you have more control over your life. If you're paying your way, you won't feel so dependent, and your parents will respect that."

2. **Lay out the terms and conditions of your stay.** Establish how long you plan to live at home, if the family is going to eat together or if you're going to buy and make your own food, and who is going to do what chores. "It's important that everyone in the family has the same expectations about what living together again means," says Claudia. "Otherwise, the old roles will fall back into place."

3. **Revise those outdated accountability and curfew rules left over from high school.** (Or at least give it your best effort.) If you don't, you'll resent living at home, and all sorts of belligerent behavior is likely to spark between you and the folks. Updating these rules can be an uphill battle if your parents are the conservative types whose automatic refrain to any suggestion of change is: "As long as you live under *our* roof, you'll follow *our* rules." But laying out a rational argument with the folks may work. Miranda used this reasoning during her summers at home between semesters at college when, for the first time in her life, she was given a curfew: "My mom started waiting up for me at night to make sure I was coming home on time, and she was furious when I'd come in late. I told

her that she was out of line to be telling me that I had to come home at a certain time when she had given me the responsibility to move halfway across the country by myself to go to school, where I had free rein." It worked.

4. **Respect your parents' need for space and privacy.** As I intimated before, Mom and Dad may have actually been looking forward to the day you would leave the nest, allowing them the opportunity to pick up their relationship and child-free lifestyle where they had left it 20-something years before. If that's how it is, respect their space as best you can until you're able to branch out on your own. If your parents don't want your boyfriend sleeping over or your girl-friends hanging out every other night of the week, suck it up and spend your evenings elsewhere, naturally keeping them posted on where you are if you want to keep the fury and fears at bay.

5. **Make an effort to be a part of the household community.** (This way, your parents won't accuse you of acting as if you're living in a hotel.) Plan fun things to do with the folks now and then. "Because I'm so comfortable around my parents, it's easy to slip into a bad mood and not make an effort to be nice around them, but it helps when you do make the effort," says Naomi, 23, of San Francisco. Along those same lines, try to avoid simple conflicts that, if you make a bigger deal out of them than need be, will blow up into big-ger fights. If you follow this rule, living with the folks won't feel as if you're sinking back into those old discouraging childhood roles, which are more likely to resurface when you're sharing turf once again.

HOME FOR THE HOLIDAYS AND OTHER VISITS

Visiting the family nest once we've established little nests of our own can be an emotionally loaded experience, and then some if our trips back home coincide with the holidays, as they usually do. "Both par-ents and adult kids are learning how to deal with the major transfor-mations going on in each other's lives," says psychologist Gerald Dugal, director of Counseling and Health at Merrimack College. "Kids are learning how to balance their independence with their desire to be nurtured again, and parents are learning to balance their delight in their child's growing up with wanting her to stay home." Add the heightened expectations brought by the holidays, and we've got a formula for familial disaster. "Anything that happens on the negative side will seem more negative," Dugal says.

Go-Girl Guidance *For better or worse, your girlhood room will probably disappear at some point in your 20s. Take the necessary precautions now if you want to preserve your privacy: pack all personal belongings in cartons ready to be moved at a moment's notice. This will avoid the otherwise horrendous prospect of Mom and Dad sifting through your drawers (and you know they'll snoop, because you never tell them anything) and boxing up your entire life when they spontaneously decide to move to a smaller house or turn your space into a guest bedroom, office, or general storage area.*

To help ease the tension during those few and far between trips back home:

Mentally Prepare for the Visit

At risk of sounding New Agey, a few days before you make the trek back home, visualize what you'd like to do while you're back in your old stomping grounds (take a walk with the folks around the lake, then see a movie; drive by the house you grew up in; rally the old high-school gang for dinner at Margaritaville just like old times). Then imagine how you'd like to interact with your parents (hold stimulating conversations about the state of Indonesia's turbulent political scene? discuss the merits of a high-risk investment plan? make cookies, eat all the dough, then feel sick for the sake of nostalgia?). And come up with some ideas on how you might circumvent problems that are likely to surface. For instance, if you've been dieting and your mom always force-feeds you at home, plan to tell her ahead of time that you're trying to lose weight, then ask her to help you stick to your diet in lieu of the usual deluge of holiday temptations. (But then don't become bitter if you find the kitchen stocked with carrots and fresh fruit instead of the usual Cokes, chips, and holiday candy you were secretly hoping for.)

Know Your Tolerance Level Before You Go

If two days is all you can enjoy back home, don't feel guilty about a limited appearance, counsels Kelly, whose tolerance for a home visit is usually four or five days. And if the holidays are just too stressful a time to visit, why not go home during a less emotionally intense time. Amanda, 24, of San Francisco, spread herself around among several family celebrations during the holidays because her parents are divorced. She's learning to avoid wear and tear: "Spending time with the family is so stressful; it often puts me in a bad mood. I don't like myself around them—I get mean and ugly. Everyone's asking the same questions, and I know it's because they just want to know what's going on, but it gets so exhausting. Sometimes it's better if I see them for a week in the summer instead of around the holidays."

If your tolerance just won't allow you to stay with your parents, options may include couch surfing with friends, or shelling out the extra cash and booking a room at a nearby hotel. If residing off-site is the only way you can enjoy a stress-free visit and not have your parents either stare at you piercingly as though they can't quite believe you are home, inquire about your daily plans the second you stumble out of bed, or act way too hyper in general, there's no reason to feel weird about your choice. Everyone will probably enjoy the visit more if you're actually happy to be there.

Reconnect with Friends

If your folks have the tendency to smother you with love and attention to the point of nausea every time you venture back to the hearth, maintain your independence (and sanity) by scheduling plans with friends ahead of time, and letting Mom and Dad know when you will and won't be able to hang with them. "I specifically pick times to go home when there are other things going on with my friends, like if one of them has a birthday," says Kelly, who adores her parents but, like the rest of us, gets annoyed when she spends too much time around them.

If your family gets resentful that you want to spend time with friends when you barely have time to see *them*, remind them that you love them (you can never say this enough during the 20s) but that you never get a chance to see your old friends either, and that it's important for you to maintain those formidable bonds. Point out the very special time you've reserved for family bonding (and if you haven't carved out some very special time, do so immediately), then stick to your agenda. Another solution may be to invite your friends along to do things with your family. With non–family members around, there's usually less direct attention on you, which could be a tremendous relief. Friends can also serve as an added incentive for everyone to behave and avoid all that conflict-provoking behavior we're all at risk of initiating when we get around each other after long absences.

Make a Conscious Effort Not to Fight

Most of us are well aware of the little things that get on our nerves when we're around our parents. Perhaps it's that tone of voice that makes us feel like a teenager again, or falling back into those old parent/child roles that don't quite work with our new and improved independence. "Since it's almost impossible to avoid those hot buttons or ignore them once they've been activated, at least try to be aware of what puts you over the edge, and learn how to respond to your reaction," says Gerald Dugal. For instance, if you blow up at your mom for guilting you out about living so far away, back off, and immediately say, "I'm sorry. I overreacted. Let's start over."

The key to familial holiday bliss is to nip our anger before it begins to escalate. "It's important to step back and not get upset over the little things," says Amanda. "I try to remind myself that this is one week out of my life, and that I can suck it up and endure. The tension really just comes from my family's wanting to be a part of my life." Also, try to register that you are not your parents—you are just *visiting* them, says Maureen, 28, of San Diego. "Remind yourself that you're home for only four days. Dig on those times, and be happy. Don't hold on to the little things that are upsetting you. Let them go, and enjoy your time together."

Don't Try to Plan Too Much

With all the shopping, social commitments, travel, and financial strain the holidays often bring, family tension can just compound the overall stress that many of us feel going home. So, heed the rule of all rules about going home: Don't overschedule. Even better, plan some down-time while you're there. In other words, think of going home as a luxurious vacation (don't laugh!), with your itinerary including the following: getting plenty of sleep, exercising every day (pay the drop-in fee at the closest gym if it's too cold or rainy for a brisk walk or jog), and eating healthy meals—not just the sweets lying around the house. Doing so will reduce the level of stress your body is being exposed to and make your stay more charming all around. Anna, 27, of Seattle has her routine down to a T: "When I go home, I take hot baths, get plenty of sleep, and make huge meals for the family, which is relaxing and something I love to do, and, of course, I get lots of praise for it."

Give Your Parents a Break

One of the difficulties in going home is that natural tendency for our family to revert back to the roles and dynamics that dominated our interactions the last time we all lived together. "Young women should remember that it's very normal for parents to slip back into their old roles when the family reunites," says family therapist Cynthia Belzer. "Parents are accustomed to interacting with their kids in a certain way, and they're often not conscious of what they're doing." The holidays may be the one time during the year that they see us, which may also give rise to feelings of loss or grief. This may be one of the reasons they're acting nervous, anxious, or annoying.

My advice: have some sympathy, and focus on the enjoyable aspects of seeing your parents again, such as being nurtured and pampered. Natalie does: "I usually let my mom take the lead when I go home. The expectations are always the same: we'll catch a movie, watch TV, eat old comfort meals, and do all those habitual, nostalgic things."

Try to remain flexible while you and the folks are working out the kinks of your ever evolving relationship. Take on responsibilities you haven't before, such as organizing family get-togethers or helping prepare meals. And don't freak out if your parents suddenly want to skip the traditional family festivities altogether and hop aboard a cruise to the Bahamas instead (unless, of course, you're not invited to join them, in which case you have every right to freak; we're not *that* grown up, after all).

THE BIZARRE ROLE REVERSAL

As these familial shifts begin to ferment, many of us find ourselves in the midst of an unfamiliar and often disturbing role switch, in which we become the adults in our family. Sometimes the change of roles simply involves something practical, such as ordering a computer for Mom and Dad and helping set it up, or navigating our parents through our new neighborhood when they come to visit.

The role reversal may also evolve into the form of giving advice to our parents, which is a trip. Ella, 27, of Portland, Oregon, for instance, has taken to giving her father advice on family matters: "Sometimes he'll bring up problems he's having with other relatives and ask me what I think. A lot of times, I can point out the other side of things for him to consider, and he'll laugh and say he never thought of that." Lily, 28, of San Francisco, even became a professional adviser to her father, who, upon her recommendation and urging, began writing CD reviews for the newspaper she worked for. "I suddenly found myself to be a hard-nosed mentor. I remember telling my dad that he's reliable and a good writer and should ask for more money," she recalls.

Another bizarre role switch that many of us encounter for the first time is a slow-growing worry about Mom and Dad getting older. Not only do many of our parents begin to show visible signs of aging as we enter our late 20s, but many of them also begin to experience ailments such as arthritis or heart disease. Our fears aren't quieted any by the fact that most of our parents are beginning to enter the age in which their risk for cancer and other fatal illnesses greatly increases. "Every time I see my parents, I get sadder leaving them. So many of my friends' parents are suddenly dying," says Ella. Rosie, 26, of Los Angeles, too, has begun to worry about her parents' well-being. She confides: "Both my parents are slowing down a bit, which makes me nervous—especially since I live far away from them. Part of me really wants to move closer to my family because of that."

I wish I could offer some reassuring advice here, but sadly, I don't have any. We are mortals, and aging is part of life, as much as the plastic surgery industry tries to deny it. We can, however, talk to our parents about our concern and urge them to live the healthiest lifestyle they can (not that they'll likely change one iota, but it's a shot).

Now that I've succeeded in *thoroughly* depressing you (sorry, won't happen again), let's move on to a happier topic.

STARTING A FAMILY OF OUR OWN

Another event that adds a new dynamic to the way we interact with our parents is starting a family of our own. Though I can't speak from experience, I've been told by those who can that having a baby creates all sorts of exciting changes within our family of origin. If our parents never treated us like adults before, our new addition to the clan may be just the ticket they unconsciously need to finally accept the fact that we have undeniably and forever irreversibly become a Woman. Having a baby, and the tremendous responsibility that goes with the territory, may also conjure up primal longings to become closer to our parents—emotionally and physically, if we've moved away—if not for the child to get to know his or her grandparents, then for us to have the desperately needed emotional and practical support. In addition, nurturing a baby may give us a newfound respect, not to mention compassion, for our mom and dad and what they must have endured in the process of raising us.

On the flip side, some parents upon becoming grandparents begin to baby us as we've never been babied before and to invade some of those boundaries we've so adamantly tried to set up and maintain through the course of fledgling adulthood. "I've always been very close to my parents, but since my husband and I had our baby, I've been struggling with their wanting to be around the baby all the time and telling us what to do," says Yolanda, 29, of Cleveland. If boundaries become a concern, don't feel guilty about adamantly reinstating them in gentle ways. Tell the folks how happy you are that they'd like to be a part of the baby's life but that you and your husband need some time alone and advance notice when they want to come over. "My dad takes a cue," says Yolanda. "He'll say, 'Be honest with us—we don't want to intrude.'"

Then, with boundaries in place, go ahead and get extremely excited by the fact that your flesh and blood want to take such active roles as grandparents, and use their combined baby-sitting power to finagle some alone time with your mate. Both of you probably desperately need it!

ON BECOMING FRIENDS

One of the more shocking (but actually kind of nice) phenomena that touches many a family flock during our 20s is a slow-brewing (emphasis on *slow*) friendship. Now I know that growing up, some girls are "best friends" with their moms or "buddies" with their dads, but the rest of us are novices in relating to our folks in an egalitarian and amicable way. It can get so unamicable that irreconcilable differences and unresolved issues make us feistier than a pit bull whenever we spend more than 24 consecutive hours back at the homestead. Even in those cases, friendship is definitely something to strive for during this decade when our previous ways of relating to the folks are in flux anyway.

It's important for us to try to maintain some sort of connection with our family as we become adults, says Zonya Johnson. "The relationship with our parents gives us a sense of continuity and identity, she notes." This is particularly true if we move away from our original stomping grounds to a city where no one knows the first thing about our upbringing. Our family thus becomes a comforting link between our youthful past and our unknown future. Moreover, close relatives are usually the most reliable and strongest supporters we'll have in life, so nurturing the changing relationship ain't a bad idea.

It also ain't that hard. In some cases, interacting with our parents as friends is easier than trying to act like family members, whatever *that* means. The reason is that we can relate to each other's lives better than ever. Now that we've entered the workforce, been in a serious relationship or two, investigated personal money management (or thought about investigating), and perhaps even entered the domain of parenthood—all of which our parents can (hopefully) relate to—there are countless more things to talk about as well as bond over. As our parents finally become free from the responsibility of raising and supporting us, they may also be more willing to accept us and our differences as they would a mutual friend (but don't quote me on that one).

Here are just a few ideas for bringing on that newfound friendship.

Inquire About Their Past

Since while you were growing up it may not have occurred to you to wonder what your parents were like when they were single 20-somethings, now's an excellent time to find out if they wore bell-bottoms, had "issues" with *their* parents, or publicly protested the Vietnam War. The interchange not only provides good bonding moments and things to laugh about but also helps you get to know them in a more holistic way, which, as I iterated before, may help you work out some of that anger you have bottled up about their inadequacies—founded or not—in raising you.

Rosie found out some heartening things about her parents when she started asking questions: "One of the things I realized is that when my parents were my age, they went through some of the same stuff that my sister and I are dealing with in our 20s. For instance, I never knew that when my parents were dating, my mom got a job offer in Oregon and had to decide between moving or staying near my dad to work on their relationship."

Getting to know our parents in a more holistic sense may also help us understand who they are and why they've made some of the choices they have in life. "It's easy to forget that our parents were real people before they had us," says Sloane. "I thought I'd figured them out, but when I told my mother that I had been dating women, she confessed that she had dated women at one time, too. It was wonderful, and it reassured me that she wouldn't think I was a freak."

Make an Effort to Stay in Touch

Without regular updates and visits, we won't have much of a relationship at all with our parents, let alone a friendship. In addition, if we never talk to our parents—especially if the lack of communication is due to unresolved conflicts—there's much more potential for sparks to fly when we do touch base, which is usually around the holidays when everyone is strung out and hypersensitive anyway. Most of the women I interviewed who have successfully moved the familial connection into friendship mode talk to their folks roughly once a week (which is way more often than I talk to mine—*guilt!*), with visits ranging from a couple times a week to a couple times a year, depending on how far away they've flown from the coop.

As for the question of who should be calling whom for those chatty updates, aim for 50-50 maintenance. (But since most of us are never home when our parents call, the responsibility of keeping in touch may fall more into our laps—*double guilt!*) "When you talk, make sure the conversation is about caring and exchanging information or advice, not about looking for problems," advises clinical psychologist Arlene Foreman. Not to insinuate that either you or your folks are bent on stirring up trouble, but if fights are part of your family tradition, bear in mind that old habits die hard, and ignore any remarks meant to push all your buttons at once.

Plan Fun Things to Do

If hanging around the house with the folks makes you seriously question your sanity, get out of the house and do something fun together. This may sound obvious, but if your parents are homebodies, you may never have related to them much outside of the hearth, where you might actually enjoy each other's company a little bit more. This may require initiative on your part, but new experiences breed new opportunities to enjoy time together.

What to do? Claire, for instance, goes to the farmers market every week or so with her mother, and then they sometimes cook a meal together afterwards. Claudia has started running and rowing with her dad. The activity has given her something for the two of them to bond over as well as opportunities to talk about more personal things, which she'd never done with him before. Lily sees movies and jazz concerts with her folks when she's back home for a visit. And Lori and her family plan trips together that they'll all enjoy, providing them an opportunity to have fun and engage in some good discussions.

Don't Forget to Laugh!

Chuckles, giggles, guffaws, and roars are magical sounds. They can change familial attitude and lighten the collective mood faster than any family discussion around the dinner table. "The secret to being close to your family is to have a good time together," says Lori. "My family and I all have a pretty good sense of humor, so we laugh all the time, and that helps things blow over when we get on each other's nerves."

Pull out those old games, like Pictionary, and let those caged *tee-hees* loose. Our endorphins can use a good collective hee-haw!

12

Our Surrogate Family

I never could have survived nine years of 20-somethingness without my friends. With family far away, they were my sole source of support when I fell down a flight of stairs during the summer between my sophomore and junior years in college, broke my jaw, and had to walk around with my mouth wired shut for two weeks, living off orange juice, coffee, and vodka, which, as awful as it sounds, wasn't drastically different from my normal diet at the time. (That was actually a very fun couple of weeks, come to think of it . . .) They were equally capable caretakers during my senior year when I had to get a surgical repair for the hernia I suffered from lifting weights a tad too heavy for my less-than-developed abs (a pregraduation attempt to transform myself into Sexy Chiseled Woman while I still had access to the college gym). They were also the ones who made me laugh so hard during my bedridden recuperation that I almost popped the stitches in my belly on more than one occasion.

Many of those same friends evolved into confidants, advisers, and steadfast comrades with whom I could commiserate during those first few torturous years of entry-level woe. The closest of my friends knew exactly how to get me out of a funk when I felt emotionally hazardous (which was a good chunk of my 20s). Most important, we all knew how to amuse each other, despite the freakish turmoil that marked our simultaneous experimentation with womanhood.

But our relationships haven't evolved without their share of "issues." Like every other aspect of the great debut into adulthood, friendships must adapt to many of the changes infiltrating our lives, and sometimes that adaptation comes with its own matched set of frustrations that require a mutual willingness (not to mention endless "friendship talks") to get over the rough spots. Remember, our friends are going through their own 20-something transitions, and, sadly, there's no guarantee that the gang will emerge postmetamorphosis with all members still speaking to each other.

What follows are descriptions of some of the typical friendship phenomena that most of us are likely to witness during this decade of change, and some advice for the taking.

THE MAINTENANCE FACTOR

One of the surprising little oddities about our adult friendships is that in order to maintain them, we must make more of an effort than ever before. Comparatively, in our younger years, they were effortless, simply due to the fact that we saw most of our friends on a daily basis at school, we all had similar lifestyles (eat, study, drink, talk about sex) and goals (graduate), and we could make plans at the spur of the moment, knowing that our friends' social agendas were either absent or of the all-inclusive sort. That all changes once we break away from school and begin to establish separate lives. Suddenly, we have to coordinate all of the orbits of our new world (the orbits being work, dating, coworker bonding, daily pilgrimages to the gym in an attempt to counterattack our daily surrender to those high-caloric sweets floating around the office), all the while trying to coordinate our free time with the equally cluttered schedules of our comrades. The deeper we settle into adulthood, the harder this juggling act becomes, mainly because most of us will be devoting more hours to work, lovers, or possibly even our own families. Even the most enthusiastic of social mechanics find the upkeep exhausting.

One way of compensating is by scaling back our repertoire of companions to a few close friends—the ones we connect with the most—and relegating the rest of the pack to the less time-intensive rank of acquaintances. We'll talk more about this downsizing reassessment in the next section. As for those friendships we *would* like to nurture, the first rule of adulthood friendships is regular contact. Without frequent updates (via phone, E-mail, or that ancient camplike practice of letter writing for those who've moved away) as well as regular opportunities to yak face-to-face and *do fun things together*, there will be no connection, no bonding, no support, no growth, and frankly, no point whatsoever to our efforts.

Maintenance requires even more dedication and effort when either you or a friend moves away. Since, odds are, at least one good friend will end up on the opposite coast at some point during our 20s, it's important to wise up to the fact that we will lose this friend if we don't make a regular effort to keep in touch. Monique, 27, of New York City, is living proof that long-distance maintenance can work. She talks to her best friend, who lives across the country in San Francisco, every Sunday night. "We've lived apart since high school, but our 20- to 40-minute weekly phone calls keep us just as close." Cynthia, 23, of Boston, stays in touch with her high school friends from Atlanta through an annual group vacation to the beach.

Get-togethers for long-distance friendships become easier once our friends all start getting married, since weddings are one event sure to assemble everyone again (or else make them suffer severe guilt trips and feel left out). My own college friends and I try to regroup at least once a year for what we've come to call Women's Weekends, in which we basically spend 48 hours retelling all our old jokes and funny stories, painting our toenails, discussing our love lives and career aspirations (in that order), and talking about women's issues just like old times (remember, I went to a woman's college).

In the case of long-distance friendships, maintenance rules differ slightly. The friend who has moved away should make more of the effort to keep the relationship alive, says friendship expert Jan Yager, Ph.D., author of *Friendshifts: The Power of Friendship and How It Shapes*

Our Lives. "When you move, you're the one who's changing things with your friends and making it harder to get together," Yager notes. On some unconscious, animal-like level, your friends may feel rejected, betrayed, sad, threatened by your sense of adventure, and even jealous of your ability to take a risk. They may also be fearful, for obvious reasons, that your friendship will end. Do keep that in mind if you're the one to leave the pack. Also try not to get resentful if you end up making more of the effort to keep in touch, says Lily, 28, of San Francisco. She left her hometown friends long ago and has visited them at least once a year, but none of them has yet visited her.

Of course, your friends must reciprocate your effort to stay connected by returning calls and freeing up time when you come to town (assuming you've given ample notice). If they don't, it may be the cue for all parties involved to reassess whether the upkeep is worth everyone's energy.

DOWNSIZING THE CIRCLE

In this decade rife with change, many of us and our friends undergo transformations that make it increasingly difficult, if not downright impossible, to relate to each other, have fun the way we used to, or even make the time to see each other. The changes may be brought on by a variety of 20-something events: one of you goes to college and the other doesn't; one is on the prowl for a man, while the other begins checking out women; one moves in with a boyfriend, the other loathes couples' lifestyles; one thinks it's fine to not return a phone call for two weeks (or until she needs a favor), the other finds that behavior intolerable; one starts making lots of money and wants to frequent fancy bars and clubs, while the other is barely scraping by on a nonprofit salary. When changes like these occur, even the closest of girlfriends are at risk of losing the passion for hanging out together as in years before, when running around, listening to music, and getting boys to buy a round of drinks was a mutually acceptable modus operandi.

"The vast majority of friendships end, but that shouldn't be considered bad or tragic," says Linda Sapadin, Ph.D., a Long Island clinical psychologist. "Some friendships carry us through a certain time in our lives, then end, but pick up again years later—for example, when the friend who moved away returns to the area, or when the kids have grown and there's more free time for socializing." Sadie, 23, of Queens, for instance, recently reunited with her best friend from college after a friendship hiatus. She explains the process: "We had a lot of baggage by the time we graduated. We weren't having fun anymore, and it became such an effort to keep in touch. We tried to talk about what was going on a couple of times, but the problems were never clear-cut, so we just took time out. She moved away, and we'd talk every now and then, but not like before. Now that she's back in the area, we've gotten close again."

If, like Sadie, you decide to scale back the intensity of a friendship for a while with hopes of reconnecting when your auras match (or at least aren't clashing), it's important to maintain *some* low-level contact, such as calling now and then for updates (and definitely on birthdays or special events), occasionally inviting each other to parties, and sending holiday cards every year if you're the organized type. Otherwise, you'll probably lose that friend for good and may regret it later on, unless there was a drastic reason for fading out the relationship in the first place.

Sometimes, however, we know exactly why we're questioning the friendship. One thing I've learned about the subject is that when conflicts arise (and they will if you're really honest with your friends), you must address them immediately. In many instances, a good talk is all you and your friend need to remind each other why you became friends in the first place. After that, minor adjustments (and, of course, mutual willingness) are all that's required to keep the friendship going full steam. If you don't talk, tension will likely simmer and then surface in ways that could annihilate the friendship. And if you don't think that's a big deal, trust me: writing off your friends (or being written off) for no good reason is a big mistake during this decade, when their support is vital to our mental well-being.

Besides, this discipline is good practice for learning to work out lovers' quarrels. Enlightened partners sit down and hash out any major or recurring problems. "You don't want to pick on every single thing, but if the problems are chronic or you're shying away from the friendship because of them, there's no point *not* talking about them, because the relationship is ending anyway," says Linda Sapadin.

If the impediments to the relationship are too huge for talk to overcome—for instance, your friend has taken yelling at you like a crazy person on speed—or if your talks haven't led to any positive changes, or if your friend becomes emotionally draining, flakes on her share of the maintenance, dodges plans, consistently dumps you for guys, makes you feel bad about yourself, or weirds out your other friends, or if her values, attitude, or interests have become so dramatically different that you can no longer trust, respect, or relate to her, it may be time to put the friendship out of its misery. Marie, 27, of New York, refers to it as "divorce."

Ending a friendship can be depressing, extremely so if we've shared formidable passages with the person in question, and if we're single and subject to loneliness. Cutting ties can also create weird tension among mutual friends, who often feel caught in the middle of the irreparable dispute. Nevertheless, sometimes, end the relationship we must. In those cases, there are typically two tactics for doing so: fade the friend out of our life, or tell her directly that we'd like to end the relationship.

For many of us, the fading-out method works best, especially if the friend has a vindictive side and would go postal if we tried to formally sever ties, and *especially* if she's vengeful and knows a bunch of our secrets that we'd rather mutual friends didn't know. To fizzle the friendship out, start by keeping yourself so busy that you're impossible to hook up with, refusing to make plans (even if you run into the fading friend on the street and she guilts you out for never having time to get together), and filling your free time with positive and supportive people who are trying to build their lives in a healthy way.

If you choose the more direct approach—which is advisable for friends who have shared a long history with you but have chosen a path you can't respect, betrayed your trust in some way, or not picked up on your attempts to fade out the relationship—talk face-to-face or write a letter explaining why you want to end the relationship. The direct approach not only is cathartic but also may give us closure and help us mourn our loss. For emotional balance, if nothing else, it's always wise to mourn the loss of a true friend, even if the ending was your idea. Accept that the friendship is over, extract the bad moments from your recent memory bank, and remember the good times you had, instead.

Then start trying to make new friends immediately, because you'll need them. In case it's been a while since you've added on to your social circle (and so we can move on to a brighter topic), let's flesh out that task right away.

FORGING NEW BONDS

Any girl who has persevered through the cruel cliques of middle school (which is pretty much all of us) has surely learned the basics for forming a trustworthy bond or two, if only out of social survival. But what's difficult about making friends in the 20s, especially the late 20s, is that many of the women who we meet through work or mutual friends are busy and don't have the time or desire to get beyond the acquaintance stage. And, to be fair, our own lives often become so hecticly divided among our jobs, catching up with old friends, and dating or mating, not to mention chilling out by ourselves to preserve a sense of sanity, that bonding with a stranger rarely takes a priority in our lives, unless, of course, we're single and attracted to the stranger, which, due to hormonal reasons, is a different ball game.

Since new friends help keep our adult support group strong and vital—with old ones moving away, becoming preoccupied with boyfriends, or turning into flakes—we must not forget how to spread our social wings. To jog our collective memory, here are five guidelines for making new friends.

#1: Seek Out the Like-Minded
To click with another, we must have similar interests (cycling, listening to obscure bands, frequenting local flea markets, monopolizing the hottest bars in town) and compatible values (honesty, trustworthiness, respect). For a friendship to really gel, we must have comparable lifestyles or else it will be impossible to see each other on a regular basis.

This is one of the cardinal mandates of friendship maintenance, as you know if you read my foregoing soliloquy on buddy upkeep.

College often provides the first platform for us to pick and choose those who will likely become our closest and most endearing adult friends. During those four (plus) years, we're submerged in a pool of intelligent peers, many of whom have similar interests and goals. We're also wading through the most formidable transition of our adult lives, finally free from parents and establishing lives of our own. This gives our school chums the unique advantage of knowing us at our most creative, idealistic, emotionally fragile, and debaucherous stage in life, making them excellent sources of support during the postcollege immersion into womanhood.

Once we graduate, the pool of friends we interact with on a daily basis drastically narrows. In order to stay social, we must make an effort to expose ourselves to many different opportunities where we might meet people with similar interests. For this, making ourselves visible at work is an obvious start. Marie, for example, acquired two close girlfriends through her first consulting job out of college: "We worked very long hours together—7 A.M. to 10 P.M.—and started to get to know each other through 20- minute I-need-to-bitch-about-my-life breaks. That evolved into drinks after work, lunch, shopping for clothes, and then wanting to meet each other's friends." If you work in an office where typical coworker recreational habits consist of chasing toddlers around the house or where the average natural hair color ranges from silver to gray, you may have to seek peer companionship elsewhere, since you'll be able to relate to those office mates on a social level about as easily as you could their toddlers or hairdressers.

Roommates, friends of friends, classes, sports teams, and volunteer opportunities are a few good ways to narrow the pool of people with whom we might hit it off. As we meet new acquaintances, it's important to aggressively pursue all those tentative plans we 20-somethings vaguely throw out, the kind that go something like: "We should totally get together sometime . . . ." Get phone numbers and call. Most people don't do this; so, if you really want to start a friendship, *you* must take the initiative. (It gets easier the more you do it.)

The best friends to make are always the ones who are going through the same life events as you. You can support and distract one another and help each other keep perspective. When you start a new job, suggest lunch with another recent hiree with whom you can brave the office initiation, or with a coworker who has a similar (but noncompetitive) job. If you have a steady guy in your life, make an effort to form friends with other couples (but, obviously, still hang out with your single friends on the side). And if you become pregnant, hit those prenatal yoga classes with gusto to find other women who are enduring the same scary body mutations as adorable you.

#2: Task Over Talk

Our gender loves to yak, but there's work to be done. That's why the fastest way to create a bond with someone you don't know very well is to share a task, project, or goal (making organized classes and sports teams ideal for forming friendships). The interaction that goes along with an activity is usually pretty natural, requires giving and receiving, and offers us a good opportunity to assess firsthand how a potential friend operates. If you're shy, having a fixed role in a shared task or activity during those early stages of getting to know someone may also help you loosen up and reveal a little about yourself, which will help an acquaintance figure out if she wants to befriend you, as well. Without the close interaction that longer-term projects usually demand, we may never get beyond the chitchat stage.

#3: Test the Bond in Unfamiliar Waters

Once we've shared a few initial exchanges at work or parties and are pretty sure that we like and respect an acquaintance enough to pursue a deeper friendship, and that the feeling is mutual (otherwise, why waste time?), a shift is in order. It's time to take the interaction out of its comfort zone, such as work-related stuff, to see if a friendship might evolve without having to rely on the circumstance or context in which you met. This, of course, requires initiation and the ability to risk rejection, but we've got to take chances if we want deeper connections.

For most of us, these initiations start naturally enough, with simple and short excursions—lunch, coffee, or drinks after work—allowing plenty of room for a quick exit if the interaction lacks verve or the person talks your ear off. If the connection seems to thrive in these noncommittal settings, initiate a more extensive activity in which you actually do something rather than just sit around and drink. Megan, 26, of Chicago, says she has made several friends through work this way—one, an office mate who initially wanted to explore Chinatown with her, and others through a weekend golf outing.

Along these same lines, be sensitive to an acquaintance's attempt to get to know you better. When a potential playmate makes an amicable gesture, such as inviting you to a party or asking you to join a group of friends to see a movie or check out a neighborhood eatery, pick up the cue. Don't blow off these overtures. You'll never make a strong tie with new blood if the initial impression you present is that of a flake.

#4: Practice the Friendship Protocol Learned at Camp

To make close friends as adults, it often becomes more important than ever for us to take on familial roles and help our friends through times of need. We all tend to be mobile and often move as far away from our family as we can (while still remaining on American soil). We therefore must come to rely on our friends for support instead of our family. Likewise, chances are we will need our friends to serve as surrogate family and fill in the role of one of our family members from time to time. In other words, help a friend move; celebrate huge events such as a birthday, a promotion, or acceptance into graduate school; overcome a horrible breakup (and *all* breakups are horrible); quit a mentally crippling job; or work through difficult family situations that often crop up these days.

#5: Give the Friendship Time to Flourish

In her research on friendships among single urban women, Jan Yager found that it takes an average of three years for an acquaintance to evolve into a close friend. She points out: "Friendships usually begin because they're convenient and easy to maintain. But it may take several years to see if two friends can resolve some of the natural conflicts that may arise over a long period of time." If a friendship can grow in spite of these major life changes that we're all undergoing, it can easily last a lifetime.

MIXING BOYFRIENDS INTO THE STEW

Strange things happen to our friendships when we're bitten by the love bug. Even our most beloved friends, whose wit and energy we cherish, often can't compete with the hormonal intoxication that overwhelms us when we're around a new amour. Balancing the two can be a tiresome task, but it should be attempted immediately after we've passed through the initial infatuation and regained hormonal control and social consciousness.

There are numerous reasons why the social stew gets so chunky:

We Have Less Time to Tinker with All the Disconnected Pieces That Make Up Our Life

Adding a boyfriend to our already frantic schedules often forces us to cut out something else, and our friends usually end up being the cut, simply because they, unlike work, are a little more flexible. This, however, should be avoided. Even though it may be exhausting, double your effort to bond with friends one-on-one at least once a week. When Molly, 27, of Philadelphia, started dating the man she ended up marrying, she says she had special "friend" time and "boyfriend" time to maintain both relationships.

Living the divided life is exhausting, but the consequence is losing these valuable friends. And if the boyfriend relationship doesn't pan out, as so often results in our 20s, as harsh and negative as that may sound, we will find ourselves alone in this time of darkness. It's not a place I would wish for anyone except my worst enemy.

Besides, if we alienate our friends, we will inevitably lose out in the long run because *no* boyfriend can supply all our entertainment and stimulation needs. If he attempts to do so, the overachiever will burn out. If he expects us to be overwhelmingly satisfied with the role of sidekick while he hangs with his friends, the arrogant idiot will eventually bore us. So, make the effort to see your girlfriends, even if all you really want to do on the weekends is curl up with your newfound lover and watch *Room with a View* for the hundredth time.

Our Friends Give Us Grief for Always Being with Him

When we're suddenly no longer free every Saturday night to see a movie or hit the nearest bar, and we're always over at the new mate's place on Sunday mornings (rendering spontaneous brunch plans next to impossible), our single friends will begin to bemoan our lack of participation in the frivolous escapades of the singles' lifestyle. They may feel rejected, jealous, or abandoned. In some cases, they might even unwittingly displace their resentment upon our poor undeserving boyfriends. But most of the time, they will warm up to him. Spending quality time with friends alone each week, as I already mentioned, will alleviate some of this added distress.

Our Idea of a Fun Night Out Changes

Smoky bars with lurking lizards slinking from one empty bar stool to another take on a new and depressing dimension when we're suddenly coupled. Once we are intoxicated by love, these characters become more revolting than ever before. Even the ones we used to tolerate (because they were friendly and wanted to buy us drinks) aren't at all appealing to those of us in love who are merely out to reconnect with our friends and could do without the meet-and-greet efforts of lonely guys. Problems arise when our single friends appreciate these friendly gestures and would like to include the characters in the conversation.

Friendships that evolved out of the nighttime search for a desirable man will surely suffer if those relationships lack other shared interests, because we won't know how to have fun with those friends anymore. We may have had similar lifestyle goals before—spend lots of money going to clubs and shopping—but entering a relationship often causes lifestyle goals and values to shift in a way that diabolically changes how we'd like to pass our time and spend our money with friends. The effect is more pronounced if the relationship is serious and may involve marriage, babies, or a down payment for a house. When this shift occurs in your life, slowly (so as not to induce withdrawal symptoms from your nightlife buddies) lure those friendships away from the clubs, and try to bond in settings of mutual interest.

Our Friends (Wrongly) Assume We're Preoccupied with Our Mates and Don't Care About Them Anymore

The false perception that we've written off our friends may become acute when we move in with our boyfriends or get married (which makes our abode less likely to be a gathering spot for girls-night-out beauty preparations). Rebecca, 23, of Chicago, for instance, says that one close guy friend stopped calling as soon as she got a boyfriend: "He just presumed I didn't want to hang out with him anymore." Since our friends often make this assumption, it's up to us to take the reins and make more of the effort to maintain the relationship.

"The friend whose life has changed by entering a relationship must reach out to the friend whose life is the same," says friendship expert Jan Yager. "Friends needs guidelines on how to approach a new couple." For instance, they need to know if it's still OK to call at 11 P.M. on a Tuesday night just to catch up, or if it's still OK to initiate plans between just the two of you now that you've become a couple.

Our Friends Don't Like Our Boyfriend and Exclude Us from Group Get-Togethers

A personality conflict between a girl's mate and friends may cause a rift among even the closest of chums. "I once had a boyfriend who tried so hard around my friends, but I found out in a roundabout way that we weren't being invited to things because he really annoyed them," says Megan. "After I discovered this, I tried to always stay with him around my friends and keep the conversation going so no one would get stuck talking to him. That was probably a clue that the relationship wasn't right."

Our friends may need time to warm up to the new fixture in our life and possibly get over any jealousy they may have related to the fact that we've found a partner and they haven't, or that we're not as available as we once were. This is where those maintenance tactics come in. Another possibility is that our boyfriend's personality needs time to find its place in the group dynamics of our pals. To help that along, create opportunities for camaraderie to develop, and make an effort to facilitate a connection. "It's sort of like being a good hostess," says clinical psychologist Linda Sapadin. "Tell each person something about the other one beforehand to find a common interest." Then work on establishing frequent get-togethers and doing things that will create shared experiences that everyone can bond over later.

Listen and learn: If your friends don't include you because your behavior changes when you're around your boyfriend (you become clingy, needy, quiet, demure, boisterous, obnoxious, or just plain annoying), try to listen objectively, hard as it may be to hear what they have to say. Your friends may be bummed that you've chosen a mate who mutes the you they love and adore. Or your object of desire maybe isn't who they imagined you'd end up with, and they are temporarily confused by the picture. Or they never would have chosen the guy as a mate for themselves and, in a myopic kind of way, can't understand what you see in him. If there's any chance your friends don't like your boyfriend due to one of these superficial reasons, ignore their opinions and advice. Most likely, not everyone will be saying the same thing about your beloved. But if *everyone* is critical, dump the guy immediately. He's not good enough for you!

Our Boyfriend Doesn't Like Our Friends

First of all, attempt to make a case for your friends, suggests friendship expert Jan Yager. "A friend may be showing an ugly side of herself around your boyfriend because she's jealous of your relationship," she says. "When you bring them together, don't set up scenarios that are likely to fail, such as threesomes. Try a double date, or party with many people."

If our boyfriend still dislikes our friends, we've got three choices: (1) Keep our friends separate from our romantic life (which is a terrible solution if you ask me, but may be the only answer if we love our friends and love our mate but don't love them together); (2) Make new "couples" friends so we'll at least be able to share some form of a social life with our chosen mate; (3) Hang out with our mate's friends (but only if we enjoy their company), and see our friends on our own time. It works for Nora, 25, of San Francisco, whose boyfriend is eight years older than she is and has a hard time relating to her friends, who are in their mid 20s.

If a boyfriend becomes jealous whenever you spend time with your friends, causing you to drift further away from them, tell him to get over it. Immediately. If he can't deal with your having a life that doesn't center around him, then he shouldn't be able to have you at all! Being jealous of your friends is a major sign that something's wrong with the guy's wiring. Don't justify his controlling behavior by thinking that it's cute that he's jealous or it's just because he loves you so much that he can't bear to spend the night without you. Don't fool yourself.

And don't ever convince yourself that he's more important than your friends. Our friends help us form our identities. Without them, we're at great risk of developing an identity crisis and depression. Besides, jealousy-riddled relationships rarely last, and if they do, they slowly but surely deplete our sense of worth.

We Become Flaky and Blow Off Our Friends

Face it, we all become flakes to some degree during those first few lovestruck months of meeting the most perfect and debonair mate on the planet. But don't let this transformation threaten your friendships. Girlfriends are valuable, especially during the early stages of a romance, when we're so excited and really *need* to talk to our friends about how great the new boyfriend is (very difficult, by the way, for those on the receiving end who are lamenting the lack of partnership in their lives; so be sensitive, and try to preserve this girly enthusiasm for friends who are in happy relationships). Girlfriends are also much in demand later on for advising us through the difficult times that many relationships must endure during this ever changing period of our lives. And, of course, we want them by our sides to share all the good times ahead, too.

If You Dislike Your Best Friend's Mate

If the guy with whom your friend has taken up is ultimately a good guy (we usually know deep down), give him a chance. Be supportive of your friend, then remove yourself from the relationship by reminding yourself that you are not dating the guy, she is. If you don't feel an intense connection with him, that doesn't necessarily mean he's wrong for her. Accept the situation, because no matter how hard we try to reason with a lovestruck friend, the decision will be hers.

If, on the other hand, your friend's mate of choice is an outright ass or potentially abusive, put on your friendship armor and, in your most persuasive and concerned manner, lay out why you're worried about the relationship and how you think it's affecting your friend's well-being. Leslie, 26, of Seattle, once confronted a friend who she believed was in a borderline-abusive relationship. Tell your friend that you're concerned, she advises, but avoid ultimatums, such as "It's either your mate or me." This will only distress your friend even more and probably steer her more toward the wretched mate. Explain your concern, telling your friend why you can't spend time with her and her mate but will spend time with her alone. "I told my friend I'd support her decision but couldn't watch her stay in that relationship," Leslie says. "That helped shape what she did, which was to eventually break up."

In addition to expressing our concern, Dee Marx-Kelly, a therapist and domestic violence specialist, suggests finding out what your friend might need—a place to stay, help moving, company on weekends—if she decides to end an abusive relationship. This is all the more problematical if she lives with her abusive mate. If you have the room, you might offer to let her chill out with you for a week until she moves back in with a parent or finds an apartment, or just let her know that you will pick her up at 3 A.M. and drive her to her mom's if she ever needs your help. If you share a group of friends, rally the gang to help encourage the one in trouble to sever the ties with her abusive lover. She may want to break up but is scared of being lonely.

GROUPING THE GANG

One more change that many of us see in our friendships as we enter the domain of adulthood is that they become more fragmented, less pactlike than they were in high school or college when we were all one massive clump of chumhood. In the 20s, we have our work friends, our college friends, our high school friends, our mate's friends, and the friends we make from the myriad other disparate activities in our lives. Many times, they're all competing for attention, which can make life a bit overstimulating.

Since it would be socially exhausting, if not impossible, to maintain each of these friendships on an intimate, one-on-one level, it's a good idea in your early 20s to learn how to pool your various groups of friends together as well as organize regular "reunions" with the old gang members. There's nothing like a solid, reliable group of friends to make us feel connected and supported in the brave new world of adulthood. Of course, organizing these weekly, bimonthly, or monthly gatherings requires diligence and persistence, so whoever in the group is most adept at that should volunteer for the position. Molly, for instance, has two monthly get-togethers with her group of friends—one in which they meet for dinner and another when they gather for an all-day outing. She explains: "My girl days are sacred. I know it's kind of contrived, but if we didn't make dates to see each other, we never would. We all work crazy hours." Sandra, 29, of Indianapolis, gets together with her girlfriends every Monday night: "Mondays are all about us. Whoever's house we meet at, the boyfriend or husband has to leave or go downstairs."

Introducing new friends to a group is always a good idea as well, though it's sometimes awkward if the newling isn't ingratiating or feels left out of the conversation. "I once had a party and invited both my college and high school friends, and it was really awkward," recalls Megan. "Some people connected, but I think most of them were psyched out from stories they had heard about each other and from wondering if I was closer to the other group than them. It didn't work out." Frequent casual gatherings may offer a way to let those connections form naturally on their own. Monique, for instance, often invites a bunch of friends from different groups to meet at a bar or have dinner at a restaurant on a certain night; she leaves it open so that whoever wants to come can just show up.

Once you've got a regular group or two in the making, the 20-something social upkeep will become easier. It takes work and time to cultivate our adulthood friendships. Along the way, don't forget to have some fun. After all, that's the whole point!

PART 5

Our Finances and Other Loose Ends

13

Financial Chaos

*O*h dear. I didn't plan for the subject of money to fall in Chapter 13. But, actually, since most of us either consider ourselves doomed to bad luck or experience terror and panic attacks when the topic of financial planning arises, maybe it is appropriate that the discussion be designated to the spooky and unsettling 13th chapter. Better money than love. At any rate, we'll ease into the workings of our finances, because if you're anything like me, money is the biggest source of denial and stress in your life. One request: Don't skip over this chapter just because you fear it will monetarily jinx you. Reading it will help you get your finances under control and determine where you need to be headed during this decade. I promise, I'm going to include only the most essential money-related subjects that merit your attention so it won't be stressful.

One of the reasons money is such a headache for us is that the whole discipline requires that we learn a new language with such esoteric concepts as CDs (which are not bonus music gifts you receive when you open a bank account, as I believed for a time), IRAS (which have nothing to do with the Irish Republican Army), junk bonds, blue chips, penny stocks, and load versus no-load mutual funds.

To add to the distress of all this financial gobbledygook, most of us have no money to spend, let alone invest in our futures. And when we do land our first jobs and pay our first rents, the monumental scope of correctly administering the deluge of cash in our checking accounts is sometimes overwhelming. The sudden responsibility literally made Abbie, 25, of Palo Alto, California, sick: "When I got my first apartment, I had to pay first and last months' rent, plus deposit. I was so nervous about handing over all that money at once that I threw up. And I never throw up."

I have learned one thing in my 20s about money: no matter how much we may ideologically wish it otherwise, money is the key to our security, future plans, and independence and, therefore, something we must respect and take seriously. This chapter aims to offer a little clarity for how to do that (without getting *too* depressed), beginning with something most of us can relate to: having none to start with.

ON BEING DIRT POOR

One common denominator among most of us 20-something girls (unless you've been recruited for some high-paying dot-com job or are living off a trust fund) is our collective poverty, or relative poverty I should say, since most of us, thankfully, aren't living on the street or eating tuna fish out of the can every night for supper. Even girls who earn higher-than-the-rest-of-us salaries have the same despair for more disposable income, especially if they're stashing a good 10 to 15 percent of their earnings in a 401(k) plan, as some financial experts tell us to. Add the stress of having to pay back student loans *and* shovel our way out of the credit card debt that we somehow accumulated between paying for our final semester of books and buying an entire new work-worthy wardrobe, and the financial chaos looks even more bleak. The good news is that if we're diligent about pursuing raises and better-paying jobs, we *will* begin to make more than the below-poverty-level salaries we started off with at the dawn of the decade. The bad news is that the more our salaries rise, the louder our consumer appetites grumble.

This is not necessarily because we are innately materialistic, though I'd be silly deny that materialism plays a role in our ever-increasing money hunger. More often than not, we genuinely lack so much when we're starting out that the minute we begin to earn more, our priorities become blinded by the need to establish a tolerable standard of living. We want our *own* apartments instead of sharing a flat with a marmot-like roommate who becomes skittish if we move her shampoo bottle from one corner of the shower to the other. We want a new car that doesn't sputter so violently that valet guys snicker when we pull up to the fancy restaurant where our chef friend has invited us to a party he's catering. We want to travel to exotic island-countries where we can be irresponsible and flirty for a week, since our carefree youth *is* sitting on a time bomb. We want to go to concerts and parties (the good ones always have cover) that are crawling with available and attractive dating prospects from which to choose. And we want *real* furniture, not a couch that we must cover with a blanket for aesthetic reasons, a '70s-chic table lamp, and a broken pine futon frame that we found on the sidewalk with a "Free" sign taped on top. It's only natural and correct that we should want these things.

Therein lies the biggest taunt of the decade: we want more than our meager means allow us to have. That leads to resentment—icing on the cake of emotional trauma that marks our great transition to womanhood. We'll discuss tactics for getting our finances all in order, but first on the agenda is how to deal with the agony of being dirt poor when the temptation to spend is probably greater than it ever will be again in our lives. The very first step is getting over that resentment we feel for not being able to afford going out to dinner more than once a week (and even then, being limited to bad Chinese), for having debts to repay before we've even *lived*, and for feeling deprived, in general, of the fun and frivolous 20-something experience we should be having like the entire cast of "Friends."

Resentment is such an individual and personal matter that there's not a whole lot I can do to help you get over it, except let you know that I can relate. One promising sign I have found is that resentment takes less of a grip when you stop comparing yourself with your friends and start owning up to some of the choices you've made, like going to a private college versus a state university that would have cost you less in student loans, or choosing a job in the nonprofit sector instead of the high-profit world of financial consulting, or even deciding to put that $300 bebe suit on your VISA, when you could have found a cheaper alternative at a discount clothing store if you really tried.

You can always make new choices to improve your financial situation, too, like getting a roommate, taking on freelance work or a weekend job, working overtime for a little extra cash, taking a class that will put you in a better position for getting a promotion and raise, or even exploring a more profitable career. It's always better to overexhaust yourself now, with the aim of getting out of a bad financial crunch, than to wallow in misery or resentment.

Another way to cope with financial distress is by making a concerted effort to get over any denial you may have regarding your current finances. When we deny the reality of our limited income and live beyond our means, our finances will spin out of control. If we have access to credit cards—and who doesn't?—the situation can lead to all sorts of problems. If we can't pay back what we owe, we develop bad credit, which is especially harmful when we need to move to a new apartment, get a car loan, or buy a house.

Creating a budget, which forces us to examine how we spend our money, is a real good start.

OUR BUDGET

To figure your budget, start with how much you make every month (not counting the 10 percent or so that your company should directly feed into your savings and/or retirement account, which we'll talk about later). Then, add up your basic monthly expenses: rent, living incidentals (groceries, gas and electricity, phone, transportation, auto insurance, the pharmaceutical stuff to which we girls must surrender part of our paycheck each month), and debt (monthly credit card payments, student loans, car payments). When you subtract what you must pay out from what you make, the money left over is what you can designate for entertainment and shopping. This little set of figures is your budget.

If you don't have any play money left or, worse, your debt and spending exceed what you make, it's no wonder you are in the financial denial to which I alluded. To remedy this problem and free up assets for your monthly entertainment fund, you will need to figure out ways of reducing your living expenses. (If you have uncontrollable credit card debt, your goal will be to get rid of that first, and then enjoy life; we'll go over the nitty-gritty of reducing debt in a minute.) For now, let's assume your credit card debt isn't living on a fault line and concentrate on trimming your monthly expenses so that you'll have more spending money.

Start with a microscopic examination of your monthly living expenses, looking for areas where you can cut back. For example, if writing your rent check every month makes you gag (most experts say that we should aim for a rent that's about 30 percent of our monthly take-home), an alternative is moving to a cheaper neighborhood, or bringing on a roommate if you live alone but have space to spare. A tiny dining room or a very large walk-in closet could conceivably be turned into another room for someone who ideally works at night and has a boyfriend with whom she stays half the time anyway. If your phone bills are beyond horrendous, switch to Internet connecting, and make your long-distance calls from work. (I didn't say that!)

....

Go-Girl Guidance *During those belt-tightening times, one way to boost your morale is to budget in a small amount of money each month purely for fun. Mary, 25, of Washington, D.C., calls this booty "me" money. The treat can be small, like a carton of Ben & Jerry's, or more decadent, like a new pair of shoes. Whatever your indulgence, make sure your "me" money is a nonnegotiable part of your monthly budget. Without this fund, you* will *go insane.*

....

If you own a car but don't drive enough to justify the monthly payments, insurance, and maintenance repairs, get rid of your wheels and start walking to work (distance allowing) or take public transit (mental health allowing). I know that chucking the car isn't a reality if you live in a sprawling city where public transportation and short distances between work, home, and the nearest store/café/bar are inconceivable, but if wheellessness is an option, getting rid of the car will free up your budget for more exciting things, like a two-week vacation to Costa Rica in February when all your friends with cars are miserable and can't get them started from the cold, anyway. As a bonus to the parsimony, walking everywhere helps keep off those pounds that start accumulating on our backsides the deeper we plow into our 20s.

A big expense for many of us is eating out, which technically should be labeled an entertainment, since sipping a latte and nibbling on a scone in a trendy café near the office is more flirtatious and exciting than slugging a cup of home brew over a bowl of Quaker Oats. But such morning excursions can add up, especially when we're buying lunch as well, which we do because a tomato, basil, mozzarella on focaccia at the nearby Italian bistro is far more delicious and engaging than the depressing pasta leftovers we could otherwise heat up in the office microwave and eat at our desk alone. Grabbing dinner with our friends after work should also be categorized as entertainment, since, let's face it, the purpose is postwork social relief and to appease the starvation that hits us like a Mack truck the second we step outside of the office, rather than about satisfying our nutritional needs, which we could do more cheaply with sautéed vegetables, beans, and couscous from the local grocery store.

While we should never completely deprive ourselves of these culinary excursions—how else are we going to exchange suggestive glances with cute men in suits sitting at the tables next to ours or get to know our coworkers outside of the office?—we should limit them to once a week each (if the budget allows even that). They *are*, after all, an entertainment, though one could convincingly argue that they help prevent depression induced by the heinous pressures of work. My advice is to spread them out, but think moderation.

And while we're on the subject of entertainment, let's probe a little deeper into that expensive beast.

THE PRICE OF FUN

Once you've set your budget and determined how much you can spend on entertainment and frivolous purchases each month, divide by four, and withdraw that amount each week from your ATM. If you're like many of us, that amount will add up to no more than a depressing $20 a week, which is why so many of us get into such horrendous debt in our young adulthood. But don't despair. You *can* enjoy life with this frighteningly paltry amount (until you manage to either make more money or drastically reduce your living expenses) if you are very, very careful about the way you spend it.

I've lived off such low entertainment funds during certain periods throughout my 20s (including the eight months it's taken to write this book!), and all the while, I've lived in two of the most expensive cities in the country—Manhattan and San Francisco. So, trust me, you can do it too, *and still enjoy youthful bliss.* Just be prepared for a few jabs to your mental health along the way, because you will occasionally feel deprived, depressed, and angry about your situation, no matter how much you tell yourself that you're living this way because of choices you've made.

If you plan to treat these emotional daggers not as proof that all universal forces are out to make you miserable, but as goads to making some changes that will improve your financial distress, they're not so bad. Then, pretend you're the starving-artist type living a glamorous and romantic lifestyle that everyone else envies, and ruminate over the following suggestions for entertaining yourself when your pockets are full of nothing but used bus ticket stubs.

Dining Out

The restaurant scene is one of our biggest entertainment expenses, but it's also one of our most popular forms of fun for several reasons: (1) Most of us don't know how to cook anything more challenging than pasta, which gets old quickly; (2) If we know how to cook, we're too exhausted at the end of the day to make the effort; and (3) Food always tastes better when we're out at a trendy spot with engaging friends, live music, and flirty waiters popping up every now and then just to see how we're doing. If you limit yourself to one dinner out each week, as I suggested in the last section, you will find yourself turning down lots of invitations to get together with friends, especially those who don't share your current frugal leanings. To avoid this fate, be prepared to suggest a few low-budget alternatives for getting together, such as going for a postwork walk, which is free, or doing the cheaper version of Friday-night dinner and movie—Saturday-afternoon lunch and a matinee.

Diane, 27, of Chicago, is always blunt with her friends when she can't afford to splurge on dinner: "I'll either suggest we do something else or meet up with everyone afterwards for drinks and enjoy only half the night with them." Sandra, 29, of Indianapolis, and her friends take turn cooking for each other as an alternative to eating out. Abbie suggests applying the home-cooked dining experience to brunch, as well: "Sometimes I'll have friends meet at my house on weekend mornings. Either they'll bring something for everyone or we'll go to the store together and get what we need to make breakfast. It's an inexpensive way to spend time with each other. Afterward, we can go on a walk or bike ride or just hang out."

When you do go out, an option is dining at the bar. My friends and I often hit restaurants that we want to try and order drinks and appetizers at the bar instead of a whole meal at a table. Doing so gives you a less expensive sampling of the food as well as a taste of the atmosphere. Plus, if your friend happens to be a knockout like my friend Nicole, you'll get freebies from the kitchen from gaping bartenders who are trying to woo her.

Also, you can economize by asking a bunch of your friends at once, suggests Bethany, 26, of San Francisco. This way, you can see the whole gang in one weekly happy-hour swoop, rather than going out with each one individually, which gets pricey for those of us on tight budgets. And don't feel bad about suggesting cheaper-than-trendy places to meet up (hole-in-the-wall ethnic restaurants sometimes have the most interesting food, anyway).

Other Venues of Entertainment

We must ward off an unending slew of threats to our bank accounts when we're young and single, since we have so much energy and (relative to our future lives) free time to enjoy all the fruits of life. We are assailed by concerts, clubs, performances, sports and fitness-related events, promising parties that, of course, charge cover unless you can convince them that you're from the local model agency and were told you were on the guest list, which works once a decade. And then there is the biggest temptation of all: travel.

Luckily, most large cities are sensitive to our moneyless existence, especially if we live near a college or university. Scout around town for fun that satisfies your cravings for stimulation but won't put you in massive debt that you'll be paying back until your mid 30s. You'll likely stumble onto free concerts in the park, discount nights at the movies, dollar martinis between 5 and 8 P.M. at the local dive, free admission to clubs before 10 P.M., standing-room-only tickets to the theater/opera/ symphony (or you can volunteer as an usher and watch performances gratis), book readings, and free or half-price days at the museum, to name a few attractions. Granted, it's a pain to schedule your life around cheap alternatives to entertainment, but it's a much bigger pain getting out of credit card debt. Take it from those of us who are slowly digging.

That said, there are certain entertainment experiences that I think are worth getting into debt. Financial advisers may heartily disagree, but I believe that traveling is so important during our 20s, and so vital to our adult development, that we should do it even if it will put us in debt for a year. As I stated in Chapter 8, traveling outside of our familiar zone (not to Club Med in Florida) is one of the best ways to figure out who we are and what we believe in, which are major aspects of becoming women and making good decisions. Besides, our workloads and famil- ial obligations will only get more hectic the older we grow, so consider travel an investment and "Charge it!"

Caution: If that trip to South America is going to spawn a flurry of creditors calling you day and night, resort to other means, such as taking a part-time job on top of your nine-to-five, and saving up for the trip the old-fashioned way. Then, travel in the most minimalistic way you can imagine. If foreign ventures are absolutely out of the question because you're afraid of planes, boats, or long train rides, look into local—but challenging—travel opportunities that don't cost so much, like camping in unknown territory.

Shopping

The ironic and painful thing about shopping is that we need so much when we're starting out (and "starting out" lasts the whole damn decade, in case you're wondering). If, according to our budget, our entertainment fund allows only $20 a week, there's no way we can buy anything more exciting each month than a semirusted pepper grinder that's trying to pass as an antique at a garage sale. And even those little purchases should be carefully watched, because they all add up and can deplete your spending cash faster than you can say, "Do you take AMEX?"

Then there's the whole topic of clothes, which we *have* to buy for work and for going out, since the sweats and T-shirts from our college days won't get us a promotion or into the nightclub everyone is raving about. Going into debt is unavoidable in some cases when it comes to getting a few things we need, such as a new pair of running shoes when our old ones are so soleless that they're giving us knee problems. And it may not always be a bad idea if what you charge is on sale and can be paid off before the interest begins to accrue (otherwise, the sale factor is worthless, since you'll probably pay more in interest than the original price if you let the balance sit on your card).

Since shopping is one of the biggest threats to overspending, there are three questions you should ask before every purchase: "Do I really need it or just want it?"; "Can I find it cheaper elsewhere?"; and "How long will it last?" If you *really* need it, you can't find a better deal anywhere else (and you *have* looked), and the item will last you for at least the next three years, then go ahead and charge it. And don't feel guilty. The only exception, as in the case of travel, is if you're in a credit card crisis. Here it's better to beg your parents for a handout than give future creditors reason to harass.

MONEY ETIQUETTE

Financial disparity within our circle of friends and acquaintances is probably nothing new as you step into adulthood. Most of us got a good taste of it growing up or while in school, where all sorts of socioeconomic backgrounds share the same awful choices at the cafeteria. But economic inequality sometimes has a more painful sting when we're out on our own, working two jobs to make ends meet and pay back those student loans, while some of our friends are making plush salaries and getting regular cash supplements on the side from their folks. Not that

Annie and Nicole's Wardrobe Tips

Because clothing is one of our biggest expenditures, I asked two of the hippest-dressed women I know—Annie, 25, a clothing designer in New York, and Nicole, 27, who works in advertising—for the scoop on their wardrobes (and they don't have exorbitant budgets to work with, either). In a nutshell: Find a pair or two of standard but *really* flattering pants (cost is no object on these as long as they are made of quality material, because you will be wearing them so often), and build on these with cheaper, funkier, more playful shirts, jackets, and accessories. Here are a few specific details, from toe to head:

Shoes

The soul of a great wardrobe is the shoes. Up-to-the-minute shoes can add character to an otherwise boring outfit. Get at least one well-made standard pair that goes with everything—skirts, pants, or going-out outfits. When you can splurge, get a couple of funkier, artistic pairs for fun. Plan to spend a little money on your shoes, since you'll be wearing them all the time.

Pants

When it comes to pants, fit is foremost. Don't fall for trends that flatter only certain types of bodies. Save the trendy stuff for shirts or accessories, and make sure the pants show off your most flattering features. Stick to basic colors that will be easy to add other items to—black, charcoal gray, or khaki—and choose materials such as cotton, wool, or that blended stretchy spandex/Lycra stuff, which is great for daytime and for going out at night. Also, every wardrobe needs a pair of really comfortable jeans; try on as many different styles as necessary to find a pair that works with your body.

Shirts

Those with limited funds can go a little wild with shirts. We can usually find cheap fun shirts and jazzy tops that are perfect for nighttime escapades by browsing knockoff stores and vintage clothing shops. Think variety when it comes to shirts (especially if you really are wearing the same pants all the time). Look for long-sleeved, short-sleeved, tank, mock turtleneck, and tube tops with bright colors, patterns, and stripes. Go for stretchy fabrics that show off your form in full glory. If you must wear suits to work, you can jazz up your conservative shell with a playful, sexy top that can be shown off outside the office doors during postwork drinks with friends.

Skirts and Dresses

If you're a skirt girl, buy your skirts as you would pants, thinking fit, versatility, and quality material and construction. If you're into keeping up with seasonal length changes, buy cheap versions at knockoff stores, and wear them as long as they're in vogue. Every wardrobe needs an all-purpose cocktail dress, but these are often funner if you can find a retro party dress in flawless shape at a vintage clothing store.

Sweaters

If you're on a tight budget, stay with basic colors (white, charcoal gray, or black) and fabrics (cotton or wool), and shop for more exciting styles and exotic materials when the cash flow is a little more fluid.

Outerwear

Jackets and coats will help you pull your look together when your clothing funds are stretched more than spandex. A funky coat, for instance, can add life to an otherwise boring outfit. Shop for these at vintage clothing stores, but purchase only if they're in mint condition; otherwise don't bother—you'll look frumpy.

Accessories

Vintage stores, again, are great sources for a few accessories that can add life to a minimalist wardrobe. Beaded, embroidered, or fringed handbags, scarves, jewelry, belts, or something wildly playful, like Nicole's red llama-fur boa, are perfect for occasions that call for extra dazzle.

we'd want their jobs (or their parents, for that matter), but the financial divide can't help but seem grossly unjust.

If you muse over this inequality too long, it will only fuel the resentment you already feel about your sordid financial situation. The first rule of money etiquette, thus, is to withdraw your nose from your friends' financial affairs (don't spend even a minute trying to figure out how they can afford those multiannual trips abroad and that brand new Pathfinder, because such ruminations will drive you crazy and are pointless anyway). Instead, point yourself in the direction of your own monetary reality, making improvements whenever and wherever you can.

The second rule of money etiquette is to devise ways of finessing certain money-related incidences that are bound to arise as you and your friends frolic through your 20s. One of the more common is figuring out how to play together when everyone has different entertainment budgets to work with. Open and honest communication about what you can and can't afford is the first step. If you're clear about your financial limits and you reciprocate with your friends in ways that satisfy everyone involved, you can avoid lots of tension, which money has a nasty habit of brewing. Likewise, you must accept (without judgment or questioning) your friends' monetary restraints and expenditures. If your closest friend suddenly can't go out every weekend because she's saving for a trip to Thailand where she plans to meditate with Buddhist monks for 10 days without speaking or eating, you've got to respect her decision—even if you can't understand her sudden spiritual awakening. Then, come up with some compromises that can keep all of your friends happy and nonstressed. Spend a Saturday taking a hike in the woods instead of meeting for brunch and then going shopping, which is miserable temptation for those who don't have the funds to participate.

Another uncomfortable scene that you may observe is dining out when everyone involved has different budgets (and appetites). After finishing off a tasty meal with a group of friends or acquaintances, we come face to face with The Bill anxiety, in which half of the group adheres to the "It all comes out in the wash" principle, preferring to divide the check equally, and the other half (who ordered only salad and water) wants to pay per order. Obviously, it's important to be sensitive to those who ordered much less than the rest of the group, since there's always a reason they did—and it's not that they prefer salad and water to grilled salmon with dinosaur kale and mango salsa. One 26-year-old woman with whom I discussed the matter handles such situations like this: "My friends who can only pay for what they ordered always put in their share, with tax and tip, first. Then the rest of us split the remainder equally."

A final source of concern regarding money-related etiquette that we'll tackle here is our parents. Three money shifts typically occur with our folks during our 20s. The most obvious is that they stop supporting us, which may enable us to get to know them more as equal adults instead of as parents who hold the purse strings. A related (and often bizarre) phenomenon is that many of us begin to pay our share when we get together with them for dining or vacations. This magnifies the shift in our evolving relationship. The third change is that if we need to ask to borrow money when we're in a pinch, we're likely to feel more shame and guilt about it than we did in college, when we had the excuse and comfort of knowing that everyone else was begging for handouts from their parents, too.

If you find yourself groveling for a few extra bucks from your parents now and then, make every effort to pay them back as soon as you can, advises Bethany. "Respect that they may be trying to save for retirement or go on vacation," she says. She further advises when you make your appeal, don't mention your recent expenditures during the same conversation. In her case, she warns: "I once made the mistake of telling my parents that I was so broke that I needed to borrow from them, and then mentioned later on that I had just been shopping and got a new pair of shoes." Oops.

GETTING OUT OF DEBT (AND STAYING OUT)

I'm going to make the bold assumption that you have incurred a little debt during your great entrance into adulthood, from either student loans, devilish credit cards, or that car loan you recently signed with its 36 easy installment payments. If you haven't tasted debt, you are abnormally perfect and un-American and can just skip on down to the next section on retirement planning and chill out until the rest of us catch up with you.

Some debt, such as student loans, is money well borrowed and an investment in your future. Because of their relatively low interest rates, manageable (though seemingly eternal) repayment plans, and reasonable deferment options, student loans should not be the source of midnight panic attacks during your second semester of senior year, even if you've incurred thousands and thousands of dollars to fund your education and still don't have a job that suggests that all the debt was worth it. If you haven't graduated yet, toward the end of your final semester, your college student loan officer will give you all the dirty details of your repayment schedule (hopefully armed with ample tissue for the tears that are certain to flood your contacts), as well as tell you how to defer paying back your loans if you aren't employed by the time your repayment grace period is up, as was my case. The cheery thing I discovered about deferring repayment is that the groovy government actually paid the interest I owed during my six-month deferment. That's not the case with all student loans, but you'll find that out when you start reading the fine print.

If you're like me, you may have several loans to repay. Again, you probably got (or will get) the skinny from your financial aid administrator at college, but in case he or she is on drugs, I'll summarize. There are a few consolidation plans that can make the whole process of paying back your loans less horrifying. Consolidating means that you will be able to merge all of your loans into one giant superloan that offers a low interest rate, as well as various options for shortening or lengthening your repayment schedule (which will increase or decrease the amount you owe each month, thereby increasing or decreasing the amount of interest you ultimately end up paying). But the best reason to consolidate your loans is that you will receive only one bill every month, which means you have to think and stress about all the student loan money you owe only once every 30 days! I highly recommend consolidation, if only for that.

If you have several loans from one financial institution, contact your lender directly about its consolidation options, or try these two programs: Federal Direct Consolidation Loan Program (800-557-7392; www.ed.gov/directloan) and Student Loan Marketing Association (a.k.a. Sallie Mae) Smart Loan Account (800-524-9100; www.salliemae.com).

Student loans are much less threatening and guilt-provoking than credit card debt, to which we 20-somethings are painfully vulnerable. There are so many things we want and need. Credit card companies seize upon our vulnerability, especially during college, sending us application after application with such enticing incentives as a *free water bottle, a two-pound bag of M&Ms, a 10% discount* on first purchases, *free checks* to spend anywhere we please, our very own *head shot* on the card, a *4.9% introductory interest rate*, and *bonus airline miles*. My first advice on the whole matter of credit card debt is to avoid it like the devil! I know many honest, smart girls who've become submerged in debt through the seductive power of plastic.

Our society once thrived without credit, so it *is* possible to stay out of debt as we begin our adult lives. But since you will probably experiment with credit despite the danger, memorize these eight guidelines compliments of those who've battled the plastic demons:

#1: No Department Store Credit Cards

In-store credit usually carries a much higher interest rate than credit cards issued by banks. If you don't pay your debt back right away, what you buy is going to cost you much more than you bargained for. The only exception is if you have money to pay off your debt as soon as the bill arrives, and signing up for a card gives you a substantial discount on your first purchase. In these cases, get the card (and discount), pay your bill in full, and immediately cancel the card and shred it into a million pieces, lest you be tempted to use it again without the discount and money to pay for it. Note: If the discount isn't more than $10 or 20, don't even bother, because when you sign on, you'll probably get put on some annoying direct-mail list that will be sold to a bunch of trashy companies who will send you junk mail every single day.

#2: One Card Only

The fewer little plastic rectangles you have, the less you'll be tempted to live beyond your meager means (and the fewer hysteria-provoking bills you'll receive). Ideally, you should use your card only for items that you know you can pay off with your next paycheck or for unavoidable emergencies, like getting new brakes for your clunker or fillings for your insatiable sweet tooth. The ideal cards have fixed annual percentage rates ranging from 9 to 12 percent, or less if you can find them, no annual fee, and a grace period that doesn't start charging interest on what you buy until the bill's due date. If you are a conscientious customer, you will be inundated with appealing offers for new cards boasting Platinum status and $25,000 credit lines. When you receive these, gingerly toss them into the recycling bin. Opening them will only lead you into trouble. There is one exception to this rule, but I'll get to that when we talk about transferring balances. First, a few more basic tips.

#3: Use Your ATM Credit/Debit Card Instead

If you're diligent about balancing your checkbook, there's no reason to fear the credit card capabilities of your ATM card, which most banks are offering these days. Keep the receipt for whatever you purchase with your card as you would had you withdrawn money from the bank, and record the amount in your checkbook ledger as you would a check. Your debit card is just as convenient as a credit card, but your purchase won't accrue interest, which will save you money. Definitely use your debit card instead of a real credit card when grocery shopping or buying little things at the pharmacy, unless you like the idea of paying 18 percent interest on cereal and tampons. Trust your elders: the interest on all the little things makes them as costly as a raging girl's night out.

#4: Pay Back as Much as You Can, as Soon as You Can

If we take the *minimum* payment request on our monthly statements to heart, we may not pay off our account in full until we qualify for social security. That's because interest continues to accrue on our balance each month. If we don't pay off everything we owe, the remainder plus the interest we've amassed will be charged interest the following month, and the month after that, which means our balance continues to grow at the speed of our card's annual percentage rate (APR) despite the fact that we pay our minimum due every month and have hidden our credit card in the closet under five shoe boxes. That's how credit card companies make so much money and why we should avoid getting into debt in every humanly possible (but legal) way.

If you have debt from several sources, pay back whatever has higher interest rates first—usually your credit cards—then tackle the typically lower-rated student loan and car loan debts. If your credit card debt is spiraling out of control, you could refinance your student or car loans so that you will owe less on them each month, using the extra money to pay off your credit cards. Then, when your costlier debts have been paid off (and cards dumped in the nearest incinerator), you can designate all your funds to paying back your temporarily neglected student and car loans as quickly as you can.

#5: Trash Those Credit Card Checks That Come with Your Statement, and Shun Cash Advances from the ATM

Both checks and cash advances will cost you dearly, since many card companies tack on an additional finance charge to your bill when you use them, plus impose an interest rate for the amount you borrow that's much higher than the rate you have for normal purchases. That means that if you withdraw $100 from your card at a bank or ATM or use one of those checks for your rent, you'll be paying back your credit card company a lot more than the amount you borrowed.

#6: Switch to a Card with a Lower Interest Rate

I said earlier that you should throw away offers for additional credit cards, and that is a good rule unless you are carrying a balance on a card (or cards) with an outrageous interest rate, say more than 12 percent. In that case, it's a good financial move to transfer your balance(s) to one card with the lowest rate you can find. Some offer temporary introductory interest rates as low as 2.9 percent on all transferred balances;

when you apply, make sure you note the expiration date for those low rates on your calendar, and have another card offer lined up and ready to take on the load when the time comes. I know this sounds tedious, but careful organization and diligence will save you money as you attempt to pay the whole balance off.

If you play credit card musical chairs, keep three things in mind. First, some balance transfer offers have associated fees or finance charges that aren't exactly highlighted in their promotions. Always inquire about transfer fees, and try to talk them out of it; many issuers are willing to waive the fees upon request. Second, even after you transfer your balance in full, the account remains open. To close it, you must officially cancel. The issuing bank won't automatically cancel a zero-balance account, so if you don't, your access to that credit line will remain on your credit report. That could be problematic later on when you're applying for a mortgage and have thousands of dollars worth of potential debt in your financial profile—something that makes lenders skittish. The other reason to cancel is to avoid the temptation to start using that clean slate of credit that your old card suddenly presents. And the third caveat: when you transfer your balance, do not use this new card to purchase new things. Declare it a debt repayment card only, and stick that shiny piece of plastic in the file where you keep your monthly statements. Here's why:

When you charge new items on a card that has adopted old debt, many card issuers apply a different (and uber-exorbitant) interest rate to those new purchases. The higher interest rate will remain on the amount of your new purchases until your entire debt has been repaid. Therefore, when you are trying to pay off a large debt, you should try to have two credit cards—one with a very low balance-transfer interest rate for your main debt, and another with a reasonable interest rate on new purchases that you will use for emergencies only, since you are, after all, trying to get out of the hole, not rack up new debt. A good resource for finding low-rate, no-fee cards is a company called CardWeb.com, Inc., which publishes a newsletter called CardTrak that lists these desirable cards. You can access the newsletter and other credit card consumer information on its website (www.cardweb.com) or by calling (800) 344-7714.

#7: Apply for a Secured Credit Card if Your Credit Is Screwed

If you have damaged your credit rating by defaulting on a loan or debt, your main priority (besides coming up with a repayment plan that suits all your creditors) is to rebuild your credit. Secured credit cards can help. You give the issuer a certain sum of money up front, which is kept in an account for you as a security deposit. Depending on the terms of your agreement, you can then charge a specified amount on that card. Once you've proved that you can repay your debts in this secured way, you may be offered a new card with real credit that doesn't require you to put up money ahead of time. CardWeb.com, Inc. (cited in the previous entry) can provide a list of secured credit cards as well as low-rate, no-fee cards.

If you are in a bad situation and creditors are calling you about monster debt that you can't currently pay off, don't pack up and move to North Dakota, thinking creditors won't be able to find you—they will. A couple of nonprofit credit counseling organizations can help with debt-repayment planning assistance: Consumer Credit Counseling Services, associated with the National Foundation for Consumer Credit (800-388-2227; www.nfcc.org), and Debt Counselors of America (800-680-3328; www.dca.org).

#8: Check Your Credit Report

I've already expounded on why a clean credit report is so important, so I won't beat that dead horse, but I will add that it's wise to check up on your report every now and then to make sure there are no surprises (or mistakes) that need mending. There are three agencies that compile credit reports, and they all get their information separately, so what one company says is part of your credit history may differ from what another company includes. You can get copies of your credit report from each company for $8 or less, depending on your state of residence. If you have had bad credit in the past but believe you've been exonerated (usually after seven years), you should make sure all three companies are showing you in the proper light.

The three agencies keeping tabs are: Experian (formerly TRW) (888-397-3742; www.experian.com/ecommerce/consumercredit.html); Equifax (800-997-2493; www.equifax.com/econsumer/pgConsumer-Products.html); and Trans Union (800-888-4213; www.transunion.com /CreditReport/).

Go-Girl Guidance *If you have several debts from different places, organization is the only way you'll survive the avalanche of monthly bills. Bethany, 26, of San Francisco, offers this solution: "Call all the companies that send you bills and ask them to adjust your billing cycle, so that all the payment requests don't come at once. Most companies have a couple of billing cycles and are willing to do that. I've coordinated mine so that two of my bills come at the first of the month, and I can pay them and my rent with my first paycheck, and two bigger bills come after the 15th, which I can take care of with my second paycheck."*

SAVING FOR RETIREMENT

The cruelest and most alarming financial factoid for those of us getting our toenails wet in adulthood is that everyone—financial gurus, the government, bosses, parents, older siblings, and financially savvy friends—is harassing us to start a retirement plan *now*!!! It is most depressing to set aside money we won't see again for 45-plus years or so when we can barely afford food, clothing, shelter, and those mandatory sanity-preserving entertainment splurges on our next-to-nothing salaries. I don't want to add depression to your money-related panic attacks, but I will say that I regret that I didn't start an official retirement savings plan the minute I was eligible.

Three reasons to do it: (1) The earlier we start contributing, the more money we make over the long haul, because our earnings (interest, dividends, and capital gains) get folded back into the pot and continue to grow along with the money we to add our plan every year. (2) There's something sexy about watching your money practically double in one year without working overtime or taking on freelance assignments. (3) When money is taken out of your paycheck before you ever see it, you really don't miss it; what happens is that you end up going out to dinner a few times less each month. That's why I, too, am going to harass you to start saving for your future, if you've been remiss, by filtering a portion of your salary into your company-sponsored 401(k) plan or, if your company doesn't offer that retirement benefit or an equivalent, to set up an individual retirement account (IRA) through a traditional broker, an on-line broker, a mutual fund company, or a bank.

Let's discuss what these plans are all about, why we need them, and which excuses for putting the whole thing off for a while aren't going to cut it.

What Is a Retirement Savings Plan?

The most common plans are 401(k)s, which are administered through an employer, and IRAs, which we can open up on our own at various financial institutions. We can then invest the money funneled into these plans in the stock market, with the idea of making our money grow faster than inflation and (hopefully) so steadfastly that we will be millionairettes by the time we're ready to retire. Retirement savings plans offer specific tax benefits, which is why we want them instead of investing our money outside of one or just sticking any extra cash we may have in a traditional savings account.

Without going into too much detail, the tax benefits are twofold. One, we don't have to pay income tax on the money we contribute to a 401(k) plan; likewise, we can deduct our yearly contribution to a qualifying IRA. Either tactic helps reduce our overall annual taxes. And two, we don't have to pay tax on the money our investments earn until we retire and start withdrawing from them. The theory holds that when we retire and are no longer earning high incomes from work, we will fall into a lower tax bracket, so the money we withdraw from our retirement savings will be taxed at a lower rate than it would had we paid taxes on our investment earnings along the way. Any way you look at it, we get to pocket more of our money if it's invested in these tax-sheltered retirement plans.

Why Do We Need to Start These Plans Now?

Aside from the tax benefits, there are, again, three reasons why we need to start a retirement savings plan in our 20s. The first is that the earlier we start investing, the more our money grows. The second has to do with inflation, which our money wouldn't be able to keep up with if it were imprisoned in a low-interest-earning bank account. If we don't invest our money aggressively in stocks with the goal of beating inflation, the money will gradually lose its value. In other words, $1,000 today may buy us a pretty sufficient fall wardrobe, but in 40 years, the same amount may barely cover a new pair of leather boots, which is a horrible thought so let's move on.

The third way these plans impinge on our future financial fitness concerns something we've all heard a lot about lately: social (in)security—and I'm not talking about party jitters. The latest government studies predict that our federally administered retirement system will run out of funds around the year 2034, which, as chance would have it, is right around the time many of us will start taking the initial steps to retire. Unless the system gets a radical overhaul, we probably won't receive much in the way of a personal payoff for all the money we've contributed to the social security program, since the taxes we pay into that fund now all go toward supporting the current generation of retirees, which is growing much more quickly than the workforce. This all means that in order to ensure that we can spend our retirement years taking painting classes at the local senior citizens center, while sending birthday and holiday checks to our grandchildren—who will no doubt be adorable, despite the fact that they'll probably snicker at our aged ankle tattoos—we must establish our own sources of retirement income.

Note: Just in case the government conjures up a way to fix our nation's social security crisis, it's wise to check up every now and then with the Social Security Administration to make sure everyone involved agrees upon how much money we've contributed, because that's partially how they calculate the amount we're due when we retire. Contact the agency to request a free copy of your Personal Earnings and Benefit Estimate Statement (PEBES): (800) 772-1213; www.ssa.gov.

Which Excuses Won't Work?

Here are a few common crocks, most of which I used during my first two years of employment, when I scoffed at the idea of setting aside money for retirement:

"I CAN BARELY LIVE ON MY MEASLY SALARY AS IT IS!"

I have no doubt this is true, but I also have confidence that you can find ways to minimize your living expenses or make extra money so that you're able to stash up to 15 percent of your earnings in a 401(k) or an IRA. If you must wait until you get your first raise, do so—that's how I eventually started my 401(k)—but commit to a retirement fund when the raise comes. If you can't contribute the maximum percentage that your company allows in your 401(k) or the maximum $2,000 per year to an IRA, put in as much as you can, especially if you're enrolled in a 401(k) plan in which your employer matches a percentage of what you contribute. In those cases, put in at least as much as your employer matches, because this is *free money*, girlfriend, and you're a fool if you don't take advantage of it! (I can say this, having been a former fool so consumed with 20-something money inertia that I didn't recognize a good deal when it was practically doing flip-flops in front of me for attention.)

"I HAVEN'T GOT A CLUE HOW TO INVEST MY MONEY!"

That's OK; neither do the rest of us who are already invested in the market and making a steady return. All you need to know are three investment strategies, which I'll get to in just a minute, and a basic understanding of the three types of investments available: stocks (shares of companies), which offer the highest potential return and, consequently, the greatest risk for losing money; bonds, which carry less risk and offer less potential profit (we get these interest-earning IOUs when we lend a company or the government a certain amount of money for a specified amount of time); and cash investments, which are the least risky and least profitable type of investments. Included in this category are U.S. Treasury bills, certificates of deposit (CDs), in which we lend money to a bank with guaranteed payback plus interest, and other short-term money investments.

These three players are often pooled together in various combinations and themes by brokers and financial professionals—who are hip to the fact that many of us don't know what we are doing—to form mutual funds. The funds are managed by their creators and are arguably the best type of investments for those of us just testing the waters. To understand why, we now proceed to those three core investment strategies I promised to explain.

Strategy #1: Risk as much as you can stomach. Since we *are* investing for retirement, which is at least four decades away, we have some time to ride the market ups and downs. The bulk of our retirement savings, therefore, should be invested in stocks, which give the highest return (i.e., the most money) for long-haul investments.

Some financial planners suggest the following general formula for figuring out how much of our savings to allocate to high-return investments: Subtract your age from 100. The remaining number is the percentage of your account that should be allocated to higher-risk investments, say, a combination of stock mutual funds that includes stocks from large and small companies, international stock funds (which invest in foreign markets), and index funds, which are composed of stocks that make up the various market-tracking indexes, such as the S&P 500 or Wilshire 5000. The rest of our retirement savings (a percentage equal to your age) should be invested in safer territory, such as taxable bonds or bond mutual funds (since tax-free bonds would be a waste in our tax-free retirement plan), or cash investments.

This may all sound confusing right now, but the more you read about investing, the more it all sinks in. The "Go-Girl Resources" section lists several books that can be a great help when you're ready to uncover all the intricacies of the market. For now, just remember that the 20s is the most opportune decade for us to take big risks in every respect, but especially when it comes to money.

Strategy #2: Diversify. Put your money in several different investments instead of just one. That way, if one company in which you've invested does poorly one year, the others in your account will hopefully balance out your loss. Or, if the whole stock market takes a dive, your safer investments in bonds and cash will help keep your entire retirement plan from looking completely worthless until the market straightens itself out. Diversification helps cut the risk we face when we invest the majority of our money in aggressive growth stocks, so it's very important for keeping our 20-something guerrilla portfolios balanced.

For those of us just getting our feet wet, the only investment vehicle we really need is either a balanced fund or an asset allocation fund, both of which include a mix of stocks, bonds, and cash investments. With this type of investment, we don't have to do any of the diversification calculating ourselves. Also, since we probably don't have much money in our accounts yet, we want to keep as much of it as possible in the same fund for maximum return; these funds are a good solution, since they incorporate both risk and variety. Index funds are other good tools for diversification, because they allow us to invest in many different companies.

Strategy #3: Don't Freak Out When the Market Is Down. Unless you're a financial guru or a wizard mathematician, you're better off bearing with the bad times, keeping your investment dollars snug in their investments, than doing what feels more natural—selling your stocks and funds the minute the market takes a downward turn. "There are no tricks to beating the market. You've got to keep your investments for a long time to make significant earnings," says financial planner Eileen Dorsey, C.F.P., author of *Lifetime Strategies: How to Achieve Your Financial Goals.* "If you keep selling your investments when prices fall, your money will never grow. It's better to ride out the fluctuations." After all, if the whole market is spiraling downward, your investment clairvoyance is clearly not the issue. Something in the economy is just inhibiting other investors from wanting your stocks, making them less desirable for the moment and driving their value down. So, when the market drops, try to look at it as a sign from the broker gods that it's a good time to invest rather than sell, because you'll get a deal. If, however, your particular investments are stagnant while everything else in the market seems to be on holiday in Pamplona, you might want to investigate why your investments aren't also running with the bulls. For instance, maybe your mutual fund got a new manager named Bubba who's better at picking his nose than stocks, or the company whose stock you own was busted for some subversive sex scandal and must direct all current and future profits into an enormous legal fund that will ultimately devastate the company's worth. Either way, you should probably sell. If nothing with your investments seems to be amiss, but 12 to 18 months go by and they still pale in comparison with the rest of the market, you should probably consider selling as well. Then, reinvest immediately in more promising stock.

"I HAVE SO MUCH DEBT RIGHT NOW!"

If you're hiding from creditors, you should pay what you owe in credit card debt and loans that you may have accumulated. But if all you have is student loan debt, you'll make out better in the long run if you refinance your loans, meaning you stretch out the time in which your loans must be paid in full, thereby reducing your monthly payments. That will liberate extra money to invest in your 401(k) or IRA. The reason this is a financially wise move, as counterintuitive as it sounds, is that the interest you earn from your investments will most likely overcompensate for the extra interest you'll end up paying on your student loans, which have exceptionally low rates to begin with. In the end, you'll make more money. Then, when you get a better-paying job or a substantial raise (not that end-of-year-cost-of-living-increase B.S.), you can go back to making higher student loan repayments. You may even be able to pay off the balance within the original time frame and save yourself that extra interest.

"MY COMPANY DOESN'T HAVE A 401(K) PLAN," OR "I WORK FREELANCE AND DON'T HAVE THE 401(K) OPTION (NOT TO MENTION HEALTH CARE!)."

Sorry, the no-401(k) excuses don't work either. IRAs proliferate everywhere you look—at banks, on the Internet through on-line brokers, at mutual fund companies, at discount and full-service brokerages—and there are massive amounts of readable literature on how to sign up. Traditional IRAs offer the same tax benefits as 401(k)s, because you can deduct what you contribute every year (there's a $2,000 maximum on most IRAS, but better options are available for self-employed people who can afford to put in more), and you don't have to pay taxes on your earnings until you retire and begin to withdraw from your pot.

One of the benefits to having an IRA is that you usually have more choice on what to invest in, since companies typically limit 401(k) investment options. Actually, having personally participated in both a 401(k) plan and an IRA, I can attest that the "more choice" aspect is more of a stress point than a benefit when you don't really understand what you're investing in anyway, but you'll eventually get the hang of the whole thing. Another downside is that no one's going to match your IRA contribution. That (and health care) is the price we freelancers must pay for getting to ditch work and head to the beach whenever we please (unless we are writing our first book, in which case, we won't see the sun or beach for eight months unless our concerned boyfriend begs us to take a break because we're beginning to look mildly deranged and our nightly lavender oil moisturizing bath isn't helping anymore).

When opening an IRA, be choosy about who administers it. Many brokerages require rather large initial investments and have unseemly commissions with each and every trade you request. Banks, though convenient, often lack a wide variety of funds to choose from. Your best bet is to look for an on-line discount broker or mutual fund company that doesn't require thousands of dollars to open an account and offers a good selection of no-load mutual funds, which means they don't charge commission every time you want to add money to your chosen fund(s). Brokering your own trades on-line also costs you significantly less in commission fees; so, if you want to put your money in mutual funds that happen to come with loads (commission fees), those are best purchased over the Net.

I do all my trading on-line; it's easy, it's secured, and it makes you feel really really cool. Give it a shot when you're ready to make a move. Many of the money magazines list on-line discount brokerages and mutual fund companies, so you can check with one of them to get some ideas on whom to call. Or go on-line and do a search for "brokerages," which'll give you hours worth of brokerages with Internet capabilities to investigate.

"I'M PROBABLY QUITTING SOON ANYWAY. I'LL START A 401(K) AT MY NEXT JOB."

I clung to the mañana excuse for a couple of years. In actuality, it may take a long time to find a new job, depending on your job-seeking karma and skills. Don't put your retirement fund on hold, because you could be getting employer matching funds *while* you're looking for that great new job. You can always roll over your 401(k) to a new company, if that company's policy allows, or to an IRA, which is what I did when I quit my editing job to become a freelancer.

The process is painless, and your company's 401(k) administrating people can walk you through everything you need to know. The most important thing to remember here is to request a *direct* rollover. This means you have the money in your 401(k) sent directly into your new IRA (which you have to open ahead of time). What you don't want is to withdraw the money from your 401(k), because you will be taxed on it *and* have to pay a 10 percent penalty to the government for cashing in your fund before you retire.

With rollovers, also be aware that in some cases, depending on the plan, you may not be entitled to some or all of the company-matched funds. This entitlement is called "vesting," and many companies require you to work for them a certain amount of time before you are vested, at which point you have full ownership of the funds they've matched and placed in your account. Ergo, before you think about quitting, check out your company's vesting schedule, and hang around a few months longer if that's all it takes to claim the extra loot.

If for no other reason, start a retirement savings plan for this motive alone: you will feel like a rock star when you get quarterly statements showing that your money has grown without your doing a single thing. Besides, if you start your retirement savings as everyone is telling you to, you will have one less thing to feel guilty about.

THE CRISIS FUND

According to most financial advisers, we should all have an emergency savings account that equals three to six months' worth of living expenses which we stash away in a forbidden zone, only to be dipped into during a crisis, such as sudden unemployment, unexpected medical bills, or the need to free your car from tow prison. If you're one to play life a little risky, however, you can hold off on setting up this safety net until you have achieved the more important financial goals of paying off your debts and starting a retirement fund. The reason it's OK to put this little fund on hold is that in dire situations, we can usually either borrow money from our parents (assuming they're able and willing) or withdraw the amount we need from our credit card account at the nearest bank. But if you have read the preceding section on credit cards, you know that the cash advance route is not advisable and should be taken only when all other resources have been tapped, since the associated finance charges and interest rates are typically out of control. That's why the experts pound away at financial discipline.

The key to starting an emergency savings pool is to open some type of savings account. If you don't, you'll never hold on to your money. Do this especially if having a savings account at your bank gives you free checking. If you're not a disciplined saver, consider forced savings. Many banks offer automatic savings plans for those of us who don't have a chunk of money with which to officially open a savings account. In these plans, a predetermined portion of your paycheck, say $50, is directly deposited to your savings account (if your employer is willing to participate) or automatically withdrawn from your checking account (on designated days that you're sure your paycheck will be there to supply the transfer.)

If your bank doesn't offer any type of automatic savings plan, try this trick that works for Mary, 25, of Washington, D.C.: "I treat my savings account like a bill that has to be paid. Every paycheck, I take 10 percent out and put it directly into savings." However you do it, for this savings tactic to work, you must vow never to touch your crisis fund unless an emergency arises.

Keep in mind that your emergency money does not necessarily need to languish in a low-interest-earning savings account. More lucrative than the traditional savings accounts are no-load money market mutual funds, which can be set up through many banks, mutual fund companies, and brokerages. Money market mutual funds are mutual funds composed of U.S. Treasury bills, CDs, and other short-term cash investments. Among financial advisers, these funds are considered just as safe as sticking our money in a traditional savings account, and in many cases, they are equally easy to dip into in the event of an emergency. The advantage is that these funds promise higher interest earnings than savings accounts or money market checking accounts that many banks offer. That means that tucked away in these funds, our money will be earning more while it sits and waits for an emergency to make its life meaningful.

If your bank offers money market mutual funds and you've saved enough for the initial investment requirements, consider moving your emergency savings into it, unless the old-fashioned savings account option gives you free checking. In that case, put the minimum amount in that account, and funnel the rest of your crisis contributions into the higher-earning money market mutual fund. Some banks offer automatic deposit or money transfers into these funds in the same way they do with savings accounts. If your bank doesn't offer money market mutual funds, you can start one up at a no-load mutual fund company. Some of these companies will let you set up an account with a low initial investment if you agree to contribute a fixed sum each month.

If you opt for the money market fund, bear in mind that the money you filter into this crisis fund should add up to only a few months worth of living expenses. Consult your budget on how much that should be, and don't reserve any more than that for a potential crisis. You can do many more fruitful things with extra cash on hand by investing in more aggressive (read: riskier) stock or index mutual funds.

If by chance you have money to play with after your debts have been paid, your retirement fund contributions are maxed out, and your emergency fund is sufficiently padded, you should think about other investment opportunities, which we will now briefly discuss.

INVESTING EXTRA $$$

If you're enrolled in a 401(k) and you make under a certain amount of money ($41,000 per year in 1999), you may be able to deduct some or all of an additional annual $2,000 contribution to an IRA that you open up on your own. If you make too much money to deduct your contributions, you can still open up a traditional IRA and defer paying taxes on your investment earnings until you retire and start dipping into your account. However, a better choice for you would be the Roth IRA. In this retirement fund, you *never* have to pay federal income taxes on your investments—even when you withdraw money from your account upon retirement. (Traditional IRAs, on the other hand, require you to pay taxes when you start dipping into the fund upon retiring.)

Other investment choices include tax-exempt bonds and short-term CDs, which are particularly helpful if you get a chunk of money and don't quite know what to do with it except hope to earn some interest for a few months until you figure that out. You can also try experimenting with more speculative investments such as penny stocks and junk bonds if you're a gambler at heart. Just remember, if you pick a winner and make some extra cash, you will have to pay capital gains taxes on your earnings. The Internal Revenue Service, it seems, wants its share of any successful gambling ventures outside of a retirement plan. And now that we're on the subject of taxes . . .

ONE FINAL TAXING MATTER

Taxes. I never hated them (or understood them, for that matter) until I became a freelance writer and suddenly had to pay huge chunks of money to the government four times a year. One very tiny perk of full-time employment is that you can, in theory, emotionally remove yourself from the whole concept of paying taxes until April 15. Then you file your annual tax return and figure out how much tax you have overpaid (in which case, you get a joyful little reimbursement check from the IRS) or underpaid, in which case you have to scrape up money from somewhere and send it to the Fed or else face a fine and interest on the money you owe.

The reason you don't have to do anything about taxes until April if you are employed and, more important, the reason your paycheck is so small, is that the company you work for sends the IRS a portion of what you owe in annual income taxes out of each paycheck you receive (or a close approximation of what you owe based on how many withholding allowances you claimed on your W-4 form and how much you are expected to earn at work that year). Those of us who are self-employed, on the other hand, must be self-disciplined and send in an estimate of the tax we owe every quarter, or else potentially face an underpayment penalty.

Pay attention to the number of allowances you claim on your W-4. These help you to figure out the tax deductions, exemptions, adjustments, and credits you're legally entitled to, which helps reduce the amount of taxes you must pay throughout the year. Review your W-4 whenever your financial situation changes, such as if you begin to take on more freelance work or get married. If you have just graduated and are starting your first job midyear, you may be a candidate for the special "part-year option" withholding tactic when you complete your W-4. If you choose this option, your employer will adjust your paycheck withholdings based on the number of months you'll actually be working that year instead of on a whole year's salary. This is designed to funnel a more accurate amount of taxes to the IRS.

Most of us will take just one or two allowances, depending on various financial situations pointed out on the W-4 work sheet. The general guideline is that the more allowances you take, the less tax you'll be paying during the year, which means you'll get more money in each paycheck but you also may end up owing the government a sizable check in April and possibly risk a fine for underpaying your taxes along the way. So, take this form seriously, and be sure to ask your employer's accounting or human resources department for help in interpreting anything you don't understand.

If you ever receive a large tax refund, you should take another look at how you filled out your W-4, because your employer is withholding too much tax money from your checks. I'm sure you have better things to do with your income than lend it to the IRS, which doesn't pay interest. Some people actually keep their withholdings purposefully high as a sort of forced savings account, but most financial consultants don't endorse such tactics because you can earn interest on this money if you place it in a savings account or money market mutual fund. And if you have debt to pay off, the money should most definitely be used for that.

Likewise, if you end up owing money at the end of the year, your best move could be to decrease the withholding allowances claimed on your W-4 form. That way, you won't be grasping for tax money next April, when you'd rather be spending any extra cash you may have on a new spring wardrobe, or at least a pair of strappy sandals.

The taxes we must pay from our wages include federal income taxes, state taxes, social security taxes, Medicare taxes (which fund the federal health care program for the elderly), and, in some parts of the country, city and disability taxes. Many of us also have to pay other taxes, such as self-employment taxes on money we earn through freelance work, property taxes if we own real estate, and capital gains taxes on invest-ment earnings that aren't protected by a tax-exempt retirement plan. Our tax system is progressive, which means the more we earn, the higher the percentage of taxes we must pay on our income, but the tax laws are always changing. Each year, Congress approves new tax credits, adjust-ments, and deductions that may reduce or increase what we owe.

Recent tax perks include the option to deduct job-related moving expenses (relevant to those of us just graduating and moving away from school to start our first jobs as well as those of us moving across the country to switch jobs), student loan interest payments (which are important to know about if you've started paying off monster student debt), and IRA contributions for those of us who qualify. If you pay tuition for higher education during a year in which you also pay income tax, you may be able to deduct qualified education expenses from the tax you owe. Because the tax laws change every year, we must keep abreast of all these changes, which are highlighted in the 1040 tax form publication packet, and take advantage of them whenever applicable. You may be able to use the simple 1040EZ form to do your taxes, which takes about five minutes and very little brain power. At any event, get used to doing your own filing (unless your tax situation is too compli-cated, in which case you should consult with your parents or find a good accountant). By doing the math yourself, you can learn what the whole system is about. And don't miss that April 15 deadline, or you'll owe a penalty fee and interest on your tax due.

14

Loose Ends

*H*ad a passing clairvoyant told me upon college graduation that my dream of becoming a writer would materialize if I could just hang in there a few years, I think I might have panicked at the thought. But here I am, teetering on the far edge of the decade, an *author*, no less, on women's issues, a subject that engages my heart and my brain. Had that same clairvoyant cornered me around age 25 and told me that toward the end of my 20s, I'd be in love and living with the man of my dreams, I might have laughed in her face. I didn't expect that to *ever* happen (not to mention during this decade). And if she had caught up with me even as little as a couple years ago and hinted that I just might feel an overwhelming pang of respect and love for my mom, I would have asked her what drug she was on. Yet, those feelings, lately, have inundated my consciousness as well. In truth, I'm glad I never came across that clairvoyant (not that I would have paid her any attention), because part of what has been so exciting about this decade is never knowing what's going to happen next. Looking back, the unexpected turns, the freak disasters, the chance encounters, and all the unforeseen changes—the jolts and bolts that make this life stage unique—have been the highlights.

You're going to love your 20s! I hope I've prepared you a bit on what to expect and given you a little guidance and reassurance about it all, too. I'm sure there are many worthy topics I've left out, and they'll hit me like a triple shot espresso as soon as I've turned in this baby and gone on to new and different things, but you can feel covered on the main points. I saved some parting thoughts to share with you, so stick with me just a little while longer. (Then we can both break out the champagne to celebrate the end of this little adventure and welcome all the big and exciting ventures ahead!)

OUR BIRTHDAYS

The 20s have three significant birthdays—our 21st, 25th, and 29th—but none of them is significant enough to get ruffled over if the event turns out to be anticlimactic. Our 21st, according to all my interviewing, is often the most anticlimactic of all, for a couple of reasons: (1) most of us have been drinking for quite some time now, anyway; and (2) half of our friends are still underage and can't legally enter bars, so we still can't always go out and celebrate with everyone in that way. As a result, most of us end up getting sickeningly drunk on Jack Daniel's at a party honoring us and make our official debut into adulthood with a happy hangover. The good news is that for this, we're absolved. The not-so-sobering rule that applies in regard to turning 21 is that we are still just kids and should *by no means* have our lives in order.

Take advantage of your youthful status, and do all the wild and crazy things to which you're inclined. You've got the excusability of being young, and that won't cut it in just a few short years. Enjoy!

I found my 25th birthday to be the most thought-provoking of all and a nostalgic time in general. That's because a young 20-something is a completely different species from an old 20-something, and the great dividing line is age 25. I guess I was kind of sad to be saying good-bye to my youthful status. I remember being 22 and thinking 28-year-olds were *soooo* old—they looked older, they acted older, and they were way too boring. When I turned 28, I remember for the first time thinking how young all the 22-year-olds around me looked. Hard to accept that as little as a few years back, I was that young. Since you're likely to hit this precipice on or around your 25th birthday, make sure you plan something fun and meaningful so that you can say farewell to your youth and hello to womanhood, because your life is about to change (and most of the changes are worth celebrating).

Having just recently celebrated my 29th (OK, it was about 10 months ago, but time flies when you're writing a book), I can say that this one wasn't as bad as I expected. You'll likely have several friends in their 30s who will kindly reassure you that you're still a baby, so you won't feel *that* old. But in case you're cowering in fret (which is totally normal), pick up a copy of Julie Tilsner's *29 and Counting*, and you'll have a good laugh and momentarily forget about your own fear of the big 3-oh!

THEME MUSIC

Ally McBeal has made the concept of theme songs famous, but there's validity to this corny idea. Music is one of the best ways to replay certain memories and feelings from the past. Because you will be establishing some of your fondest memories during the 20s (take it from me), you should listen to lots of music during landmark events (travel, falling in love, moving, starting a new job) so that the songs can bring on total recall of those times later on.

I will forever recall the feeling of what it was like to explore San Francisco for the first time whenever I hear Lloyd Cole ballads, which I was listening to all the time when I first moved to the area. When I hear Seal, I'm right back in Thailand, lying on the beach reading Fitzgerald and dreaming about becoming a writer. I'm whisked back into my first apartment in the city (and all the excitement that went with that) whenever I hear Bjork or Blind Melon, while R.E.M. and Sting bring me right back to the time when I moved into a studio and was living alone for once. John Coltrane floods the memory bank of my first Christmas with my boyfriend and the trip we took right after, cross-country skiing through an ancient forest of giant sequoias. The Brand New Heavies, Erykah Badu, and Massive Attack will forever remind me of my year in New York. And I'm sure I'll get panic attacks and flashbacks from here on out whenever I hear Lenny Kravitz, whose music has kept me from going nutty throughout the writing of this book.

I could go on, but you get the point: Make sure you've got *some* type of music to coincide with all those formidable memories in the works. You'll thank me for it in your late 20s, when you start getting nostalgic about such things.

THE THREE-MONTH MARKER

Several of the women I interviewed cited three months as being the amount of time required to figure something out, so I thought I'd pass it along. One woman said she knew after three months that the graduate program in which she was enrolled was completely wrong for her. Another woman said that after three months of being in her first job, she knew she was in the wrong field. A relationships expert I consulted said if you have doubts about a guy after three months of dating, move on. So, here's a good rule of thumb when you're adjusting to new events and all those changes happening around you: If three months have gone by, and your doubts are soaring, trust your instincts, and make appropriate changes.

TOP 10 LIST OF THINGS TO DO IN YOUR 20S

I could hardly write a guide to the 20s without a top 10 list of prerequisites to turning 30, could I? Here goes:

10. **Learn the guffaw.** My friend Jennifer and I rather innocently discovered the guffaw once when we were bored and trying to amuse each other with various laughs while waiting in line to get on a ferry. Here's how to do it: Take a deep breath, open your mouth wide, and scream, "*Bah, ha, ha, ha, ha!!!*" Do this as loud as you possibly can, using the full force of your diaphragm. When done properly, it will give you a complete head rush and scare the people around you, who will then (after their momentary fright has passed) begin to chuckle at your cartoonish laughter. Afterward, your throat may hurt a smidge, but you'll feel so relaxed that you'll want to do it all over again. It's a great mood lifter, especially if you've gotten into the adult habit of muffling your laughs.

9. **Have a wild and passionate fling.** The older you get, the less inclined you'll be to have a crazy love affair with someone who's not right for you in any other way but physically. If you've always had a secret desire for a scandalous affair, act out those fantasies now. (Best to be carried out with a firefighter, motorcycle mechanic, or similar icon of masculinity.) Don't forget protection!

8. **Travel far and wide.** I know I've said this before, but I can't resist repeating myself here. Travel is just so wonderful during our 20s when we're so open to new experiences and so impressionable. Our future changes every time we venture out into the unknown. It's also best to travel now when you probably have fewer obligations.

7. **Fulfill those lifelong fantasies.** You know that *thing* you've always wanted to do? (Scuba dive, sky dive, dye your hair platinum blonde or velvet red, get a tattoo?) Do it *now*, because you probably won't have the guts to do it in your 30s.

6. **Run a marathon, do a triathlon, or bike a century ride.** We are at our physical primes, ladies. Now is the time to challenge our bodies as we never have before. (Plus, training for an event is just plain cool.)

5. **Take a woman's self-defense class.** An effective self-defense class is not the same thing as taking a martial arts class, such as judo, or some gym-born cardiokick class. No matter what martial artists (or gym promoters) profess, when you're under attack, a karate chop or roundhouse kick isn't going to get you out of a bad situation unless you've been practicing for more than 20 years. Take a woman-oriented self-defense or rape-defense class that will teach you real-life defense strategies that can save your life. Such skills can't possibly be learned from punching or kicking the air once a week on blue mats.

4. **Reform dietary inadequacies.** If your childhood memories consist of sugary cereal, boxed mac & cheese, and frozen pizza dinners, start the dietary overhaul early on in the decade. Changing bad eating habits only gets harder the older we get.

3. **Keep in touch with at least one high school friend.** Remember, our high school friends are the ones who knew us during our experimental Flock of Seagulls hair days (and hung out with us despite it!). Besides, they're some of the most steadfast and loyal friends you'll ever have. Don't let distance or busy work schedules get in the way.

2. **Don't work too hard.** Our professional lives are only *part* of who we are. Chill out!

1. **Dig on these times.** I know it can be awfully hard to keep perspective when we're constantly broke, relationship challenged, and hating our jobs, but we've got the rest of our adulthood to right all the wrongs. As the 10,000 Maniacs once wrote: *These are days you'll remember.* Food for thought. The even greater thing to remember is that the 20s are only the beginning. Life becomes more and more amazing every single day!

KEEP ON MOVIN'

Throughout this book, I've made several analogies involving transportation. There was the soul-search train, analogous to figuring out our purpose in life. Then there was the car race that typifies dating. And let's not forget the bumpy airplane ride in the Introduction that represents the whole turbulent decade. Either I'm seriously due for a vacation that involves one or more modes of transportation (maybe a Christmas present to Hawaii from someone near and dear?), or else my subconscious is trying to tell me something to the effect of this: The 20s are a *total* trip!

In fact, this decade is the most exciting voyage you'll ever experience. You've got so much ahead of you to enjoy, freak out about, and (hopefully) laugh about hysterically after the panic has passed. I almost wish I could join you and do it all over again (*almost*). Many exciting opportunities await you. Welcome them wholeheartedly as they come—the scarier the better—and many of them will change the course of your future. And, on that note, there's just one thing left to say: You *go*, girl; you *go*!

Go-Girl Resources

WORK
To Read

JobSmarts for Twentysomethings: A Street-Smart Script for Career Success, by
　　Bradley G. Richardson (Vintage, 1995).

*College Grad Job Hunter: Insider Techniques and Tactics for Finding a Top-
　　Paying Entry Level Job*, by Brian Krueger (Quantum Leap, 1995).

What Color Is Your Parachute?, by Richard Nelson Bolles (Ten Speed Press,
　　1999).

*Sexual Harassment: A Practical Guide to the Law, Your Rights, and Your Options
　　for Taking Action*, by Tracy O'Shea and Jane LaLonde (St. Martin's,
　　1998).

To Surf

Monster.com; CareerPath.com; Internet Career Connection
　　(www.iccweb.com); Career Mosaic (www.careermosaic.com);
　　WetFeet.com; VAULT.com; The Riley Guide (www.rileyguide.com or
　　www.dbm.com/jobguide/salary.html for salary surveys); Equal
　　Employment Opportunity Commission (www.eeoc.gov/)

LOVE AND SEX (BUT MOSTLY SEX)
To Read
Sex for One: The Joy of Selfloving, by Betty Dodson, Ph.D. (Crown, 1996).
For Yourself: The Fulfillment of Female Sexuality, by Lonnie Garfield Barbach
    (New American Library, 1991).

To Surf
Coaltion for Marriage, Family and Couples Education
    (www.smartmarriages.com); Good Vibrations Catalogue: (800) 289-8423
    (www.goodvibes.com); Swoon.com

Videos to View
The Incredible G-Spot, hosted by Laura Corn, author of *101 Nights of Great
    Sex* (can be ordered through Good Vibrations); Betty Dodson's
    Selfloving: Portrait of a Women's Sexuality Seminar
    (www.bettydodson.com)

MIND AND BODY
To Read
The Harvard Guide to Women's Health, by Karen Carlson, M.D.; Stephanie
    Eisenstat, M.D.; and Terra Ziporyn, Ph.D. (Harvard University Press,
    1996).
*The Complete Home Healer: Your Guide to Every Treatment Available for over
    300 of the Most Common Health Problems*, by Angela Smyth (Harper
    Mass Market Paperbacks, 1995).
The Artist's Way: A Spiritual Path to Higher Creativity, by Julia Cameron (G. P.
    Putnam's Sons, 1992).
Premenstrual Syndrome Self-Help Book and *Menstrual Cramps Self-Help Book*,
    by Susan M. Lark, M.D. (Celestial Arts, 1989 and 1995).

To Surf

American Institute of Stress (www.stress.org/)

To Contact

Eating Disorders Awareness and Prevention (EDAP), a nonprofit clearinghouse of information and referral center for eating disorders: (800) 931-2237 (www.edap.org/)

FAMILY STUFF
To Read

When You and Your Mother Can't Be Friends: Resolving the Most Complicated Relationship of Your Life, by Victoria Secunda (Delacorte, 1990).

Women and Their Fathers: The Sexual and Romantic Impact of the First Man in Your Life, by Victoria Secunda (Delacorte, 1992).

OUR FINANCES
To Read

Get a Financial Life: Personal Finance in Your Twenties and Thirties, by Beth Kobliner (Fireside, 1996).

The Wall Street Journal Guide to Understanding Personal Finance, by Kenneth M. Morris and Alan M. Siegel (Lightbulb, 1997).

The Wall Street Journal Guide to Understanding Money and Investing, by Kenneth M. Morris, Virginia B. Morris, and Alan M. Siegel (Fireside, 1999).

To Surf

For tax information: Internal Revenue Service (www.irs.gov); for investment information and research: Charles Schwab (www.eschwab.com); E*TRADE (www.etrade.com)

Index

Acne, 215–16

Adult education, 182–83

Aerobic exercise, 177–78. *See also* Exercise

Aging
    parents, 263–64
    in the 20s, 201–2

AIDS, 137

Am I Thin Enough Yet?: The Cult of Thinness and the Commercialization of Identity (Hesse-Biber), 196

American Association of Sexuality Educators, Counselors, and Therapists (AASECT), 131

American College of Obstetricians and Gynecologists, 227

American College of Sports Medicine, 230

Androgen, 215, 221

Anger-management workshops, 191

Assertiveness, 53–55

Associations, 22–23

Astroglide lubricant, 152

ATM credit, 305

Baby, 264–65

Baggage. *See* Unresolved issues

Belzer, Cynthia, 252, 254, 262

Benton-Jones, Allison, 171, 199, 202, 203, 251

Benzoyl peroxide, 216

Bergfeld, Wilma, 218

Berson, Diane, 216

Bicycling, 327

Birth control, 123, 132, 140–44

Birth control pills, 142, 228

Birthdays, 324–29

Blood cholesterol screening, 239

Body hair, 221–22

Body image, 130–31, 195–209, 212
    advertising and, 198–99
    bloating and, 204
    clothes and, 203–4
    media and, 197–98
    obsessions and, 202–3

Body issues
  digestive system, 222–24
  faces, 214
  feet, 229–30
  hair, 219–22
  resources, 330–31
  shape, 212–14
  size, 212–14
  skin, 215–19
Bone density, 230
Bonuses (work), 41–42
Boundary issues
  couples and, 106
  identity and, 171–72
  parents and, 249–51, 264–65
  sex and, 124, 128–30
  siblings and, 256
Breast exam, 238
Brottman, Martin, 223
Brown, Susan, 115
Budgets, 292–94

Calcium, 223, 233
CardTrac, 307
CardWeb.com, Inc., 307, 308
Career assessment tests, 7–8
Career centers, 7
Career counselors, 7–8
Career goals, 3–6. *See also* First job
  emotions involved, 4
  list-making, 6
  nonprofit organizations, 6
  purpose in life, 4, 16, 64
  questions to ask, 4
  resources, 329
  soul-searching, 4–6
  trial-and-error approach, 16–18
Career insiders, 13–16
Cars, 293
Cellulite, 213
Cervical cap, 141
Childhood trauma, 252–54

Clitoris, 146, 147–48
Clothes. *See* Fashion
Clubs and organizations, 188
Cochron, Melissa, 110
Commitment
  job offers and, 36–37
  relationships and, 94
Communication issues
  conflict resolution, 98–101
  dating and, 89–92
  on the job, 51–52
  orgasm and, 149–50
  relationships and, 95–98
  speaker-listener technique, 97
  "x, y, z" formula, 97
Compatability issues, 79–85, 121
Complete Idiot's Guide to Amazing Sex,
    The (Locker), 126
Condoms, 139–40
  female, 140
  reliability, 141
Conflict resolution, 98–101
  humor and, 102
Constipation, 222
Consumer Credit Counseling Services,
    308
Cooney, Theresa, 245
Cover letter, 25–28
Coworkers, 48–50, 61–62
Cramps, 225–26
Credit cards, 292, 302–9
  billing cycles, 309
  interest rates, 306–7
  secured, 308
Credit report, 308–9
Culture shock, 46–48
Curfew rules, 257

Date rape, 87, 88–89, 129
Date rape drugs, 88
Dating
  age of partners, 70–71

assessing compatability, 79–85
dating around, 89
first dates, 77–79
initiating a date, 76–77
internet, 75–76
meeting people, 72, 73–76
mutual interests, 72–73
protocol, 70
reasons for, 69–70
relational definition, 89–92
R.E.M. test, 84
safety, 73, 76, 88–89
scar test, 84
telephoning, 78
using friends for setups, 73–74
vacation test, 84
warning signs, 86–88
Debit card, 305
Debt, 302–9
billing cycles, 309
consolidating, 303
repaying, 305–6
Debt Counselors of America, 308
Decision making, 16–18
Denial, 292
Dental dams, 139
Depression, 35, 189–90
Dermatology, 215–18, 221
Diabetes, 240
Diaphragm, 141
Diarrhea, 222
Diet (nutrition), 222. *See also* Nutrition
Diets (losing weight), 235–36
Digestive systems, 222–24
Divorce, 99, 109, 115, 245
Dodson, Betty, 147
Dress code, 46
Dugal, Gerald, 258, 261
Dysfunctional families, 244

Eating Disorder Resource and Information Guide, The (Hartline), 205

Eating disorders, 209
Education funds, 42
Education, higher, 11
Elders, 48–49
Emotional issues, 163–93
depression, 189–90
envy, 191–93
identity crisis, 164–72
loneliness, 181–85
rage, 190–91
self-loathing, 172–75
stress, 175–81
Entertainment, 294–98
Envy, 191–93
Equal Employment Opportunity
Commission, 64
Estrogen, 213
Etiquette, 46–47, 60, 85
interviewing, 30
money, 298–302
Exercise, 177–78, 206, 213–14
flexibility, 231
muscle mass, 230
stress and, 230
variety, 231
weight-bearing, 230
Eye examination, 239

Fad diets, 236
Family. *See also* Parents; Siblings
dysfunctional, 244
starting a, 264–65
Fantasies, 327
Fashion, 29–30, 46, 203–4, 212, 299–300
Favors, 184
Female orgasm, 145–60
different types, 152–54
faking, 157
mind-body connection, 154–56
movie versions, 145–46
multiple, 153

Fiber, 222, 232–33
"Fighting to win," 100
Financial issues
  budgets, 292–94
  cars, 293
  crisis fund, 317–19
  eating out, 294, 295–96
  entertainment, 294–98
  investing money, 312–15
  living at home, 257
  "me" money, 293
  parents and, 251
  poverty, 290–92
  resources, 331
  retirement, 309–17
  shopping, 297–98
Finder's fee, 24
First impressions, 29–30
First job
  advancing, 52–59
  bonding with elders, 48–49
  communication issues, 51–52
  coworkers, 48–50, 61–62
  culture shock, 46–48
  hazing, 44
  induction, 44–46
  insecurities, 43–44
  office gossip, 47–48
  personal problems, 47
  reasons for disliking, 59–64
  training programs, 44–45
Flattery, 86
Flings, 327
Foreman, Arlene, 247
Fortgang, Laura Berman, 48, 60
401(k) plans, 40–41, 310, 315–16, 317
Frankel, Lois, 51–52, 54–55, 56
Friendship
  after a relationship breaks up, 111–12
  ending, 272–75
  highschool, 285, 328

influenced by boyfriends,
    279–84
  long distance, 271
  maintenance factor, 270–72
  new bonds, 275–79
  nights out with friends, 280–81
  parents as friends, 265–68
  reunions, 285–86
  sex with a friend, 136
  as surrogate family, 269–70
  at work, 276
*Friendships: The Power of Friendship
    and How It Shapes Our Lives*
    (Yager), 271–72

Garage sales, 182
Gender roles, 170
GHB drug, 88
Girlhood room, 259
Gossip, 47–48
Graduate school, 11–12
Grafenberg spot, 146, 147–48
Grandparents, 264–65
Grief, 109
Grocery shopping, 234
Guffaw, 326
Gum probing, 239

Hair
  body hair, 221–22
  gloss, 219–20
  gray, 219
  thinning, 220–21
Hartline, Christine, 205, 209
Headhunters, 24
Health care, 39–40
Health issues. *See also* Body issues;
    Exercise
  screening tests, 236–40
  smoking, 234
Herpes, 137, 138

Hesse-Biber, Sharlene, 196
Hillman, Carolynn, 148–49, 150, 201, 207
Hıv, 137
Hoff, Holly, 209
Holidays, 258–63, 262
  avoiding arguments, 261
  stress, 262
  time commitments, 260–61
  visualizing visit, 259–60
Holmquist, Virginia, 254
Hormones, 215, 224
  balding and, 220
  body hair and, 221
  implants, 142–43
  injections, 142
Humor, 80

Identity issues, 94–95, 96, 106, 164–72
  identity crisis, 164–72
  voice, 170–71
Insomnia, 179–81
Internet dating, 75–76
Internships, 8–10
Interviewing
  answering questions, 31–32
  asking questions, 33–34
  career insiders, 13–16
  dress, 29–30
  etiquette, 30
  first impressions, 29–30
  follow-up, 34–35
  for jobs, 20–21, 28–35
  for promotions, 56–57
  thank-you letter, 33, 34
Intrauterine device (IUD), 143
Investing money, 312–14, 319–20
  diversifying, 313–14
  risk, 313
IRAS, 315–16
  Roth, 320

traditional, 320
Irritable bowel syndrome, 223

Jerry Maguire, 95
Job benefits, 39–42
Job description, 45
Job hunt, 19–42. *See also* Interviewing
  duration of, 20
  interviewing, 20–21, 28–35
  networking, 21–23
  references, 34
  rejection, 35
  researching companies, 23–25
  resources, 329
  stress and, 20–21
Job offers, 36–37
  commitment, 36–37
  negotiation, 37–39
Job satisfaction, 62
John Holland Self-Directed Search (SDS), 7
Johnson, Zonya, 172, 174, 265
Jump-Start Your Career (Frankel), 51–52

Kegel exercises, 153
Ketamine hydrochloride, 88

Lactose, 223
Levine, Josie, 193, 247
Lillak, Dale, 171–72
Living situations
  living alone, 171
  living with boyfriend, 115–19
  living at home, 257–58
Locker, Sari, 126, 130, 137, 149, 153
Loneliness, 181–85
Love Your Looks: How to Stop Criticizing and Start Appreciating Your Looks (Hillman), 148, 201

Marathon, 327
Marriage, 115–16, 119–22
   compatability, 121
   personal readiness, 120
   relational readiness, 120–21
Marx-Kelly, Dee, 87–88, 100, 252
Masturbation, 125
Materialism, 290–91
Mattox, Marty, 213, 231
Menopause, 245–46
Menstrual period, 224–25
Mental-health checkup, 193
Mentorship. *See also* Role models
   careers and, 15, 49, 50–51
Metabolism, 213, 235–36
Mind-body connection, 154–56, 171,
   208
Mission statements, 25
Money etiquette, 298–302
Morning-after pills, 144
Morwessel, Rosemarie, 230
Motherhood, 165, 264–65. *See also*
   Pregnancy
Moving, 185–89
Myers-Briggs Type Indicator test, 7

National Foundation for Consumer
   Credit, 308
Negotiation
   job offers, 37–39
   raises, 57–58
Neighborhood involvement, 183, 188
Networking
   for jobs, 21–23
No-load money market mutual funds,
   318–19
Nutrition, 177, 206, 231–36, 327
   diets and, 235–36
   fiber, 222, 232–33
   folic acid, 233–34
   iron, 233

junk food, 234
milk, 223, 233
multivitamins, 234
variety, 232

Occupational guidebooks, 10–13
Occupational Outlook Handbook, 10, 57
Oedipal issues, 86
Olson, Michele, 212
Opportunities in Psychology Careers, 12
Oral sex, 139, 150–51
Orgasm. *See* Female orgasm
*Overcoming Job Burnout: How to Renew
   Enthusiasm for Work* (Potter),
   25, 49

Pachter, Barbara, 30
Pap smear, 237
Parents, 243–52
   aging, 263–64
   controlling, 253
   divorce after children leave, 244
   empty nest euphoria, 244
   financial independence from, 251
   friendships with, 265–68
   having fun with, 267–68
   menopause in mothers, 245–46
   moving out of house of, 249–50
   need for privacy of, 258
   parental advice, 247–48
   past of, 266
   resources, 331
   role reversal, 263–64
   separating from, 246–52
   staying in touch with, 267
Parrott, Leslie, 95, 97, 98, 108, 120, 121
Personal problems at work, 47
Platt, Riska, 235
Pms (premenstrual syndrome), 227–29
Potter, Beverly, 25, 49
Pregnancy, 125, 202, 221

Prentice Hall Complete Business Etiquette Handbook, The, 30
Privacy, 250–51
Problem-solving skills, 100. *See also* Conflict resolution
Profit sharing, 41
Progesterone, 215
Promotions, 58–59, 64–65
Psychics, 6
Purpose in life, 4, 16, 64, 95

Rage, 190–91
Rebound relationships, 113
Recommendations, job, 60
Recovering Your Self-Esteem (Hillman), 201
References, 34
Rejection
  for a date, 77, 78
  for a job, 35
Relationships, 93–94
  abuse, 107
  breaks from, 114–15
  communication and, 95–98
  living together, 115–19
  long-distance, 103–4
  maintaining romance, 101–3
  patterns, 252–53
  quitting relationships, 104–14
  rebound, 113
  self-preservation and, 94–95
Reproductive systems, 224–29. *See also* Birth control
  cramps, 225–26
  PMS, 227–29
Resentment, 291–92, 301
Resources
  body issues, 330–31
  career goals, 329
  financial issues, 331
  job hunt, 329

  parents, 331
  sex, 330
Résumés, 25–28
  format, 27–28
  scannable résumé, 28
  slanting, 26
Retirement, saving for, 309–17
Reviews, 56
Rhythm method of birth control, 143
Risk-taking, 16–18
Rohypnol, 88
Role models, 169–70, 198. *See also* Mentorship
Roommates, 186
Routines, 187
Rules, The, 85
Rust, Paula, 127

Salary, 14
  negotiating, 37–39
Sapadin, Linda, 272, 273, 282
Saving Your Marriage Before It Starts (Parrott), 120
Savings plans, 317–19
Scott, Joyce, 13, 15, 29, 38, 47
Screening tests, 236–40
Self-defense, 327
Self-esteem, 172–75
  parents and, 248
  sex and, 134
Self-promotion, 55–57
Sex. *See also* Female orgasm
  birth control and, 123, 132
  body and, 125
  body image and, 206–8
  boundary issues, 128–30
  casual sex, 134–36
  differing opinions about, 125–26
  esteem and, 134
  foreplay, 132, 150–51
  inhibitions, 130

intimacy and, 135–36
libido, 158–60
lust and, 133
painful intercourse, 152
resources, 330
sexual positions, 151
Sex for One: The Joy of Selfloving
    (Dodson), 147
Sex partners, 131–36
Sexual harrassment, 63–64
Sexual health, 138–44
Sexual history, 132, 136–38
Sexual orientation, 126–28
Sexually transmitted disease (STD), 125,
    137, 139, 141, 144
    screening tests, 237
Shopping, 297–98, 299–300
Siblings, 254–56
Silence, 38
Skin
    acne, 215–16
    circles under eyes, 218
    dryness, 216–17
    enlarged pores, 218
    wrinkles, 217–18
Skin cancer check, 238–39
Smoking, 234
Social Security Administration, 311
Sollee, Diane, 97, 99, 121
Sommerstein, Judith, 9, 16, 33
Speaker-listener technique, 97
Spending time alone, 171, 184
Spiritual groups, 183–84
Sports, 182
Steele, David, 76
Stock options, 41
Stress, 175–81
    cramps and, 225–26
    at holidays, 262
    job hunt and, 20–21
Stretch marks, 218

Strong Interest Inventory, 7
Student loans, 303
Sugrue, Dennis, 130–31, 151, 152, 156
Sunblock, 217–18
Supervisors at work, 59–60

Tannen, Deborah, 97–98
Taxes, 320–22
Telephoning, 184
Thank-you letter, 33, 34
Theme music, 325–26
Three-month marker, 326
Tilsner, Julie, 325
Travel, 167–69, 296–97, 327
Triathlon, 327
29 and Counting (Tilsner), 325

Unresolved issues, 252–54

Vacation, 41
Vacation test, 84
Varicose veins, 218

Walking, 213–14
Wardrobe. *See* Fashion
Weight, body, 199–201, 204–5
Weishaar, Shirley, 30, 38
White, Lynn, 244, 250, 254
Woman Doctor's Guide to Skin Care, A
    (Bergfeld), 218
Work. *See* Career goals; First job; Job
    hunt
Work environment, 62–64
Wrinkles, 217–18

"X, y, z" formula, 97

Yager, Jan, 271, 278, 281, 282
Yoga, 177–78
You Just Don't Understand (Tannen),
    97–98